The American Monomyth

The American Monomyth

By Robert Jewett
and John Shelton Lawrence

Foreword by Isaac Asimov

1977
ANCHOR PRESS/DOUBLEDAY
Garden City, New York

Library of Congress Cataloging in Publication Data
Jewett, Robert.
The American monomyth.
Includes bibliographical references and index.
1. United States–Popular culture. I. Lawrence, John Shelton, joint author. II. Title.
E169.12.J48 973
ISBN 0-385-12203-9
Library of Congress Catalog Card Number 76-18354

PRINTED IN THE UNITED STATES OF AMERICA
FIRST EDITION

Grateful acknowledgment is made to the following sources for the use of photographs and excerpted material:

The Steve Austin cartoons are reprinted by permission from *Scholastic Sprint*, copyright © 1975 by Scholastic Magazines, Inc.

The Star Trek® convention photograph of George Takei, Leonard Nimoy, and James Doohan is reprinted by permission from the photographer Jeff Maynard, New Eye Studio.

The Costume Call photograph is reprinted by permission of the photographer Neal Slavin.

The *Rider on the Rain* poster is reprinted courtesy of Avco Embassy Pictures Corp.

The Laocoön photograph is reprinted courtesy of The Bettmann Archive, Inc.

The Superman® cover copyright © 1970 by National Periodical Publications, Inc. Superman and Mr. Meany copyright 1940 by Superman, Inc., copyright renewed © 1968 by National Periodical Publications, Inc. Superman and Lois Lane copyright 1943 by Detective Comics, Inc., copyright renewed © 1971 by National Periodical Publications, Inc. Reprinted by permission.

The photographs of the Adamsville sign and Buford Pusser's grave are reprinted by permission from the Des Moines *Register* and *Tribune*.

The illustration from *Heidi* by Johanna Spyri was drawn by William Sharp. Illustrations copyright 1945 by Grosset & Dunlap, Inc. Illustrations copyright renewed © 1973 by Grosset & Dunlap, Inc. Used by permission of Grosset & Dunlap, Inc.

The illustrations from Laura Ingalls Wilder's *By the Shores of Silver Lake* were drawn by Garth Williams. Pictures copyright 1953 by Garth Williams. Reprinted by permission of Harper & Row, Publishers, Inc.

The photograph from the motion picture *Jaws®* is reprinted courtesy of Universal Pictures.

The Lone Ranger® pictures are from The Lone Ranger Silver Anniversary Issue, copyright © 1958 by Lone Ranger Television, Inc. Reprinted by permission.

The picture of Buck Rogers' atomic gun and the *Daisy* magazine advertisement are reprinted by permission of Robert C. Dille, Glenview, Illinois.

The Flash sequence copyright © 1971 by National Periodical Publications, Inc. Reprinted by permission.

The photograph from the motion picture *The Virginian* is reprinted courtesy of Universal Pictures and The Museum of Modern Art/Film Stills Archives.

The Wonder Warthog cartoons from *Zap* magazine #4, copyright © 1969, are reprinted by permission of Gilbert Shelton, artist.

The Americans: The Democratic Experience by Daniel J. Boorstin. Copyright © 1973 by Daniel J. Boorstin. Reprinted by permission of Random House, Inc.

Angel in Armor: A Post-Freudian Perspective on the Nature of Man by Ernest Becker; reprinted with the permission of the publisher, George Braziller, Inc. Copyright © 1969 by Ernest Becker.

"The Apple" by Max Ehrlich and Gene L. Coon, from *Star Trek 6;* James Blish novelization copyright © 1972 by Bantam Books, Inc., and Paramount Pictures, Inc. Reprinted by permission.

The Art of Walt Disney by Robert D. Feild. Copyright 1942 by Western Publishing Company, Inc. Copyright renewed © 1970 by Robert D. Feild. Reprinted by permission of Western Publishing Company, Inc.

The motion picture, *The Bible*. Courtesy of Twentieth Century-Fox Film Corporation.

Buffalo Bill: The Noblest Whiteskin by John Burke. Copyright © 1973 by John Burke. Reprinted by permission of G. P. Putnam's Sons and Cassell & Company Ltd.

Carrington by Michael Straight. Copyright © 1960 by Michael Straight. Reprinted by permission of Alfred A. Knopf, Inc.

Charles Bronson, Superstar by Steven Whitney. Reprinted by permission of Steven Whitney, represented by Peter Miller.

Death Wish by Brian Garfield. Copyright © 1972 by Brian Garfield. Published by David McKay Company, Inc. Reprinted by permission of David McKay Company, Inc., the author, and Henry Morrison, Inc., his agents.

The motion picture, *Death Wish*. By permission of Dino De Laurentiis Corporation.

The Disney Films by Leonard Maltin. Copyright © 1973 by Leonard Maltin. Used by permission of Crown Publishers, Inc.

The Disney Version by Richard Schickel. Copyright © 1968 by Richard Schickel. Reprinted by permission of Simon & Schuster, Inc.

Earthquake: The Story of a Movie by George Fox. Copyright © MCA Publishing, 1974. Published by New American Library. Reprinted by permission of MCA Publishing.

"The Epic of Creation" from the *Larousse Encyclopedia of Mythology*. Reproduced by permission of The Hamlyn Publishing Group Limited.

Flash Comics and *Action Comics* sequences reprinted by permission of DC Comics, Inc.

The Great Comic Book Heroes by Jules Feiffer. Copyright © 1965 by The Dial Press. Reprinted by permission of The Dial Press.

Hair: The American Tribal Love-Rock Musical by Gerome Ragni and James Rado. Copyright © 1966 by Gerome Ragni and James Rado. Reprinted by permission of Simon & Schuster, Inc., and Nat Shapiro.

Helter Skelter: The True Story of the Manson Murders by Vincent Bugliosi with Curt Gentry. Published by W. W. Norton & Company, Inc., New York, New York. (Published in England by The Bodley Head as *The Manson Murders.*) Copyright © 1974 by Curt Gentry and Vincent Bugliosi. Reprinted by permission of W. W. Norton & Company, Inc., and The Bodley Head.

The Hero in America by Dixon Wecter. Copyright © 1963 by The University of Michigan. Reprinted by permission of The University of Michigan.

"The Intellectual in Videoland" by Douglas Cater. Copyright © 1975 by *Saturday Review*. Reprinted by permission of *Saturday Review*.

The Lives and Legends of Buffalo Bill by Don Russell. Copyright © 1960 by The University of Oklahoma Press. Reprinted by permission of The University of Oklahoma Press.

Inclusion of Lone Ranger material authorized by Lone Ranger Television, Inc., a subsidiary of Wrather Corporation, owner of all rights, title, and interest in and to the Lone Ranger property.

The Making of Star Trek by Stephen Whitfield and Gene Roddenberry. Reprinted by permission of William Morris Agency, Inc. Copyright © 1968 by Stephen E. Whitfield.

Part 2 Walking Tall by Webster Carey, based on the original screenplay by Howard B. Kreitsek. Copyright © 1975 by Bing Crosby Productions, Inc. Reprinted by permission of Bantam Books, Inc.

Popular Culture and High Culture: An Analysis and Evaluation of Taste by Herbert J. Gans, copyright © 1974 by Basic Books, Inc., Publishers, New York. Reprinted by permission of Basic Books, Inc.

Quest for Paradise by Charles L. Sanford. Copyright © 1961 by The University of Illinois Press. Reprinted by permission of The University of Illinois Press.

Regeneration Through Violence: The Mythology of the American Frontier, 1600–1860 by Richard Slotkin. Copyright © 1973 by Richard Slotkin. Reprinted by permission of Wesleyan University Press.

Space Guardians by Brian Ball. Copyright © 1975 by Futura Publishers, Ltd. Reprinted by permission of Simon & Schuster, Inc., and Futura Publishers, Ltd.

"Spock's Brain" by Lee Cronin, from *Star Trek 8;* James Blish novelization copyright © 1972 by Bantam Books, Inc., and Paramount Pictures, Inc. Reprinted by permission.

Star Trek Lives! by Jacqueline Lichtenberg, Sondra Marshak and Joan

Winston. Copyright © 1975 by Jacqueline Lichtenberg, Sondra Marshak and Joan Winston. Reprinted by permission of Bantam Books, Inc.

Virgin Land: The American West as Symbol and Myth by Henry Nash Smith, Cambridge, Mass.: Harvard University Press. Copyright © 1950 by the President and Fellows of Harvard College; reissued, with a new preface, 1970.

Walking Tall by Doug Warren. Copyright © 1973 by Buford Pusser Enterprises. Reprinted by permission of Pinnacle Books, Inc.

"Welcome Home, Jaime," an episode of the television program *The Bionic Woman*. Reprinted by permission of Martin Caidin.

"What Westerns Are All About" by Walter Karp. Copyright © 1975 by American Heritage Publishing Co., Inc. Reprinted by permission, from *Horizon* (Summer 1975).

"Who Mourns for Adonais?" by Gilbert A. Ralston and Gene L. Coon, from *Star Trek 7;* James Blish novelization copyright © 1972 by Bantam Books, Inc., and Paramount Pictures, Inc. Reprinted by permission.

The World of Star Trek by David Gerrold. Copyright © 1973 by David Gerrold. Reprinted by permission of Ballantine Books, a Division of Random House, Inc.

Zap Comics and *Arcade: The Comics Revue*. Copyright © 1967, 1969, 1975 by R. Crumb. Reprinted by permission of R. Crumb.

TO

Ellen, Jennifer, and Eric

Contents

The Mysterious Stranger:

A FOREWORD BY ISAAC ASIMOV

This fascinating book by Robert Jewett and John Lawrence begins by spending two chapters on *Star Trek,* and I suppose it is for that reason that it fell into the charming head of the editor of the book to get me to do an introduction. It seemed an obvious connection.

And yet the book is about a lot more than *Star Trek*. It is about what the authors call "The American Monomyth."

We know what a "myth" is; it is a tale that is fanciful, usually of unknown origin, a tale that is tied in with religious beliefs and that serves to explain the origin or purpose of some natural or social phenomenon.

For instance, the most popular character in the Greek myths was Herakles ("Hercules" to the Romans), the strong man. Herakles was condemned to perform twelve labors of increasing difficulty before he could find rest. It is rather tempting to suppose that Herakles represents the Sun, that fierce and strong heavenly object that must, in the course of the year, pass through the twelve constellations of the zodiac.

Herakles proved to be so popular to the ancient Greeks that he began to intrude in other tales that had nothing to do with the Sun's path across the heavens and, like so many other fictional characters, began to assume a life of his own beyond the intent of the original creator. (There was a proverb, in fact, that went "Nothing without Herakles"–meaning that no great mythical feat would carry conviction if Herakles were not somehow involved.)

Consider, then, the case of Admetus of Pherae. The time had come for him to die, and the Fates were ready to snip the thread of his life. Admetus, however, was a favorite of the god Apollo, and Apollo persuaded the Fates to let him live. –But there was a condition. The remorseless Fates would not be altogether deprived, and they demanded that some member of Admetus' family must die in his place if he were to live.

Admetus, apprised of this, turned to his children, and appealed to their filial devotion. One and all refused. They had had so little life so far that they could not give it up.

He turned to his parents then and appealed to their parental love. Both refused. They had so little life left that they could not bear to give it up.

Admetus was in despair, but his beautiful wife, Alcestis, loving him more than her own life, offered to take his place. He accepted the sacrifice and at once she faded, died, and went down to Hades in his place–and Admetus lived.

As told in this fashion, the story emphasizes the great love and the beautiful sacrifice of Alcestis. –And yet surely Admetus, in contrast, is a miserable creature to wish to save his life at the expense of those whom he should have loved more than his life.

Perhaps because of the imbalance between Admetus' poltroonery and Alcestis' courage, many people were uneasy at having Alcestis end in Hades, and a new ending was attached.

It seems that Herakles was just happening to pass by in the course of one of his labors while the court at Pherae was in mourning. Hearing of Alcestis' sacrifice, Herakles entered the Underworld and by brute strength forced Hades to relinquish the shade of Alcestis. The woman's corpse revived, and Herakles restored the living Alcestis to Admetus. –Fadeout! Happy ending!

Herakles just happened by–he came from nowhere. With no thought of personal gain, he made the cause of sympathy and justice his own, fought the villain, rescued the fair maid, and restored the happiness of the King. Then, scarcely pausing for thanks, he vanished into nowhere.

How convenient it would be if, whenever the world is too much for us (and when is it not?), some mysterious stranger would pass by–coming from nowhere, going to nowhere, asking nothing in return, and putting everything to rights.

The desire is so strong that every culture invents such a figure. The Greeks had Herakles; the medieval Christians had their knights-errant, their Lancelots and Tristrams; even the medieval rabbis went to the trouble of inventing tales of Elijah coming from heaven to rescue pious Jews fallen on hard times.

This is the "monomyth," the myth of the one man serving as rescuer for no reason but his devotion to abstract justice.

Why the *American* monomyth? –Because what the myths of other nations and cultures have had in small, the American forms of popular literature have raised to an overpowering institution in a dozen different directions. So overpowering, in fact, that the myth stands almost alone–hence *mono*myth, the single story we do deeply believe in, and repeatedly rewrite with new characters in new settings.

Read the book and see how this has been done and in what way. I assure you that you will look on all the tales you read, hear, and view in a new way after reading this book, and perhaps consider the significance of the monomyth to our society in a new, and rather upsetting, way, too.

Introduction

In the bleak Bicentennial winter of 1976, fans of the American monomyth were rejuvenated by a miraculous birth. Jaime Sommers was restored to life as The Bionic Woman. It all started in the summer of 1975 during a two-part program dealing with the romance between Jaime and her six-million-dollar fiancé, Steve Austin. They had been playmates in idyllic Ojai, California. She became a tennis champion while Steve was in the Air Force being retooled as a bionic superman, and when they found each other again, it was love at second sight. For American audiences who seem ill at ease with married superheroes, this produced a titillating dilemma. They accepted decades of Superman's impasse with Lois Lane and resigned themselves to the serialized deaths of marriage prospects for the men of *Bonanza.* They are confident that the Lone Ranger will continue to be satisfied with Silver. Hence, it was not surprising that Jaime was critically injured during the second episode while sky diving with Steve. Although he arranged for bionic repairs, her body rejected the powerful spare parts, and the life indicators flickered away on schedule at the program's end.

Then the miracle occurred. Fascinated by the prospect of a superwoman who would help redeem the nation from its enemies, fans of *The Six Million Dollar Man* demanded that the bionic woman be revived. The network responded to weeks of devoted nagging by concocting a plot in which Jaime would be resurrected. But since her existence would be more threatening than all the conspirators that Steve so neatly subdues each week, the romantic connection had to be placed in limbo. Jaime develops mysterious difficulties remembering anything connected with Steve, but even this barrier offers too little protection. The suspicion seems to linger that the lovely Miss Sommers will recover the memory of her affection and lure him into marriage. So The Bionic Woman is deported from Sunday to Wednesday night, a safe distance from Steve Austin, thus permitting each redeemer figure to remain sexually intact. The OSI, television's version of the CIA, becomes a ministry of love as chief Oscar Goldman passes romantic messages between the pair stranded on their separate programs.

In the first episode of *The Bionic Woman,* Jaime nostalgically returns to her hometown to become a teacher. She gives up championship tennis because her bionic strokes chip the concrete and drive the balls through steel fences. She moves into a garage apartment, cleaning out the place with bionic speed surpassing that of Walt Disney's Snow White. Taking a position with a class that has terrorized its last three teachers provides a perfect opportunity for superpowers. She intimidates the rowdies by tearing a huge telephone book apart while telling them sweetly:

> I'm here to stay, and if we're going to get along, you're going to learn a little bit about respect. Some teachers feel that the best way to get respect from their students is to threaten them. (Rip) I don't like to make threats because most of the time they're not really carried out, you know? And, I've always felt that the best way of teaching was the gentle approach. (Rip, rip) I feel that respect for a teacher should grow naturally through friendship and through trust. And I expect you to be able to develop and to understand and have that kind of respect for me. (Rip, rip, rip; terrified amazement among pupils)

On the way home Jaime saves a victim from a car accident by ripping off the door just before the explosion–a setup, as it emerges, for the enemies to determine whether her powers are intact so they can use her in their vile plans. And so it goes in the weeks that follow. The class becomes a loving encounter group bringing apples to the teacher while villains from around the world plot to misuse Jaime's bionic powers.[1]

Puzzles abound in this resurrection tale. Why would such an event seem dramatically credible in the twentieth century? Why does a secularized audience display such fascination with more-than-human powers and accept bionic deeds of leaping over buildings and running at sixty miles per hour? Why are the destructive effects of such powers so consistently suppressed by the slow-motion film technique that turns brawls into ballet? How is it plausible that "the gentle approach" of incredible force could throw villains so benignly into the bushes or pools of water? And why the elaborate efforts, requiring corporate machinations of the highest order, to keep the bionic lovers apart? If Hercules, the mighty predecessor of all superheroes, was allowed to enjoy his productive night with the fifty daughters of King Thespius, why can't the cool American strongman in the liberated seventies be joined with even one daughter of Ojai?

These puzzling motifs would not be so interesting as points of departure in tracking the American monomyth except that they have become so predictable. As John Cawelti suggests, ". . . Strongly conventionalized narrative types . . . are so widely appealing because they enable people to re-enact and temporarily resolve widely shared psychic conflicts." Invention in the dramatic realm strives after a statement of unique personal vision while conventions ". . . assert an ongoing continuity of values. . . ."[2] Our concern lies with these ritually predictable plots because they provide some of the best clues to tensions and hopes within the current American consciousness.

It appears that conventional formulas are often linked together in a single recurrent pattern, and that the current pattern differs sharply from traditional ones. In *The Hero with a Thousand Faces,* Joseph Campbell depicted the archetypal plot of heroic action in traditional myths. The plot of the *classical monomyth,* as he called it, is as follows:

> *A hero ventures forth from the world of common day into a region of supernatural wonder: fabulous forces are there encountered and a decisive victory is won: the hero comes back from this mysterious adventure with the power to bestow boons on his fellow man.*[3]

One can find this plot in the stories of Prometheus stealing fire from the gods to benefit mankind, of Ulysses undergoing his adventurous journey, of Aeneas visiting the underworld to discover the destiny of the nation he would found, of St. George and the dragon, and of Hansel and Gretel. Campbell incorporates myths, legends, and fairy tales of many cultures into this framework, showing that the archetype is molded upon rites of initiation, in which persons depart from their community, undergo trials, and later return to be integrated as mature adults once again. Since this kind of plot is not typical for popular materials in America, many analysts of myth have concluded that ours is a postmythical culture.

The acceptance of materials like the bionic tales, however, indicates that Americans have not moved beyond mythical consciousness. On the contrary, there has emerged in place of the classical monomyth a distinctively *American monomyth.* Its impress may be seen in thousands of popular-culture artifacts:

> *A community in a harmonious paradise is threatened by evil: normal institutions fail to contend with this threat: a selfless superhero emerges to renounce temptations and carry out the redemptive task: aided by fate, his decisive victory restores the community to its paradisal condition: the superhero then recedes into obscurity.*

Whereas the classical monomyth was based on rites of initiation, the American monomyth derives from tales of redemption. It secularizes the Judeo-Christian redemption dramas that have arisen on American soil, combining elements from the selfless servant who impassively gives his life for others and the zealous crusader who destroys evil. The supersaviors in pop culture function as replacements for the Christ figure, whose credibility was eroded by scientific rationalism. But their superhuman abilities reflect a hope of divine, redemptive powers that science has never eradicated from the popular mind. The presentation of such figures in popular culture has the power to evoke fan loyalties that should be compared with more traditional forms of religious zeal; among those who resist overt fandom, the superheroes seem to offer a *mythic massage* that soothes and satisfies. It imparts the relaxing feeling that society can actually be redeemed by antidemocratic means.

We cannot look long at monomyth material without raising questions about its symptomatic meaning. What is the significance of the contradictions between modern sexual liberation and monomythic renunciation, between the hope of supernatural redemption and the claim of secularization, and between the depiction of impotent democratic institutions and the reliance on extralegal superheroes? Whether one accepts these paradoxes or not, and whatever the intent of their creators, the power of the popular media by which they are conveyed is undeniable. We are not at all convinced by Marshall McLuhan's facile claim that the medium alone is the message.[4]

In the chapters that follow, we examine individual artifacts from popular culture, providing what Harvey Cox calls an "iconography of popular culture" to decipher the moral and social meanings of recurrent symbols.[5] Piece by piece, the fragments of the American monomyth are serially assembled. Links among *Star Trek, Playboy, Snow White,* and *Jaws* are initially elusive but prove to be mythically coherent. We do not claim that every item in popular culture is monomythic since some do, in fact, transcend conventional formulas. But such inventions do not negate the dominant conventions nor detract from the mythical coherence that holds disparate materials together. The prevalence of the American monomyth remains in spite of exceptions.

In seeking a precise grasp of monomythic content, we occasionally compare pop materials with items drawn from "high culture"—usually the pop culture of an earlier era. We do not feel that classical literature is always superior in its insights to current pop material or that the two realms should be kept in hermetically sealed compartments. Both high and popular culture share a concern with the myths of their time, each revealing them in distinctive ways. For the vigor of each and the health of the larger culture that contains them both, it is preferable that they be responsive to one another. In any event, our concern is with content and mythic relevance rather than aesthetic merit.

For the past several years we have sat, so to speak, at the feet of monomythic schoolmarms like Jaime Sommers. We have found ourselves getting rowdy as we listened to the ripping noises of their "gentle approach." We confess that we have committed several acts of vandalism against the media center at the monomythic schoolhouse. We hope that others will join our gang.

The American Monomyth

I

"Star Trek" and the Bubble-gum Fallacy

> ". . . The *Enterprise* IS a cosmic 'Mary Worth,' meddling her way across the galaxy, solving problems as she goes."—David Gerrold, *Star Trek* scriptwriter[1]

In popdom's frantic realm, lasting popularity is always sought but seldom achieved. Pop fame can be as ephemeral as any fashion—in the top ten this week, off the charts next week, never to be heard or remembered again. But occasionally pop productions achieve a sliver of immortality that stretches into months, years, or decades. These are the bronzed monuments, standing out amid mountains of evanescent cotton candy. Such artifacts must surely resonate with the psyches of their pop audiences, offering significant clues to the human fears and yearnings of their time. Yet the source of enduring popularity remains puzzling, even to the experts whose performances attract mass adulation. One of the more enduring and mysterious masterpieces of current pop culture is *Star Trek*.

Seventy-nine episodes of *Star Trek* were produced by Gene Roddenberry between 1966 and 1968. They have since been replayed by local stations all over the country to viewers numbering in the millions. There is even a cartoon version of *Star Trek,* which plays to the kiddies on Saturday mornings. When NBC first thought of canceling the program in 1967, they were inundated with protest mail that forced a renewal for one more year. In an unprecedented manner the series has evoked the spontaneous development of fan clubs and locally produced fan magazines dedicated to keeping the *Star Trek* vision alive. William Shatner, who played the lead role of Captain Kirk, commented on the strange "fanaticism" of these fans.

> I really don't understand it. . . . I recently attended two of the "*Star Trek*" conventions in New York—they have them all over the country, Chicago, Los Angeles, and San Diego. Frankly, it was an experience that was perhaps unique. I was asked to appear in an auditorium of some 8,000 to 10,000 people, there just because of "*Star Trek*." They were crazed. I don't know why the fanaticism has attached itself to the show. You wouldn't believe what they have at these conventions. . . . Why this is happening defies rational explanation.[2]

When one discusses the appeal of *Star Trek* with its less dedicated viewers, the term "bubble gum" is frequently used. Although college students across the country reportedly watch the replays with addictive regularity, even forsaking science labs for TV lounges, their explanation of its appeal tends to be cryptic: "It's just entertainment. Just bubble gum." Which leads to the question of this chapter—and the book. How could material that exercises so powerful an appeal be mere entertainment? What does "fanaticism" have to do with "bubble gum"?

I

The serious investigation of bubble gum has not advanced very far. But we can report the following. The term "bubble gum" is used to describe a type of teen rock music that is supposed to lack significance. It is music devoid of message, musical innovation, or any other sign of serious intent. This seems analogous to the experience of chewing bubble gum, a genuinely diversionary activity unable to impart mythic vision or alter the chewer's consciousness. Hence the response, "It's just bubble gum," implies that material such as *Star Trek* is pure diversion. It has no message or significance.

The most eloquent and learned exponent of the bubble-gum approach among recent analysts of popular culture is Herbert J. Gans. He contends that ". . . people pay much less attention to the media and are much less swayed by its contents than the critics, who are highly sensitive to verbal and other symbolic materials, believe. They use the media for diversion and would not think of applying its content to their own lives." The Columbia sociologist feels that while people may be glued to the TV watching a program like *Star Trek,* they are not thinking about it any more than they would about the bubble gum they are chewing. He concludes that ". . . popular culture . . . tends to go in one eye and out the other. . . ." Since these materials never lodge in the brain, they must be harmless: ". . . popular culture does not harm either high culture, the people who prefer it, or the society as a whole." Indeed, it plays a positive role, providing ". . . temporary respite from everyday life. . . ."[3]

Above all, Gans insists, it is wrong to ascribe harmful effects to media fantasies. In contrast to alarmists who suggest that "bubble gum" with violent content may be harmful, Gans implies there are no influential models of destructive behavior in popular culture. The violence, social tensions, and public irresponsibility that some have linked to popular culture are actually not widespread. "If the media had as significant an effect on aggressive behavior as the critics and some researchers charge, a constantly increasing tide of violence should have manifested itself in America since the emergence of mass media, but historical studies suggest that violent crime has declined over this period." That would be news to the FBI. Actually, the murder rate is now ten times higher than it was in 1900 and has doubled in the years between 1968 and 1974. But even if there are a few problems in bubble-gum land, Gans insists that popular culture has nothing to do with them: ". . . Popular culture content does not have the effects attributed to it, except perhaps on a minority of people who consume it in other than the accepted ways. Because of its lack of overall effect, it cannot be considered a source of danger to the society or to a democratic form of government."[4]

The oddity of Gans' argument is that while popular-culture materials are seen as harmless, they nevertheless perform socially beneficial functions.

> Popular culture has played a useful role in the process of enabling ordinary people to become individuals, develop their identities, and find ways of achieving creativity and self-expression. . . . The issues are rarely presented as they appear in ordinary life, and problems are solved much too easily, but still, they offer ideas to the audience which it can apply to its own situation.[5]

This contradictory union of qualities is puzzling. Popular-culture artifacts like *Star Trek* are too trivial to cause harm, yet capable of effecting good. Programs that "go in one eye and out the other" can help our citizens gain self-identity and true creativity.

We would like to label this line of argument *the bubble-gum fallacy.* It paradoxically ascribes trivial and instrumental qualities to popular-culture materials possessing psychically resonant themes. It suggests that popular culture, while powerfully influential in benign areas of behavior, lacks the power to corrupt and destroy—an obvious contradiction. This stance discourages any investigation of the power of such materials to shape consciousness and thus indirectly influence behavior. Above all, the bubble-gum fallacy obscures the mythic qualities of popular-culture materials that render them attractive to the deeper levels of consciousness. Audiences can thereby be hooked on a program or comic strip without ever knowing or asking why. Perhaps a look at the world of *Star Trek,* with its thousands of dedicated fans, will offer some clues to this curious phenomenon.

II

Does *Star Trek* have a message? Are its concept of the universe, its scheme for the mission of the *Enterprise,* and its array of characters essentially trivial and meaningless? Does it have a message beyond the brilliantly entertaining presentation of space travel?

The United Starship *Enterprise* is on a five-year mission to explore the galaxy. She is one of twelve starship-class spaceships under orders of the United Federation of Planet Earth, with a crew of 430 men and women and a gross weight of 190,000 tons. Since her speed on space-warp drive far exceeds that of light, the *Enterprise* explores and carries out assignments, making only infrequent contact with Federation authorities. Given this format, the episodes permit the *Enterprise* to intervene on her own initiative in the affairs of other planets, playing the role of cosmic sheriff, problem-solver, and plenipotentiary.

The leader of this semi-autonomous space probe is Captain James T. Kirk, the youngest man ever to be assigned a starship command, and a brilliant, irresistibly attractive and hard-driving leader who pushes himself and his crew beyond human limits. He always leads the landing party on its perilous missions to unexplored planets but, like a true superhero, regularly escapes after risking battle with monsters or enemy spaceships.

Kirk's main cohort, Mr. Spock, is cut even more clearly from superhero material. He is half human and half Vulcan, which gives him ". . . extra-keen senses, prodigious strength, an eidetic memory, the capacity to perform lightning calculations, telepathy, imperturbability, immunity to certain diseases and dangers, vast knowledge–especially of science." As played by Leonard Nimoy, Spock is a strong, ascetic character of pure rationality, his emotions kept strictly under control by his Vulcan temperament. The emotional tension is hinted at by his slightly Satanic appearance, including pointed ears. A Spock feature that has fascinated the female writers of the stories is *pon farr,* the periodic rutting season which renders all Vulcan minds powerless and threatens death if union with an appropriate partner is not achieved. Nimoy reported that the question of Spock's extraordinary sex appeal emerged ". . . almost any time I talked to somebody in the press. . . . I never give it a thought . . . to try to deal with the question of Mr. Spock as a sex symbol is silly."[6] One wonders whether even television stars use a little bubble gum on occasion.

All the remarkable powers of Spock, Kirk, and his crew are required to deal with the adversaries of the good ship *Enterprise.* The *Star Trek* universe is populated by two vicious races of bad guys. The "Romulans" are similar to the Vulcans in ability and technological development but are ". . . highly militaristic, aggressive by nature, ruthless in warfare, and do not take captives." The "Klingons" are even worse, though less intelligent. David Gerrold's description is delightful: "Klingons are professional villains. They are nasty, vicious, brutal, and merciless. They don't bathe regularly, they don't use deodorants or brush their teeth. . . . A Klingon is a good person to invite to a rape–or even a murder, provided it's your own. . . . Klingons build their battlecruisers without toilets . . . drop litter in the streets . . . pick their teeth in public. And those are their good points. . . ." Clearly such villains are ". . . more symbolic than individual,"[7] threatening the peace of the galaxy in a way that requires constant vigilance by the *Enterprise.*

To counter these threats and to cope with the weird, aggressive powers that seem to inhabit all earthlike planets of the universe, the *Enterprise* acts as galactic redeemer in episode after episode. As Gerrold explains, ". . . The *Enterprise* IS a cosmic 'Mary Worth,' meddling her way across the galaxy . . . to spread truth, justice, *and the American Way* to the far corners of the universe." The format of *Star Trek* accentuates this role by keeping Kirk and his ship out of communication with Earth. The captain becomes ". . . the sole arbiter of Federation law wherever he traveled . . . a law unto himself." The story thus fits into the genre of the isolated zealous hero or nation, answerable only to a higher law and fighting for right whenever called to do so, a theme America has tried to act out in recent times. And like a sophisticated American, Captain Kirk does not allow himself to become "paranoid" about the enemies who are out to get him or the planets he must destroy in the fray. In a spirit worthy of Halberstam's "The Best and the Brightest," Kirk's ". . . enemy is an adversary to be met with strength and even destroyed, if necessary, but not necessarily a villain with whom no reconciliation is possible. Peace really is his [Kirk's] profession."[8]

The moral vision of *Star Trek* thus partakes of the spirit and rhetoric of the *Pax Americana.* Its basic moral principle is zeal for the mission. This is in effect what authors Lichtenberg, Marshak, and Winston celebrate in their comprehensive fan book, *Star Trek Lives!* They affirm an admirable ". . . equality of moral stature" on the parts of Spock and Kirk. "Each of them is that rarest of all things among men: a man of unbroken integrity . . . each remains dedicated to the striving, extravagantly willing to pay the price." But when one measures this moral quality against standards forbidding deceit, adultery, and violence, the lack of restraint is striking. What we have here is moral zeal attached solely to the mission and to their own vision of what amounts to "the American Way." It is a zeal transcending both due process and the moral code of the Federation's "noninterference directive," which Kirk has sworn on pain of death to uphold. This directive is consistently broken in *Star Trek* episodes when "necessary" for the fulfillment of the mission. It is an effective format for reinstating in the realm of fantasy some of the American values that floundered in the sixties against ugly obstacles in Vietnam. Dedication to the ideals would alone suffice, in fantasy if not in reality. Zeal for one's own value system justifies the intervention in someone else's. One episode that Gerrold claims is patterned after the *Pueblo* incident bears the message ". . . that the ends justify the means; because our ends are just, then no matter what means we choose, our means will be just too." Thus it is understandable that fans Lichtenberg, Marshak, and Winston would admire this kind of ". . . fierce dedication, each to his own philosophy and vision of life, and the integrity of character that supports that dedication." The impact of this kind of uncompromising zeal on other cultures is worth noting. Gerrold writes that the cumulative message of *Star Trek* is that ". . . if a local culture is tested and found wanting in the eyes of a starship captain, he may make such changes as he feels necessary."[9]

The correlations between the *Star Trek* format and recent tragedies in American history are troublesome and painful, especially for those who happen to enjoy the élan and imagination of this series. It would be foolish to blame programs like *Star Trek* for the debacle of Vietnam. What fascinates us is the connection between these correlations and the peculiar commitment a series like this evokes from its most dedicated fans. Richard Slotkin's concept of "National Mythology" provides an important clue.[10] He shows how the historical experience of a nation provides metaphors and stories which assume mythic proportions in literature and art, so that the resultant myth exercises a reciprocal pressure on succeeding generations. It shapes the sense of reality and is itself reshaped by subsequent experience. Thus a national mythology may come to exercise the same unconscious appeal as the archetypal myths of which they are variants.

It is perhaps characteristic of our current mood, having experienced the collapse of *Star Trek*'s dynamic sense of mission, that its successor in the demoralized 1970s should be *Space 1999*. Its setting is *Moonbase Alpha,* which originally had the task of monitoring lunar storage sites for atomic wastes shuttled from Earth. When the garbage mysteriously explodes, the Moon is blasted out of its orbit and careens through space. So rather than playing the galactic sheriff role, the drifting base repeatedly suffers siege from fan-tastic, malevolent life forms. In "The Last Sunset" episode there is a critique of the kind of zealous internationalism that marked *Star Trek,* as a crew member goes berserk and raves dangerously about establishing a new urban civilization that could colonize the galaxy. But the mythical scheme of redemption through violence is retained as the madman is beaten into sensibility by "Sheriff" Koenig, *Alpha*'s commander. The saloon brawls of the cowboy Western are transposed to outer space as the antidote to galactic crusading.

The "Guardians of Space" title assigned to a collection of *1999* programs is hardly descriptive: The fumbling technicians are hard pressed to keep from falling off the Moon. In one of its episodes a mysterious force sucks up the moonbase's energy sources. Lightbulbs dim, appliances stop functioning, and crew members freeze. Technician Anton Zoref has mysteriously been taken over by some unknown force, his body absorbing energy at a most improbable rate. Koenig demands that the force be ". . . rooted out of Zoref's body! While we've got a chance of controlling it, we'll destroy it—immediately." This zealous resolve does not have to be enacted because Zoref stumbles into a nuclear furnace and suicidally consumes its energy, ending the crisis. The chilly, de-electrified base seems to stand for Britain or America running out of fuel, and only violence can redeem the situation. The line "An alien force is loose somewhere on *Alpha*" expresses the mood of the series quite aptly. Interplanetary redemption has been succeeded by a tedious quest for mere survival in a paranoid universe, with Commander Koenig as the only one capable of managing even that.[11]

Despite the discrepancies in their quality and sophistication, both *Space 1999* and *Star Trek* appear to be traditional reworkings of American ideology. But as one might expect, there is a hitch to this burgeoning mythic theory of ours.

III

At the surface level *Star Trek* stories seem to defy interpretation as mythic material with powerful unconscious appeal. The entire series takes a singularly dim view of myths, not to speak of legends, fables, and their primitive religious accouterments. *Star*

Trek celebrates the freeing of the human spirit from superstition and narrow-mindedness. It wears the cloak of empirical science. It purports to be a future chapter in what Joseph Campbell called "the wonder story of mankind's coming to maturity." Campbell, the famous historian of world myths, argues that with the coming of the scientific age, mankind has been set free from myths. "The spell of the past, the bondage of tradition, was shattered with sure and mighty strokes. The dream-web of myth fell away; the mind opened to full waking consciousness; and modern man emerged from ancient ignorance, like a butterfly from its cocoon, or like the sun at dawn from the womb of mother night." Producer Gene Roddenberry would surely agree. The antimythic bias in *Star Trek* is clearly visible in the following episode.[12]

"Who Mourns for Adonais?"

The U.S.S. *Enterprise* is approaching an unexplored M Class planet when an immense, masculine face appears on the scanner screen and stops the ship in midspace by a tremendous exertion of energy. Captain Kirk leads the exploration party of Spock, Chekov, McCoy, Scott, and the ravishingly beautiful archaeologist Carolyn Palamas. They find themselves in a Greek-like temple complex. A magnificent, muscular man whose face they had seen on the scanner rises to greet them with the words, "I am Apollo. . . . You are here to worship me as your fathers worshipped me before you." When Kirk asks what he requires, he insists he is Apollo and demands "loyalty," "tribute," and "worship" in return for a "human life as simple and pleasureful as it was those thousands of years ago on our beautiful Earth so far away." Kirk replies, "We're not in the habit of bending our knees to everyone we meet with a bag of tricks." When they refuse obeisance, Apollo's wrath melts their phaser guns and injures Scott, who has attempted to protect Carolyn from amorous advances. She volunteers to go with Apollo and quickly falls in love with him.

Captain Kirk theorizes that an unknown race capable of space travel had come to ancient Greece with the ability ". . . to alter their shapes at will and command great energy." This theory is corroborated by Apollo's explanation to Carolyn:

"Your fathers turned away from us until we were only memories. A god cannot survive as a memory. We need awe, worship. We need love."

Carolyn replies, "You really consider yourself to be a god?"

He laughs, ". . . In a real sense we were gods. The power of life and death was ours. When men turned from us, we could have struck down from Olympus and destroyed them. But we had no wish to destroy. So we came back to the stars again."

After making love to Carolyn, Apollo returns to the other members of the crew. The enraged Scott attacks him, only to be struck down with the blue-hot streak that lashed from Apollo's finger. This provokes Kirk to declare war on the god, and Kirk too is struck down. When Apollo disappears to recharge his power source, they decide to attack him in hopes of wearing him down. The *Enterprise* crew meanwhile prepares to fire phasers against Apollo's force field. When Carolyn appears again, Kirk tries to cope with her infatuation.

The lovely archaeologist relates Apollo's message, "He wants to guard . . . and provide for us the rest of our lives. He can do it."

Kirk reminds her, "You've got work to do."

"Work?" Carolyn replies.

Kirk insists, "He thrives on love, on worship. . . . We can't give him worship. None of us, especially you. . . . Reject him! You must!"

"I love him!"

"All our lives, here and on the ship, depend on you."

"No! Not on me."

"On you, Lieutenant. Accept him–and you condemn the crew of the *Enterprise* to slavery!"

She stares at him blankly.

Kirk pleads with her to remember ". . . what you are! A bit of flesh and blood afloat in illimitable space. The only thing that is truly yours is this small moment of time you share with the rest of humanity. . . . That's where our duty lies. . . . Do you understand me?"

Carolyn comes to her senses when she discovers Apollo will not accept her liberated intellectual interests. This time the god lashes out in fury at her. But the incandescing phaser beams from the *Enterprise* strike his power source just in time, reducing him to a "man-size being."

"I would have loved you as a father his children," Apollo says, in anguish. "Did I ask so much of you?"

Kirk's reply is gentle. "We have outgrown you," he says. "You asked for what we can no longer give."

Denied the worship so necessary for his being, Apollo's body begins to lose substance, and for the first time he admits the time of the gods "is gone. Take me home to the stars on the wind."

This episode bears a clear message that the era of myths is over, that retreating into slavery to the gods of the past would be terrible. Moreover, the episode suggests that the ancient myths can be scientifically explained by assuming that space travelers played the role of gods. This theme has enormous appeal, judging from the popularity of works such as *Chariots of the Gods*.[13] The episode implies that meaning is purely of this world, any threshold to mysterious, transcendent reality firmly denied. In contrast to the illusive message of myths and religions, the meaning of Carolyn Palamas' life is simply her "duty" to the only reality of which she can be sure, the "humanity" she shares. This conviction of Captain Kirk fits the spirit of the entire series. It is unthinkable that he or his crew, not to speak of the strictly scientific Spock, would give credence to myths for a moment.

Yet the story line of this and other episodes follows a mythic pattern. David Gerrold, one of the writers of *Star Trek* scripts, defined *Star Trek* as ". . . a set of fables–morality plays, entertainments, and diversions about contemporary man, but set against a science-fiction background. *The background is subordinate to the fable.*" This can be documented at those points in which dramatic coherence–that is, hewing to the mythic story line–caused scriptwriters to depart from the standards of scientific accuracy. For instance, the attractive young crew of the *Enterprise* never ages despite journeys through the light-year distances of outer space. Members of the bridge crew are regularly shaken off their seats by enemy torpedoes despite the fact that shock waves would not carry past a spaceship's artificial-gravity field. The scientific liberties are taken for dramatic effect, creating ". . . action, adventure, fun, entertainment, and thought-provoking statements."[14] These are actually mythical elements that appeal to an audience schooled in a particular mythical tradition.

When one compares the themes of the series with the content of classical myths, similarities are immediately apparent. Isolating such content from the genesis and function of myths, we mention three patterns visible in "Who Mourns for Adonais?" The first is *saga,* which features a protagonist journeying to unknown and dangerous regions, undergoing trials to test his strength and wit. In the classical monomyth delineated by Joseph Campbell, a journey is undertaken in response to the requirement for each human to move from childhood to maturity through "the crooked lanes of his own spiritual labyrinth." But in materials embodying the American monomyth, the saga of maturation tends to be replaced by the defense against malevolent attacks upon innocent communities. Gene Roddenberry's original prospectus for *Star Trek,* featuring the format of "Wagon Train to the Stars," aims at saga. He planned the series to be ". . . built around characters who travel to other worlds and meet the jeopardy and adventure which become our stories." This correlates with the announcement at the beginning of *Star Trek* programs, that the mission of the *Enterprise* is ". . . to explore strange new worlds, to seek out new civilizations, to boldly go where no man has gone before."[15] Thus in the saga of Apollo's planet, the *Enterprise* had to be mortally endangered by the gigantic face on the scanner, and it was essential for the protagonists Kirk and Spock to leave their command post and come face to face with the foe. It was obviously bad military and space-travel strategy, as many critics have pointed out. No sensible commander would send himself and the key technical officers on a landing party like this. But it is essential to the saga format and thus is characteristic of almost every episode.

The second mythic pattern visible in *Star Trek* is *sexual renunciation.* The protagonist in some mythical sagas must renounce previous sexual ties for the sake of his trials. He must avoid entanglements and temptations that inevitably arise from Sirens or Loreleis in the course of his travels. Thus Lieutenant Palamas is tested in the episode with Apollo, her sexual liaison endangering the survival of the *Enterprise.* After she renounces her passion, the saga can get back on course. In the classical monomyth this theme plays a subsidiary role in the initiation or testing phase. The protagonist may encounter sexual temptation symbolizing ". . . that pushing, self-protective, malodorous, carnivorous, lecherous fever which is the very nature of the organic cell," as Campbell points out. Yet the "ultimate adventure" is the ". . . mystical marriage . . . of the triumphant hero-soul with the Queen Goddess" of knowledge.[16] In the current American embodiments of mythic renunciation there is a curious rejection of sexual union as a primary value.

In *Star Trek* each hero is locked into a renunciatory pattern closely related to the mission. On long expeditions in outer space, there is, for example, no intrinsic reason why the captain would not be accompanied by his wife and family. This was customary for the masters of some large sailing vessels in the era of extended voyages. But that would violate the mythic paradigm. So Roddenberry describes the renunciation pattern: "Long ago Captain Kirk consciously ruled out any possibility of any romantic interest while aboard the ship. It is an involvement he feels he simply could never risk. In a very real sense he is 'married' to his ship and his responsibilities as captain of her." In numerous episodes Kirk is in the situation Carolyn Palamas faced, forced to choose between an attractive sexual partner and his sense of duty to his mission. The authors of *Star Trek Lives!* report that female fans

> . . . vicariously thrill to Kirk's sexual exploits with gorgeous females of every size, shape and type–from the stunning lady lawyers, biologists and doctors who have loved him, to the vicious and breath-taking Elaan of Troyius, who ruled a planet but was willing to risk destroying her entire solar system for him. . . . Many see Kirk's loves as having a tragic element. There is affection and warmth in his response, and evidently the capacity for deep love. But very often the situation is impossible. He loses not through his faults but through his virtues, because of the demanding life he has chosen.

They go on to describe the renunciation of sexual bonds for the sake of loyalty to the *Enterprise* and its crew. "Time and again, he had to make a choice between a woman and his ship–and his ship always won."[17]

This renunciation of sexual love for the sake of loyalty to one's comrades goes far beyond the classical monomyth. It is seen perhaps most clearly in the person of Spock. He is loyal to Kirk and his comrades at the expense of risking his life for them again and again, but he persistently resists the temptation of entanglements with the opposite sex. Nurse Christine Chapel, a beautiful, talented crew member who is hopelessly in love with Spock, receives the cold shoulder in story after story. Here is a man ". . . capable of the prodigious outpouring of passion triggered by the irresistible *pon farr* and yet incapable of lasting emotional ties" with women.[18] Sex is an autonomous force here, distinct from Spock's personality and capable of destroying his ability to reason. Since he cannot integrate it with his personality, it must be rigidly repressed until it overpowers him in the rutting season. Spock bears within his person the temptation threatening every saga with disaster—it must be fiercely renounced for the mission to succeed. Such a motif may not be true to life, and it is certainly improbable that there are sophisticated planets with *pon farr* rites derived from Puritan fantasies, but it is true to the mythic paradigm.

Star Trek's successor, *Space 1999,* presents an even less subtle renunciation pattern. In an episode taking place on Piri, the illusory Planet of Peace, which lures the entire crew into imminent destruction, Commander Koenig must first resist Dr. Helena Russell. She nuzzles close to him at the prospect of finding an Earth-like habitation that will allow them to leave the seemingly doomed *Alpha.* Koenig, not trusting his crew to carry out an adequate investigation, is then confronted by the lovely girl of Piri.

> She walked towards him, loose robe open so that he saw the rosebud nipples. She kissed him on the lips. It was a rebirth. All the bitterness of loss and regret ebbed away. All doubts vanished. "Piri the beautiful," he said. "Piri the end of our voyaging."

Koenig resists this temptation and returns to *Moonbase Alpha,* where his entire crew is about to depart for the sexual paradise. The girl of Piri comes, tempting him to descend, and when he joins the rest of the crew, a final temptation confronts him. Dr. Helena Russell is waiting in readiness:

> Her robe was open to the waist. She smiled as he looked down at

> her well-shaped breasts. "I've waited so long for this, John!" she sighed. She held him possessively.

Despite these open smocks, John has a redemptive plan. Leading Helena into the bushes, he administers a shock with his laser gun, and the hypnotic spell of Piri is broken. The lovely doctor ". . . looked down and saw that her robe was open. . . . She covered her breasts. Her face was crimson. Memories were returning fast."[19] It is an interesting comment on the mythic contrivance of these roles that Martin Landau, who plays Koenig, is married to Barbara Bain, the Dr. Helena Russell who must be so fiercely resisted. One of the curious features of modern monomythic drama is that even marriage, a perennial form of real sexual relationships, must be renounced by superheroes to gain redemptive powers.

The third mythical pattern in *Star Trek* is *redemption.* In the classical monomyth the beautiful maiden must be redeemed from the clutches of the sea monster, the endangered city spared from its peril, and the protagonist redeemed by fateful interventions in the nick of time. This pattern is much more diffuse in the classical monomyth than in modern materials standing closer to the American pattern. The classical hero may experience supernatural aid as he crosses the threshold into the realm of initiatory adventure and then returns, and he may confront trials embodying the redemption of others. But his own redemption takes the form of gaining mature wisdom, achieving atonement with his father, enjoying union with the goddess, and returning home with benefits for his people. The redemption scheme in materials like *Star Trek* has nothing to do with the maturation process. It fits rather the pattern of selfless crusading to redeem others. This form of selfless idealism has been elaborated most extensively by Ernest Tuveson in *Redeemer Nation.* As so frequently in American history, the *Enterprise* sense of high calling leads to violations of its "noninterference directive." If Kirk and his crew encounter an endangered planet, their sense of duty impels them to intervene. It may not be legal, or right, or even sensible, but the zealous imperative to redeem is all-pervasive. While Gerrold may have overstated in claiming that among the seventy-nine *Star Trek* episodes, ". . . there never was a script in which the *Enterprise*'s mission or goals were questioned,"[20] he has accurately described the series as a whole.

While the *Enterprise* regularly plays the mythic redeemer role, Mr. Spock embodies it in a particularly powerful way. His half Vulcan origin makes him a godlike figure, peculiarly capable of effecting redemption. Spock consults his computer with superhuman speed to devise the technique of saving galaxies and men from prodigious threats, leading the audience to view him with a kind of reverence that traditionally has been reserved for gods. Leonard Nimoy's interview, approvingly cited by the authors of *Star Trek Lives!*, points toward audience yearnings for an omniscient redeemer. The viewer sees Spock as someone

> . . . who knows something about me that nobody else knows. Here's a person that *understands* me in a way that nobody else understands me. Here's a person that I'd like to be able to spend time with and talk to because *he would know what I mean when I tell him how I feel.* He would have insight that nobody else seems to have. . . .[21]

In short, Spock is perceived as a god, which matches the requirements of the mythical pattern, namely that without a superhuman agency of some sort, there is no true redemption.

The central character of *Space 1999,* Commander John Koenig, is presented with no less redemptive facility. "His sometimes icy detachment had persuaded terrified men and women that they could still hope in spite of the cataclysm that had blotted out all thought of normal life. His essential humanity radiated throughout *Moonbase Alpha,* a visible lifeline for the weak and a constant source of reassurance for the strong." In episode after episode Koenig is the only crew member who understands the demands of the redemptive task. He is constantly surrounded by a community of 310 associates who become utterly unrealistic and softhearted in times of threat. In the Piri episode he finally redeems the entire crew by taking the beautiful, screaming temptress and throwing her body against the idolatrous altar, shouting, "See what passes for life on Piri."[22] In the massive explosion that follows, the entire crew is returned to its senses. And to relieve the cruelty of this brutal redemption, the program reveals that the girl of Piri had really been nothing but an automaton. But the point remains: Violent redemption, achieved at the cost of renouncing sexual temptation, is eloquently expressed in both *Space 1999* and *Star Trek*.

These mythical themes help us to focus sharply on a paradox evident in *Star Trek*. While its themes occasionally contest the mythical world view, its format and stories are thoroughly mythical. To use Joseph Campbell's terms, it is as if space-age man, having emerged from the "cocoon" of mythic ignorance, awoke to find himself still enmeshed "in the dream-web of myth." This paradox of *Star Trek* reveals a *myth of mythlessness*. Its implicit claim to be antimythical and purely scientific is itself a myth—that is, a set of unconsciously held, unexamined premises. The *Star Trek* format may be a new set of wineskins, but the mythic fermentation within is as old as Apollo.

IV

How can this paradoxical myth of mythlessness be sustained? How does *Star Trek* convince its audience, consisting of an unusually high proportion of scientists and technologists, with stories that are so brazenly mythical and unscientific? Consider the episode "Spock's Brain" as an example. The beautiful Kara is mysteriously transported to the *Enterprise,* touches her bracelet to knock everyone unconscious, takes Spock to the operating room, and removes his brain. When Dr. McCoy reports that no known surgical technique could restore the brain and that within three days Spock's body would deteriorate, Kirk responds that he will find the woman with the incredible knowledge: "I'll force it out of her!" He instinctively decides which unlikely planet to investigate and encounters Kara in her underground city, which worships "the Controller," now Spock's brain, which maintains the vast life-support system. The dull-witted women hold their men in primitive subjugation on the cold surface of the planet. A marvelous message helmet inherited from the men of ancient times gave Kara the directions for the brain transplant. The *Enterprise* landing crew breaks free from their guards and, directed by Spock's computer voice, enters the control room. Kirk wrests the bracelet from Kara, touches the proper blue button, and disables the painful electronic headbands by which the Amazons hold men in bondage to "pain and [sexual] delight." McCoy uses the magic helmet to reconnect Spock's brain. The sobbing Kara is certain that her domineering cohorts will die without a "Controller" maintaining their luxurious environment below, but the *Enterprise*'s technical-aid teams bring the sexes together on the cold surface of the planet. Kirk is certain that the sex war is over now because ". . . cuddling is so much warmer than wood fires."[23] This sexual version of *Pax Americana* is as wildly improbable in plot and timing as the mythical elements of Amazons and magical knowledge would lead one to suspect. But it is mythically coherent, combining the risk of saga with a timely redemption in the form of resurrection, weaving in the motif of sexual renunciation as Kirk and his crew avoid falling prey to the sexual delights of the Amazons. All this helps sharpen the question: Why doesn't the audience discern the transparency of the myth of mythlessness in an episode like this? Why do science students desert their labs for such Amazonian fare?

One key to the acceptance of *Star Trek* seems to be its emphasis on technical exactitude in the details of production. Roddenberry called this the "Believability Factor" and felt that it would be crucial to the acceptance of the show. "Our audiences simply won't believe that this is the bridge of a starship," he stated, "unless the characters on it seem at least as coordinated and efficient as the blinking lights and instrumentation around them." The effort paid off in the enthusiasm of audiences composed of scientists, technicians, even space-center personnel, in the inclusion of a *Star Trek* program in the Smithsonian archives, and in the display of an *Enterprise* model adjacent to *The Spirit of St. Louis*. Highly educated fans like Lichtenberg, Marshak, and Winston speak of "the atmosphere of believability" in *Star Trek:* ". . . The ship lived. It flew. It went to real places. Where other science-fiction shows tried to gloss over scientific inaccuracies, *Star Trek* fought to create a wholly believable technology and a real universe." *Star Trek Lives!* extends this confusion between fact and fantasy to a conflation of the actors and their roles. Kirk's nobility of character is reflected in Shatner's ". . . real life in the tireless dedication to his work. . . ." Leonard Nimoy's battles with directors to retain a valid characterization of Spock led fans to ask, "Does this sound like Spock? It does to us."[24]

But at least one crucial caveat is called for here. While exactitude and gadgetry are parts of science, they do not constitute the degree of scientific objectivity capable of calling one's own myths into question. The essence of the scientific outlook is a critical state of mind, which is willing to examine all dogmas, including those of science itself. Karl Popper, a major interpreter of science, has even argued that ". . . what we call 'science' is differentiated from the older myths, not by being something different from a myth, but by being accompanied by a second order tradition—that of critically discussing the myth." This is conspicuously lacking in *Star Trek* because the mythical formulas so crucial to the plots are never called into question. Indeed, the myth of mythlessness ensures that they not even be acknowledged. Instead of a rigorously self-critical scientific outlook, *Star Trek* offers *pseudo-empiricism,* an empirical veneer of gadgetry, and crew talk applied to a mythical superstructure.[25]

One of the most interesting elements of pseudo-empiricism in *Star Trek* is the "Idic" philosophy that Spock brings from Vulcan. It is a vague series of ideas, including repression of sexual energies into a rut cycle, concentrating on deriving personal profit from competition rather than being obsessed with winning, and placing one's energies in technological manipulations. But the authors of *Star Trek Lives!* are impressed by the fact that ". . . the optimism of the Idic is implicit in the fact that this philosophy is practiced, lived, *realized* by a planet-wide culture, the Vulcans, and it works!" Whoa! Works where? Realized by what planet-wide culture? On television or in reality? The writers go on: "The Vulcan nature is said to be more violently warlike than that of humans, but their world has enjoyed peace for hundreds of years. A large part of *Star Trek* fandom is energized by the belief that this Vulcan concept of peace is the only one which will help our world survive. . . ."[26]

The language of this citation deserves close scrutiny. Under its pseudo-empirical cloak, *Star Trek* is presenting an alternative reality system so powerful and credible that a "belief" is "energized." And it is, of course, the "only one" capable of world redemption.

This is the language not of science or technology, but of religion. The appropriation of this kind of belief system by individuals is described at great length by the authors of *Star Trek Lives!* They cite examples of individuals deriving a sense of courage and meaning from encountering this reality system. "In *Star Trek,* the fan escapes not from reality but to reality—to a reality where failure is only a prelude to success, where strength, determination, and integrity can earn triumph just as Spock has won his battle by virtue of his strength."[27] In other words, there is a reality in the *Star Trek* fantasy that transcends petty problems, and it thus provides a means of salvation. The television programs communicate this higher reality to the audience, evoking faith and courage. Such language, suitable for inclusion in William James' *Varieties of Religious Experience,* leads us to the pop-religion theme of the next chapter. Before continuing, however, it is necessary to suggest the need for a new theory of communication.

V

Despite the bubble-gum fallacy and the myth of mythlessness, pop-culture artifacts like *Star Trek* are developing visions of life and destiny capable of evoking powerful loyalties in at least some audience members. Pseudo-empiricism allows this to take place, convincing the audience that it is witnessing advanced science. As we confront the strange believability of such materials, there is need for a critical theory capable of cutting through the scientific veneer to the core, which unsuspectingly gives religious vitality to pop-culture artifacts. This veneer is growing denser and more difficult to penetrate.

When modern television was in its pilot stages in 1938, E. B. White wrote perceptively about the way the alternative reality in the picture box would someday threaten to displace the real world. "A door closing, heard over the air, a face contorted, seen in a panel of light, these will emerge as the real and the true. And when we bang the door of our own cell or look into another's face, the impression will be of mere artifice." In the very year that White uttered these prophetic words, an alarming confirmation was provided by Orson Welles' radio drama, "Invasion from

Mars." Welles and scriptwriter Howard Koch had taken H. G. Wells' *War of the Worlds* and adapted it for the *Mercury Theatre* by presenting it as a series of radio bulletins. Koch chose Grover's Mill, New Jersey, as the site of the fictional Martian invasion. The program opened with the announcement that a fictional play would follow. The play itself was interrupted three times to reiterate the fictional character of the "news bulletins." But thousands fell into panic and fled from their homes. Police received reports that Martians on their giant machines had been sighted wading the Hudson to occupy Manhattan. Hysteria spread across the nation, giving rise to bizarre incidents: One husband found his wife listening to the broadcast with a bottle of poison in her hand screaming "I'd rather die this way. . . ." A church service in Indianapolis was dismissed when a woman announced that the world was coming to an end. A man in Oakland, California, volunteered to fight the Martians. Evaluating the resultant hysteria, the New York *Daily News* applauded the simplistic solution pledged by the broadcast system: "Let all chains, all stations, avoid use of news broadcasting technique in dramatizations where there is any possibility of any listener mistaking fiction for fact."[28] The problem of "mistaking fiction for fact" was far more subtle than avoiding broadcast techniques, as White was surely aware, when he predicted that a new sense of reality would be shaped by the media.

The technical wizardry of *Star Trek* has traveled impressively toward the fulfillment of White's prophetic statement. And more is yet to come as film companies seek new means of smothering sensory channels with an ever-increasing surfeit. We now have "Quintaphonic Sound" in the movie *Tommy,* which produces an acute sensation of being in the middle of the orchestra. There is "Sensurround" in movies like *Earthquake,* producing rumbling noises that evoke the sensation of earth tremors. "Totalvision" is reportedly coming soon, on a gigantic screen five times larger than Cinemascope, confronting the puny viewer with a terrifying, gargantuan image. The perfection of Huxley's "feelies" will nicely round out the repertoire of illusions. The cumulative effect of these technomythic advances threatens to further inhibit the critical process, accentuating and broadening the trend of which *Star Trek*'s and *1999*'s pseudo-empiricism is merely a minor theme.

Who can doubt that the sound and sight and bracelets of the next generation of Amazons are real? That the odor seeping from under the seats is really a love potion capable of overpowering the inhibitions of the audience?

It is appropriate to develop a *technomythic critical theory* that will sensitize audiences to mythic content and the techniques of presentation that lend them credibility. It would thereby provide critical armor against the powerful sensory assaults by which pop culture conveys its mythic images. It would draw pop artifacts into the evaluation process from which no area of culture should ever be exempt. This might correct the curious anomaly by which the ideas of pop culture remain virtually aloof from the critical process that has painfully engaged every other area in current society. Apart from occasional and ineffective concerns over violence or sex, the media most frequently encountered by the public seem least subject to thematic examination. Public debate is warded off by the incantation, "It's just entertainment."

Douglass Cater calls for such a new theory of communication: "We must now be concerned not with Gutenberg-based concepts of truth, but with the effects of electronic communication." The technomythic critical theory we develop here will carry us in this direction. It will fulfill Cater's suggestion that attention should be given to the best, as well as the worst, in pop culture, ". . . not simply laudatory attention but a systematic examination of style and technique and message." We share his hope to ". . . raise the viewers' capacity to distinguish truth from sophistry or at least their awareness . . . of the resonance being evoked from them." This resonance is closely related, we shall argue, to basic mythic substructures that have developed over the course of time in America. One of these we choose to call the American Monomyth, a coherent plot that binds thousands of pop-culture artifacts like *Star Trek* into a single, appealing package. To piece this together out of the materials we have studied may help throw light on the way modern man ". . . chisels his little statues of perceived reality"[29] out of the new electronic environment.

II
Trekkie Religion and the Werther Effect

"The anthropologist must . . . characterize our culture as profoundly irreligious."—Clyde Kluckhohn, *Mirror for Man*[1]

Visiting a Gothic cathedral, one encounters the popular art and religion of an earlier era. From the menacing gargoyles on the exterior to the stained glass and glittering altars within—all was emblematic of the religious and social order of the public. Some of these cathedrals were under construction for as many as two hundred years, longer by far than the intended life of most modern artifacts. They aroused powerful feelings in worshippers for centuries more. Historians, theologians and philosophers have documented the gradual waning of the emotional energies which sustained the life of the great cathedrals. Their vaulted aisles will doubtless survive for years to come, but more as pilgrimage sites for the new secular tourists than as generators of the sort of vital faith which led to their construction. As Henry Adams said, "The art remained, but the energy was lost. . . ."[2]

A popular belief has thus arisen that the religious impulse is dead. It presumably lies entombed alongside pagan mythological consciousness—both victims of a patricidal, secular science. Phenomena like *Star Trek*'s popularity suggest an alternative hypothesis. Religion may have merely changed its theater and neglected to place its name on the marquee. The move from cathedral to the tube, screen, or stereo offers the faithful many of the values sought in traditional religion. Yet pseudo-empiricism's sleight-of-hand ensures that neither the new believers, the producers, nor even the sponsors comprehend that a strange, electronic religion is in the making.

Discerning the pop religion of *Star Trek* presents a dilemma similar to the one encountered with the myth of mythlessness. An antireligious bias is present in *Star Trek* materials, and in several instances one finds explicit attempts at smashing idols. It is strange that iconoclastic episodes like "The Apple" should have the power to evoke the kind of religious response from fans we cited toward the end of the previous chapter. This instructive episode inverts the Garden of Eden premise and justifies a technologically motivated "Fall," an eating of the mythical apple, as an advance from religious superstition toward human freedom. In fact, "The Apple" features Captain Kirk actually destroying the religion of a paradisal planet for the sake of a progressive, secular outlook.

I

"The Apple"[3]

A *Star Trek* landing party materializes in the lush garden of Gamma Trianguli VI, an unexplored planet that seems as close to an earthly paradise as they would ever see. When Chekov notes that it is "just like Russia," McCoy replies, "It's a lot more like the Garden of Eden, Ensign."

The idyll is destroyed when one of the security guards examines a thorn pod which explodes and kills him. Spock picks up a unique rock specimen which explodes when thrown to the ground. At this point he dramatically throws himself in front of Captain Kirk to save him from one of the thorn pods. Spock's Vulcan constitution proves immune to the lethal missiles. They decide to abandon this dangerous paradise when they discover that a mysterious power field is inhibiting the transporter. Within a few moments other security guards are killed.

Enraged by their deaths, Kirk and his landing party capture a humanoid who claims, "I am the Eyes of Vaal. He must see." Vaal turns out to be a great dragon god that requires periodic meals of explosive rocks to keep its underground power source humming. But the citizens of the planet are kept in a state of sexual and technological innocence by this god, who makes "the rains fall, and the sun to shine. All good comes from Vaal," as they say. The planet lacks bacteria, and its inhabitants do not age so they need no "replacements." It is truly a "paradise" like the mythical Eden, a "splendid example of reciprocity." But Dr. McCoy is appalled: "These are humanoids–intelligent! They've got to advance–progress! Don't you understand what my readings indicate? There's been no change here in perhaps thousands of years! This isn't life, it's stagnation!" In other words, a stable, primitive culture cannot be tolerated.

Kirk allows the young romantics, Chekov and Martha Landon, previously warned against their "field experiments in human biology," to engage in public necking, so that the citizens of Gamma T. will get subversive ideas. But Akuta receives the word from Vaal to kill the landing crew. The force that threatens the *Enterprise* and its crew must somehow be destroyed. But Spock retorts to Kirk, "This may not be an ideal society, but it is a viable one. . . . If we are forced to do what it seems we must, in my opinion, we will be in direct violation of the noninterference directive."

Kirk replies, "These people aren't living, they're just existing. It's not a valid culture." There is, in other words, a duty to interfere.

"Starfleet Command may think otherwise," Spock suggests.

Kirk replies, "That's a risk I'll have to take."

Moments after Akuta and his men attack the crew and are subdued, the *Enterprise* phasers are directed to destroy Vaal. There is a tremendous series of explosions.

Akuta comes forward, "But it was Vaal who put the fruit on the trees, who caused the rain to fall. Vaal cared for us."

"You'll find that putting fruit on the trees is a relatively simple matter. . . . You'll have to learn to take care of yourselves," replies Kirk. "You might even like it. . . . You will be able to think what you wish, say what you wish, do what you wish. You will learn many things that are strange, but they will be good. You will discover love; there will be children."

Back on the bridge of the regenerated *Enterprise* the officers are debating the correctness of smashing idols. Kirk insists, "We put those people back on a normal course of social evolution. I see nothing wrong with that."

Kirk draws the moral, "It's a good object lesson, Mr. Spock, in what can happen when your machines become too efficient, do too much of your work for you."

Spock points out the analogy to the Garden of Eden story: "In a manner of speaking we have given Adam and Eve the apple, the awareness of good and evil, if you will, and because of this they have been driven out of paradise."

That brings Kirk up short. "Mr. Spock, you seem to be casting me in the role of Satan. Do I look like Satan?"

"No, sir. But–"

"Is there anyone on this ship who looks even remotely like Satan?"

There was a grin on McCoy's face as Spock replied in an even tone: "I am not aware of anyone in that category, Captain."

"No, Mr. Spock. I didn't think you would be."

It may strike one as paradoxical that seemingly enlightened episodes like this would produce a "crazed" following whose "fanaticism" appears thoroughly religious. To be sure, all of the now familiar mythic patterns are here: the saga of the *Enterprise*'s dangerous mission, the sexual renunciation of its leaders, and the redemption scheme through which the inhabitants of Gamma Trianguli VI are freed from their superstitious captivity. Given the proximity of such mythic patterns to the perennial concerns of religion, one wonders whether an unconscious process is taking place here that the producers and audience neither intend nor understand. Could it be that the myths, in their pseudo-empirical garb, are creating a new pop religion, capable of powerfully affecting the thoughts and actions of fans?

II

The evidence of such a pop religion, strewn throughout *Star Trek* fan literature, is described most extensively in *Star Trek Lives!* This book is written in the spirit of the religious devotion that it so meticulously documents. In most religions, individual revelatory ecstasies and redemptive experiences evoke a sense of wonder before a numinous, divine reality. Fans as well as actors seem to have this sense in discussing *Star Trek*. George Takei, who played the role of Sulu, admits, "I hate to deify any human being, but Gene Roddenberry . . . really is like a god to us because he did bring us together." Lichtenberg, Marshak, and Winston convey a numinous sense in describing Spock. "Spock is *utterly capable* of dealing with any sort of threat . . . total master of any situation that technology can create." A letterwriter asserts that ". . . in episode after episode we have satisfied for us mankind's age-old yearning for a superman . . ."[4]–that is, Mr. Spock. Such attributes owe more to divinity than to humanity.

Both Spock and Kirk play the role of superhuman redeemer figures in *Star Trek* episodes, as we have seen. In "The Apple," Spock saved Kirk's life by throwing himself in the path of the exploding thorn pod, an act of selfless redemption on a superhuman scale. He evinces an

> . . . aura of tightly leashed, restrained power . . . enough power . . . to destroy the *Enterprise* and take half the galaxy with it if he so chose. . . . But if power, personal efficacy, is the pure good, and it is the good in us which selects the goals toward which that good power will be used, then also Spock contains more good than any earthly human we are likely to meet.[5]

In traditional theology God alone possesses unlimited power, and his goodness consists in using it responsibly. Within this frame of reference, Spock has definitely supplanted God in the pop religion of *Star Trek*.

If Spock has displaced God, it is Kirk who plays the role of a Christ without passion, and in this role he, even more than Spock, consistently appears as a superhuman redeemer. In "The Apple," he takes it upon himself to redeem a people even at the peril of his own life. Not only does he risk the missiles and explosive rocks of Gamma Trianguli VI, but he also voluntarily accepts the burden of violating the directive to avoid ". . . interference with the normal development of a viable culture. It comes very close to forbidding *any* interference whatsoever, and it forbids it very strongly. A starship captain takes an oath to die rather than violate it." Kirk thus risks his own life for the sake of redemption.

This kind of willingness to "lay down his life for his friends" (Jn. 15:13), to offer his "life as a ransom for many" (Mt. 20:28), is the mark of divine and semidivine redeemer figures. But it is also characteristic that they are somehow able to inspire others with the same goals. Captain Kirk seems to be in view when fans write that "*Star Trek* is about one man's love for his goal . . . about that man's ability to communicate that goal to his co-workers, and to evoke in their hearts a similar love, a burning passion of total devotion to this image of how Man could and should be."[6]

A special kind of discipleship arises from those who confess the pop religion of *Star Trek*. "Love" radiates from the redeemer figures and is transmitted in real life, primarily to other fans within the movement. The fans write, "Spock and Kirk and the whole realm of *Star Trek* speak to us eloquently of knowledge and efficacy and hope, of striving and prevailing, of seeing each other. And the sum of the message is love. Love of life . . . Here is the supreme optimism of a primary kind of love which is *not* sexual and yet may find expression in sexual terms. . . . To experience the concrete sense of that love and that hope, people watch *Star Trek*." In content, mood, and motifs, this is indistinguishable from what is commonly called "religion." Joan Winston, one of the organizers of the first *Star Trek* convention, describes the mood pervading the bedlam of unexpected throngs. "With all these people crushed into this too-small area, there were no incidents, no fights, just love. Miles and miles and tons and tons of love."[7] Here is the Woodstock Nation for the straights, a *Star Trek* universe in which true love replaces skinny-dipping, dope, and sexual show-and-tell.

Perhaps the ultimate proof of the religious nature of *Star Trek* fandom is in its outbursts of ecstasy. The authors of *Star Trek Lives!* state, for example, that ". . . the depth of William Shatner's Kirk leaves us speechless. But only figuratively, for throughout this book we have tried *heroically* to restrain the outpourings of boundless admiration that Mr. Shatner's achievement has aroused in us." When Joan Winston received a phone call from Leonard Nimoy, she gave way to this kind of ecstasy: "Oh bliss, oh frabjous joy." It was beyond normal human joy, calling forth words and expressions like "frabjous" from Lewis Carroll's *The*

Jabberwock, evidencing an effort to express the unexpressible. This kind of ecstatic feeling is reflected in the title and mood of *Star Trek Lives!* To say that a program "lives" of its own accord seems patently absurd, especially one that has been out of production for years. But here the fans' convictions are decisive. Their yearning for a "resurrection" has produced a religious sleight-of-hand.[8]

Lichtenberg, Marshak, and Winston report that they have received hundreds of letters from secret fans who are ". . . respectable, solid citizens who know their own family situations to be such that they dare not confess the depth of their feeling for *Star Trek.* They have tried, perhaps, and have run into such derision, teasing, or outright rage that they now feel compelled to hide their love like a secret vice." Many fans actually report personal redemptive experiences resulting from their encounters with the programs. A woman who is vice president of a fan club writes, "*Star Trek* has changed my life . . . opened my world to new thoughts and drained my pocketbook trying to keep up with everyone. . . . It's made me a much more real person, a lot easier to live with. I don't try to explain myself too much to outsiders." Another woman reports that after being hospitalized for depression she ". . . started again to believe in the future of mankind." Her ". . . mental outlook vastly improved." A man from Ohio writes, "*Star Trek* has been, and always will be, the biggest influence in my life."[9]

These redemption experiences seem to be closely related to the "Goal Effect" of *Star Trek,* challenging a tired mankind to strive once again for goals that seem unreachable at the current moment in American history. The series ". . . gives us the energy and the fuel to make the effort. By its mere existence–by the kinds of things it is saying and the kind of effort it took to say them, it gives us the sense that great efforts are possible and can succeed. It gives us the courage to tackle goals of our own. . . ." A form of inspiration is clearly evoking discipleship here. In explaining their faith, the authors cite approvingly Ayn Rand's theory of art: Art ". . . answers the question *why* . . . why go on. The function of art, to me, is to give answers . . . to give reason to have courage." The creation of this kind of hopeful courage was evident in a letter

Roddenberry received from a University of Wisconsin science student who was saved from being a high school dropout by seeing *Star Trek*. "For him it rekindled an interest in the future and in machinery."[10]

Professor Herbert J. Gans would undoubtedly discount this kind of interpretation. Convinced that popular-culture materials do not really motivate people or alter their value systems, he argues that ". . . content choice is affected by selective perception, so that people often choose content that agrees with their own values. . . . Thus the prime effect of the media is to reinforce already existing behavior and attitudes, rather than to create new ones."[11] This has a rather hollow ring, given the experiences reported by confessors of the *Star Trek* faith. To an extent popular religion has always had a reciprocal relation with human needs and cultural values. Only in the rare instances of higher, prophetic religion are new values created. But this should not lead one to overlook the powerful effect a particular pop religion may exert. Ordinarily the more conformist and the less self-conscious a religion, the more powerful its hold. Gans' mistake is to view popular-culture materials as mere entertainment rather than as powerful, ritualistic forms of a pop religion.

III

A popular religious movement usually produces an explicit theology over the course of time. At least this has been the pattern for religious groups in the Western world. It is not surprising, then, that a *pop theology* has emerged which elaborates and explains the assumptions and experience of *Star Trek* faith. Much of this material is in the form of fantasy literature, spinning out *Star Trek* episodes and characters to see what happened beyond the revelational scope of the original television series. This "fanzine" literature includes series like *Eridani Triad, Star Trek Showcase, T-Negative, Grup, Impulse, Babel, Spockanalis, Alternative Universe, Tricorder Readings,* and *Tholian Web*. There are hundreds of different issues of these magazines, in a development strikingly similar to the growth of apocryphal literature in the biblical tradition. This kind of writing answers essentially theological questions, amplifying and illustrating a faith.[12]

The authors of *Star Trek Lives!* ask why so many thousands of hours have been devoted to writing, editing, and publishing this fan literature. They ascribe it to ". . . the sheer love of *Star Trek.* People have become so entranced with that world that they simply cannot bear to let it die and will re-create it themselves if they have to. . . ." By writing stories, they produce the feeling that they are in effect knowing the gods. Fanzine writers confess that "we want to know all about these *Star Trek* characters–their innermost thoughts, the most trivial details about them. They have become *friends* in a way that few flesh-and-blood people are, and almost no fictional characters are."[13] There is a ritualistic, confessional quality to this writing. The writers' expression of personal experience is largely subordinated to mythic conventions. In a ritual fashion, the fictional characters are kept alive. They enter into personal relationships with their devotees. They live on in faith. It all sounds very much like the practice of dogmatic theology in a traditional religion.

A particularly good example of the theological activity in fan magazines is *Kraith,* with its writers' guide and its collection of stories, published thus far in four volumes, with six more planned. It develops a "Demanding Fantasy" that ". . . is a combination of the need for a demanding pleasure with the need to work out answers to certain fundamental human questions. . . . 'Whither man?' and 'Why?' and 'What's it all about?' and 'What is the proper relationship of man to himself, to his group, to the universe?' " Here within premises of faith provided by the *Star Trek* format and characters a new theology is developing. Its scripture is embodied in the seventy-nine television episodes; its task is to unfold the meaning of that revelation for the basic human questions. The theological impulse in this kind of publishing program is unmistakable. *Kraith* claims that *Star Trek* is ". . . a staggeringly effective model for dealing with deep human questions,"[14] the kind of sentiment shared by many religious and occult groups in the current period.

The theological message of *Star Trek,* judging from these fan materials, relates to world redemption in general and redemption of individual audience members in particular. The "Optimism Effect" referred to in *Star Trek Lives!* confirms the hope that despite the present malaise, mankind ". . . can overcome the problems of today." The television stories cultivate this hope by bringing into our living rooms imaginary cultures of the future, even on this planet Earth, that have transcended problems that look lethal today. George Takei (Sulu) attributes this redemptive effect in the television series to Gene Roddenberry. "I think he's the one who felt, very seriously and deeply believes, that we *can* overcome the problems of today." Fans extol with fervor " . . . the optimism of *Star Trek*–its vision of a brighter future of man, and of a world characterized by hope, achievement and understanding. . . ."[15]

The origin of this pop optimism is typically American, as betrayed by a peculiar competitive terminology. "But the deepest conviction of the creators of *Star Trek* was, and is, that triumph is possible, that we can *win.*" This reminds one of the Reverend Norman Vincent Peale's power of positive thinking and his book, *You Can Win.*[16] *Star Trek*'s innocent optimism conceals the unexamined premise that the "American Way of Life" will somehow prevail in the universe. Here is a package designed to appeal to the innocent, a theology oblivious to its essentially religious premise, a philosophy sure that the fantasy values of a particular culture will appeal to galactic inhabitants everywhere. The lack of critical principles, so essential to either theology or philosophy in the classical tradition, helps protect such convictions and values from the incursions of reality.

There is also a profound appeal in the so-called Vulcan Philosophy which shaped Spock and presumably led that planet into centuries of peace. This philosophy adds up to an optimistic, nonviolent (except for holy causes), sexually segmented individualism. It urges the repression of sexual energies for the sake of larger causes, a renunciation of sexual commitments, an animalistic expression of sexual instincts at the appropriate rutting season, and in the meantime, a sublimation of sexual energies in the form of technological zeal. Projecting traditional American values and repressions onto imaginary planets where their workability can be fantasized apparently enhances believability. What has failed in American experience is nevertheless affirmed to be "true" because it is depicted operating successfully in outer space. Clearly this is uncritical religious faith rather than rational thought.

IV

Among the evidences of *Star Trek* pop religion are voluntary behavior alterations. Some fans model their actions after those of the stars just as disciples in traditional Christianity imitate their Lord. A sixteen-year-old youth resembling Leonard Nimoy has had his hair cut and his eyebrows shaped in slanted Vulcan style. He almost always wears a blue velour shirt and has taken on so many of Spock's mannerisms that he seems to be a second Spock. Another young man, studying physics at the graduate level, ". . . went to court and legally changed his name to 'Spock'—no last name, just 'Spock.'" A man in Los Angeles is busy constructing an *Enterprise* shuttlecraft, the small spacecraft used for short voyages. He has reproduced *Star Trek* equipment and uniforms and works at building the complicated *Enterprise* bridge seen on the television series. Two men from Poughkeepsie, New York, have constructed their own bridge set and transporter room in order to make their own amateur movies.[17] Such examples could be multiplied many times. The motivations for these actions are probably as complex as those associated with the Christian imitation ethic. The desire to be like one's redeemer, to achieve union with him, or to gain self-identity by copying his appearance or actions, often seems to coalesce in such imitation.

The pattern of behavior alteration on the part of female fans seems to be quite different. It is visible in part in the fanzine literature. The stories written about *Star Trek* characters, spinning out their life stories and debating about whether the new fantasies correspond to the established patterns, seem to be written almost exclusively by women. While male fans write mainly about technological details, the females write about Kirk and Spock. Many of the stories featuring Spock remind one very much of the ancient mystery religions in which union with the god provides the ecstatic high point of the ritual. As in the mystery religions, one does not enter into a normal marriage with gods like Spock. *Star Trek Lives!* reports that a ". . . favorite theme is the 'no strings attached' meeting of his peculiarly urgent need. Various females have volunteered for that with alacrity. (Practically everybody, it sometimes seems.)"[18] But unlike the mystery religions, the actual achievement of redemption through sexual union with the body of the god is available only in fantasy form because suitable temple rites are not available—yet!

There are instances in which women actually attempted to carry out such rites of union with *Star Trek* actors. Gerrold reports that ". . . one girl ran away from home to go to Hollywood and try to move in with Leonard Nimoy. She chased after him for months, in general making his life miserable. In the process she managed to interfere with shooting schedules . . . and the nerves of everyone she came in contact with." One enterprising group of girls tried black-magic rituals to make their *Star Trek* heroes fall in love with them. They reportedly ceased their efforts in this direction when told that every hour of black magic takes away a year of one's personal beauty, for how could one ever hope to attract a god when one's beauty is gone? One little old lady from California achieved union with the god in an ingenious way. She tape-recorded the *Star Trek* programs ". . . for the express purpose of later dubbing in her own voice over the leading lady's."[19]

These kinds of voluntary behavior alterations, deriving from complex webs of motivation and fashion, are typical of pop culture as a whole. The crazy antics of movie star fans and rock fans have long been observed and parodied. But the religious quality of such behavior has not been taken seriously, in part because the artifacts of popular culture that inspire such behavior are not explicitly religious. The result is that effective analytic tools are lacking. In an attempt to construct a suitable analytic category, we turn back in history to consider an appearance of pop religion strikingly reminiscent of what we are currently witnessing.[20]

In 1774 Goethe published a novel that became an important landmark of popular culture in the era of mass-produced literature. Its title was *The Sorrows of Young Werther,* a story in which a sensitive young man, thwarted in his passion for a young woman, committed suicide. Within a decade this novel became an international sensation, published in many versions and translations, and evoking hundreds of imitations. As S. P. Atkins explains,

> Novelists, playwrights, poets, composers, choreographers, and iconographers ranging from reputable painters and illustrators to anonymous wax workers, all unrestrained by laws of copyright and inspired by their own or others' interest in Goethe's popular novel, quickly appropriated its themes to their peculiar talents. In addition, the cult of Werther was exploited by the trade: *eau de Werther* was sold, and Charlotte and Werther figures . . . as familiar and ubiquitous as Mickey Mouse or Donald Duck today, appeared on fans and gloves, on bread boxes and jewelry, on delicate Meissen porcelain. . . .[21]

The imitation of *Werther* characters also led to more alarming results in that romantic era. Walter Kaufmann relates that ". . . all over Europe large numbers of young people committed suicide with a copy of the book clutched in their hands or buried in a pocket." Suicide notes referred explicitly to Goethe's novel. In one particularly dramatic case, the young Fanni von Ickstatt leaped to her death from the tower of the Munich Frauenkirche. The unfortunate Goethe was accused of responsibility for this death by a host of preachers and lecturers. A lecturer, Johann Georg Prandl, wrote verses bemoaning her death and condemning Goethe. Goethe was alarmed at the incredible uproar over his novel and its unforeseen impact. During his first trip to Italy, when he was both feted and condemned as the author of *Werther,* he expressed the wish that he could destroy his creation.[22] It had seemingly taken on life of its own. Although no one wrote a *Werther Lives!,* as far as we know, it would have been completely appropriate.

When an artifact enters the arena of popular culture and assumes its own existence in the imagination of fans, a powerful though elusive process begins. It is extremely difficult to sort out the causal and motivational influences in the *Werther*-related suicides. But they illustrate an interesting interplay between fantasy and reality that obliterates any clear distinction between mere entertainment and seriously contemplated life purposes. The novel was inspired by an actual suicide, that of K. W. Jerusalem, and also by Goethe's own frustrated passion for Charlotte Buff. The novel in turn inspired public interest in the life of K. W. Jerusalem, leading to the publication of Jerusalem's biography by another author. But once the novel captured the popular imagination, a fantasy process began, which resulted in a wide variety of imitations and personal identifications with the heroes. This process of behavior alteration has its closest analogues in religious ethics, but the particular artifact inspiring it is not itself religious.[23]

We propose to call this paradoxical and elusive result a *Werther effect*. In the Werther effect a member of an audience (a) experiences a work of fantasy within a secular context that (b) helps to shape the viewer's sense of what is real and desirable, in such a way that (c) the viewer takes actions consistent with the vision inspired by the interaction between his own fantasy and popular entertainments. A Werther effect is the form of voluntary behavior alteration produced by interaction with a powerful artifact of popular culture. It is a religious type of ethical scheme within a nonreligious context, occurring regardless of the intent of the artifact's creators. It characteristically embodies a redefinition of the boundary between fact and fantasy.

V

Having designated a series of behavioral changes inspired by materials like *Star Trek* as Werther effects, we do not intend to take the line of Goethe's critics. One does not eliminate fantasy processes by banning works that may have inspired them. And who is to say whether some of the effects may not be positive? The complex interaction between individual imaginations and popular artifacts should instead be brought to consciousness and subjected to criticism. One must avoid both the Puritanical ban and the bubble-gum cop-out.

The religious aura of pop culture has been faintly sniffed in the past by Puritanical types with keen noses for idolatry. Savonarola intoned against popular entertainments with the same arguments as the Puritan divines in revolutionary England. They fervently hoped to ban the festivals and theatrical troupes that they felt popularized subversive forms of behavior, polluting the imagination of the faithful. "Christian" in *Pilgrim's Progress* received his most severe testing at "Vanity Fair," where worldly diversions and illicit relations were hawked. Religious zealots throughout American history promoted the ban against the insidious influences of pop culture. From the prohibitions against theaters and pictorial art in colonial days to the recent book burnings in West Virginia, the ire of the faithful has burned against what was perceived as a corrupt, competitive religion. This perception was in one sense correct, especially in sensing the presence of formative influences wearing the innocent guise of mere entertainment. These raging reformers tasted a fragment of truth, but their repressive strategy simply rendered them powerless to deal with the fantasies resident in the popular mind. This approach eliminated the possibility of public discussion about fantasy and behavior essential to the health of both the individual and society.

The bubble-gum fallacy, however, is an equally inappropriate response in dealing with pop religion and its strange Werther effects. Herbert Gans should be applauded for his attempt to defend popular culture against the snobbist campaigns of critics representing "higher" tastes. But his refusal to cope with the connections between pop culture and its Werther effects stifles the truth about fantasy life as surely as the Puritans would. Gans believes that the effects of pop culture on individuals are not worthy of serious study. His inclination is to draw inferences only if large numbers are involved. "Successful ads produce sharp increases in sales curves, but often these reflect the behavior of only a few hundred thousand people, and no one yet knows the relative impact of ad and product on buying decisions." Antisocial behavior results from improper conditioning prior to the encounter with pop culture, which prevents people from experiencing it as bubble gum. He writes, ". . . The media encourage violent attitudes and acts only for some people at some times. . . . 'Loners' may resort to aggression partly because they do not belong to any group and because they find substitute satisfaction in media fiction. . . ."[24] He seems to assume that so long as one conforms to his group, he will behave properly since the conditioning social milieu is benign.

In contrast, we believe that significant subjects for investigation occur at the individual level, and furthermore that pop culture shapes the allegedly benign milieu, sometimes offering destructive models for behavior. Social science cannot afford to ignore the effects of "loners" on society. The big-number bias should not obscure the fact that loners influenced by pop culture sometimes make decisions of great social magnitude. Evans and Novak report that Richard Nixon made the decision to invade Cambodia after several viewings of the movie *Patton:* "The impact of *Patton* on Nixon's Cambodian decision was felt by every close advisor who was aware of the President's repeated viewings. . . . A few weeks later, Secretary of State Rogers told a friend that the movie 'comes up in every conversation' with the President."[25]

Charles Manson found inspiration for the Tate and LaBianca murders in the song "Helter Skelter" from the Beatles' *White Album,* whose apocalyptic significance he ranked with the Book of Revelation. As described by Susan Atkins, one of his disciples, ". . . Helter Skelter was to be the last war on the face of the earth. . . . You can't conceive of what it would be like to see every man judge himself and then take it out on every other man all over the face of the earth." The cultic slayings at the Tate and LaBianca residences were meant to precipitate a racial Armageddon from which the blacks and the Manson Family would emerge victorious. Paul Watkins, second in command in the Family, described the crucial role of the *White Album* in the formation of this vision of redemptive violence. "Before 'Helter Skelter' came along . . . all Charlie cared about was orgies." Although the Werther effect was not intended by the Beatles, and in fact the album contained material rejecting violent revolution, it nevertheless contributed to Manson's plans for bloody, symbolic executions. In the song "Revolution 9" he enjoyed the sounds of machine-gun fire, screaming victims, and the faintly heard call, "Arise! Arise!" Manson used the title of the song "Piggies" as a term for establishment types needing a "damned good whacking." The words "Pigs," "Rise," and "Helter Skelter" were written with the blood of the victims at the scene of the gruesome executions. At his trial, Manson commented on the powerful influence he attributed to this music.

> Is it a conspiracy that the music is telling the youth to rise up against the establishment because the establishment is rapidly destroying things? . . . The music speaks to you every day, but you are too deaf, dumb, and blind. . . . It is not my conspiracy. It is not my music. I hear what it relates. It says "Rise," it says "Kill." Why blame it on me? I didn't write the music.[26]

Lynnette Fromme acted out of loyalty to Manson's peculiar pop religion in her attempt to assassinate President Ford. Though the choice of victim was shocking, her profession of zealous faith contains elements of sexual renunciation and world redemption similar to those in *Star Trek*. "We're nuns now and we wear red robes. We're waiting for our Lord and there's only one thing to do before He comes off the cross and that's clean up the earth."[27]

It would be foolish to directly blame *Patton* for the Cambodian invasion or the Beatles for murders and assassination attempts. Strong influences other than pop culture are undoubtedly present. But with events of such magnitude, the refusal to explore the formative role of pop culture seems like a suicidal evasion of responsibility. If researchers can avoid the unproductive avenues of snobbery, bans, or bubble gum, the most positive result might be to bring these matters to public consciousness. Only as the powerful interaction between fantasy and the electronic-age pop artifacts comes to open debate can it be evaluated according to democratic ethical guidelines.

III
The Golden Way to Violence in "Death Wish"

". . . The heroes of all time have gone before us; the labyrinth is thoroughly known; we have only to follow the thread of the hero-path."–Joseph Campbell, *The Hero with a Thousand Faces*[1]

"VIOLENCE IS GOLDEN WHEN IT'S USED TO PUT DOWN EVIL."–*Dick Tracy Comics* on the day following Robert Kennedy's assassination[2]

The heroic path has beckoned to travelers in every generation, offering clues about proper responses to threatening circumstances. The present, violent age is no exception. Heroic forms from the past give shape to popular materials and invite emulation by current audiences. The approach of Rollo May, a leading theorist of contemporary consciousness, offers a suggestive point of departure. He believes that rising violence in our society is directly related to the abandonment of the mythic road system. Convinced that there are no modern equivalents of the classical myths, May points to resultant apathy and impotence as the sources of aimlessly destructive actions. Violence arises when myths and symbols, which provide maps of order and meaning, fall into disrepair. The self, deprived of the myths that confer meaning upon its existence, feels an impotence and frustration that easily boil over into rage. Violence results from a lack of mythic coherence.[3]

Our analysis of *Star Trek* and *Space 1999* indicated that popular entertainments contain mythical elements comparable with the classical myths whose demise May laments. In these materials violence is presented in carefully wrought golden imagery. The presence of such images, not the absence of older myths, accounts for some of the destructive turmoil in our midst. Violence, we submit, increases when a mythic system, intact though perhaps unacknowledged, channels frustration and aggressive impulses into destructive avenues. Mythical violence suggests to its audience the possibility of achieving a negative form of integration through zealous retribution.

The movie *Death Wish* reveals the technomythic processes by which violent images are conveyed to contemporary audiences. It is archetypal in that it adapts the dominant American myth of the western vigilante to the modern urban situation. Moreover, the transformation of Brian Garfield's novel *Death Wish* into this monomythic film points toward an equally significant process. It indicates how a traditional paradigm becomes a mythic prism through which both the story and the audience response are refracted, throwing a golden aura onto the path of violence.[4]

I

The story of *Death Wish* opens with Paul Kersey and his wife vacationing in Hawaii, enjoying themselves in a paradisal setting. On the deserted beach, they defer the urge to make love until they can return to the hotel. "We have become too civilized for that," says Kersey with regret. Upon their return to New York, vacation over, they encounter a traffic jam in miserable winter weather and fall exhausted into bed. When he resumes work at his architectural firm the next day, Kersey is stricken by tragedy. His wife and daughter-in-law are attacked by three hoodlums who force their way into their East Side apartment. Kersey's beautiful wife is brutally murdered, and his daughter-in-law is raped. He buries his wife and returns to work with stoic coolness. He inquires at the police station about the killers only to be told that they may never be apprehended. While fretting about his powerlessness to cope with this anonymous malevolence, Kersey purchases several rolls of quarters and puts them in a sock. Before long, he has to use this primitive weapon to beat off a mugger. Returning home shaken, he exultantly tests his weapon again. It shatters on a living-room chair, indicating the need for a more reliable weapon.

Kersey's boss sends him on an assignment to Tucson, hoping to relieve him of his trauma. There Kersey encounters a successful real-estate developer with frontier attitudes. He takes Kersey, a conscientious objector, to a gun club for an encounter with the West's tradition of pistol firing for self-defense. In a pivotal episode, the two men visit Old Tucson and witness a staged shootout between good guys and bad guys. Impressed more than his liberal biases can admit, Kersey returns to New York after brilliantly completing his architectural assignment. On a visit to the hospital where his daughter-in-law is recuperating, he discovers that she has moved from shock into an incurable psychosis. Upon opening his suitcase in the now lonely East Side apartment, he finds a gift from the Tucson developer–a pearl-handled revolver in a velvet-lined case.

In a conversation with his son while returning from a hopeless visit to his daughter-in-law in the sanitorium, Kersey secretly resolves to take up the "uncivilized means" of vigilante defense. It is preceded by a significant conversation that takes place with his son. "What do you call people who just sit by and do nothing when attacked?" Kersey asks. "Civilized?" responds his son. From this point on, Kersey systematically offers himself as a target for muggers. When they attack, he responds with the six-gun. Reluctantly and with sickened revulsion at first, he becomes a cool executioner who gains a sense of personal fulfillment and manhood. He redecorates his apartment in bold colors as a sign of rejuvenation. Meanwhile, his campaign to redeem the city from muggers produces a worldwide sensation. An enormous outpouring of sympathy from the public and even from the Police Department wells up, producing reduced crime statistics. As the vigilante marksman attempts his eleventh killing, he is wounded and taken to the hospital, where the police captain promises not to reveal his identity if he will simply leave town. The movie closes with Paul Kersey arriving at O'Hare International Airport to witness four Chicago toughs harassing a comely girl. Helping her pick up her parcels, Kersey responds to the obscene gestures from the retreating thugs by aiming down his trigger finger at them with a gleam in his eye. The traveling vigilante in the businessman's suit has arrived in yet another desperate, lawless community.

II

This story of rape and vigilante vengeance has numerous variants, including films like *Straw Dogs* and *Billy Jack*. If such a story appeared in a primitive culture, it would undoubtedly be classified as mythical. We use the term "mythical" here to refer to dramatic narratives told to convey a people's sense of reality. In classical and primitive cultures such narratives dealt with the interaction of men and higher powers, disclosed ultimate realities and norms, and offered adherents models for behavior and answers to agonizing questions. As noted in *Star Trek,* such narratives contain themes like saga, sexual renunciation, and redemption. These myths need not be explicitly religious. Henry Tudor notes that ". . . there are many myths in which the sacred plays no role whatsoever. . . ." An essential mark of mythic thinking is the ordering of present experience as ". . . an episode in a story, an incident in a dramatic development. . . ." A story from the past is presented as a model of how life should be understood and lived, and is generally accepted uncritically as a kind of revelation. Richard Slotkin has offered a valuable summary of how the narratives of a particular culture produce a mythology capable of channeling subsequent behavior.

> A mythology is a complex of narratives that dramatizes the world vision and historical sense of a people or culture, reducing centuries of experience into a constellation of compelling metaphors. The narrative action of the myth-tale recapitulates that people's experience in their land, rehearses their visions of that experience in its relation to their gods and the cosmos, and reduces both experience and vision to a paradigm. . . . The believer's response to his myth is essentially nonrational and religious . . . he feels that the myth has put him in intimate contact with the ultimate powers which shape all of life. . . . Myth . . . provides a scenario or prescription for action, defining and limiting the possibilities for human response to the universe.

In these terms, *Death Wish* is unquestionably mythical, even though it does not feature duels with dragons or struggles among the gods. It explicitly offers an "Old West" prescription for understanding and dealing with modern crime.[5]

The plot of this myth is distinctly American. It belongs to the genre described by Richard Slotkin, the "myth of regeneration through violence" that developed out of the Puritan colonists' tales of Indian wars and captivities. Seeing the alien Indian culture as a demonic threat, these stories depicted violence as the means both of cleansing the wilderness and regenerating true faith in the believing community. They reveal an ambivalence about the western paradise that is similar to the Eden-civilization theme in *Death Wish*. The wilderness was both the source of licentious temptation and the stage for the millennial drama of world redemption. It is in post-Puritan materials like *The Leatherstocking Tales* and the later cowboy stories that the West came increasingly to be viewed as the unspoiled source of vitality and regeneration. Cooper's deerslayer derives his identity and power from the wilderness, becoming the self-reliant killer that nature presumably has taught him to be. Like Charles Bronson in the character of Kersey, the deerslayer remains true to his own private standards despite pressures, remaining the isolated, celibate figure his heroic tasks demand.

As in *Star Trek,* the "myth of cool zeal" embodied in countless cowboy Westerns features a superhero who redeems the threatened community from bad guys. A cool, dispassionate zeal for traditional values marks such superheroes. They are selfless, sexually unattached, and committed to justice though not to restraints of due process. With idealism shaped in part by the ideology of the "Battle Hymn of the Republic," they are willing to "die to set men free," but fate invariably directs their aim so they can exact divine retribution at little cost to themselves or the community. The suffering victim becomes the violent redeemer. This paradox is caught by Michael T. Marsden, who describes the Western hero combined from ". . . the most useful qualities of the Old Testament God and the New Testament Christ . . . a Sagebrush Savior who is kind, yet strong; who is just, yet firm." This kind of hero ". . . must be suprahuman . . . invulnerable to the human weaknesses shared by those whom he must defend and protect. If he is to be the answer to the dreams and prayers of the troubled, he must ride tall, shoot straight, and remain eternally vigilant for the causes of right."[6] In this secularized drama of redemption, the redeemed remain passive. The *Death Wish* victims are inactive, and the government is ineffective; but the superhero and those who emulate him are able to eliminate the threat by vigilante action.

Victor Turner suggests that mythical material provides the community "symbolic enrichment" in adapting to threatening new circumstances. The mythic instruction is therefore ". . . essentially a period of returning to first principles and taking stock of the cultural inventory," and ". . . often the cultural knowledge is transmitted by the recital of mythical narratives." Thus in *Death Wish* the urban hell is cleansed by the adaptation of the Old West ritual, but not through a conscious process on the part of the audience. Most viewers simply feel captured by a film like *Death Wish*. They are not aware of being ritually instructed, because myths derive from and appeal to the unconscious rather than the conscious mind. Although the process within an individual may be largely unconscious, the mythical paradigms of his culture have already been implanted, so that an American responds to one kind of mythical plot and a Chinese to another. Ernest Becker's definition of "the unconscious" seems most appropriate in this context: ". . . The Unconscious is not a reservoir of animal drives; rather, it is the unexamined residue of our early training and feeling about ourselves and the world."[7] In the case of the American viewers of *Death Wish*, we would suggest that the impact of the modern myth is largely determined by the "unexamined residue" of the Old West and superhero paradigms.

According to Becker, the unconscious mind provides the unreflective, uncritical motivation for subsequent behavior:

> Since the Unconscious represents our basic organismic conditioning about the kind of world we are comfortable in, the kind that is "right and true" for us, we must understand that it comprises the gross and deep going *motives* of our behavior–motives which are not amenable to reflective, symbolic scrutiny. Since our Unconscious is our basic emotional identification with the kinds of feelings and acts which make us comfortable, we can say that it contains the motives that *determine* our behavior, whether we consciously will it or not.

Now, if traditional myths play a role in shaping the unconscious mind, and if a film like *Death Wish* serves as a transitional bridge for adapting an archaic myth to current needs, the entire process has immense cultural significance. The ever-recurring fantasy of redemptive violence may provide a key to the high incidence of violence on the part of virile males and the passivity on the part of the general public, both of which seem to be characteristic of current American society. Donald Lunde reports, for example, that ". . . most murders in the U.S. are committed by young adults, predominately males. More than half of all murderers are under age 35, whereas less than one tenth are over age 50." And it must be remembered that this is true in a country whose ". . . murder rate has been almost 20 *times* as high as England's" throughout the twentieth century. The connection between these arresting facts and the violent mythic images in pop culture deserves more careful scrutiny than it has received.[8]

In discussing *Star Trek* we noted that its believability derives from the scientific credibility of space travel portrayed in a precise and gadget-filled style of production. Within these conventions, outer space seems to pose few obstacles to the credence of fantasy. When the story shifts from the least-known galaxies to the inner city, the creation of mythic credibility is a much more difficult task. Surface realism alone cannot compel assent to absurd images of action in a familiar terrain. Something else must account for the power of the violent mythic images in a movie like *Death Wish*. We detect here a mythic paradigm that includes the subtle use of three components: *mythic selectivity, Werther invitation,* and *mythic massage.* It is these processes that allow the audience's encounter with urban hell to be mythically productive, offering appealing patterns for thought and action.

III

Mythic selectivity is a process by which an artifact defines the factual realities in a given situation. *Death Wish* has struck audiences as highly realistic in its depiction of urban violence and pastoral tranquillity. But an examination of the selectivity with which the film presents "the facts" reveals substantial elements of distortion. For instance, paradise is supposed to be located in Hawaii and Tucson, whereas New York and Chicago are simply urban hells. Selective elimination of contrary features is required to sustain such a conclusion. New York is pictured only during the most miserable part of the year–its neighboring beaches and parks, its beautiful buildings and cultural facilities are overlooked. Muggers lurk in every alley. Couples drop exhausted into bed, too overburdened by urban chaos for sexual enjoyment. Arizona and Hawaii are pictured as idylls of safety, whereas their actual crime rates per 100,000 population were roughly comparable to New York's in 1974. The rape scene in *Death Wish* was made to look routine in New York, whereas the actual incidence per 100,000 population is 42.8 for New York City, 27.4 for Honolulu, and 49.3 for Tucson. If Kersey had been pictured as traveling to locations that are relatively safe compared with Manhattan, he should have gone to the Albany, New York, area–there the murder rate is about one fourth that of Tucson's (3.2 vs. 11.6) and one third that of Honolulu's (9.0). The rates for rape are equally discrepant, leading one to suspect that western landscape and gunmen do not produce a crime-free paradise.[9] In *Death Wish* the beach is so isolated during the high tourist season that Kersey and his wife are tempted to make love in the open. The beach presumably has only one hotel, no other visitors, and no "natives." Tucson likewise has neither smog nor non-white Americans. Its housing developments are idyllic. Its developers presumably care nothing about profit, unlike those in the New York office, because they are motivated by love of the "natural" way of life. However, this benign developer is a big-game hunter with trophy horns in his home and even on his car, clad with cowhide seat covers. The predator here becomes the model saint, naturally lacking in wife, family, or other tainted associations.

The muggers are pictured with equal selectivity. The first three villains appear stereotypically like thugs in older cowboy movies, knocking over groceries in the supermarket and bumping innocent damsels, just as maidens were pushed off the boardwalks. The thugs leer at Kersey's lovely wife and daughter-in-law, their appetites as close to the surface as those of the bad cowboys in the saloon scenes of old Westerns. The muggers insolently lift the home address from the women's grocery cart so they can stalk their helpless prey. After the terrible rape and murder scene, they dash off and are never seen again, their malevolent behavior influencing the audience's response to all the other muggers in the story. With the exception of the first one Kersey slays, the bad guys fit the stereotype to the letter—bullies when they pull a knife on a presumably unarmed victim, but cowardly when they find he is ready for self-defense. They always draw first but never mortally wound our hero. John Cawelti has described this conventional "last-minute precision" of the cowboy films. "The hero never engages in violence until the last moment and never kills until the savage's gun has already cleared his holster. Suddenly it is there and the villain crumples."[10] In one instance a *Death Wish* mugger with a drawn weapon cannot even manage to get a shot off before our vigilante draws and kills him with the neat predictability of the baddies dropped by the sheriff's shotgun in Old Tucson. No Peckinpah realism here.

The police are portrayed as mediocre at most, the beat policemen better than their overseers. The chief is an overweight, clumsy degenerate, his burned-out cigar and chronic wheezing corresponding to the bumbling of the force as a whole. They cannot even effectively stake out Kersey's house after warning him to stop his killings. He slips out the back door with ridiculous ease while the chief himself is parked out front. The district attorney and police commissioner chew candy with the chief and indulge themselves in walnut-paneled offices rather than biting the bullet on crime. They want only to disguise their incompetence and avoid making Kersey a martyr, but they do not really wish to enforce the law. One policeman averts his gaze from an obvious mugger, apparently out of cowardice, so that Kersey has to face the assailant alone in an empty subway car. The characterization is as selective as the depiction of the worthless sheriffs in the black-hat Westerns. Finally, a veritable army of cops descends on our wounded vigilante, stumbling over each other to open the door for the chief, as incompetent as the bluecoats who have to be saved by scouts in old wagon-train stories.

In a world of cunning predators and incompetent law-enforcement officials, *Death Wish* offers a hero selectively pictured as larger than life. Despite his urban attire, he is really a superhero in

Steve smiles.

People have been dreaming up supermen for millennia, starting with the Greek gods Atlas and Hercules. Six Million Dollar Steve Austin is a recent version whose destructive strength conquers evil without hurting anyone.

Steve uses his bionic arm. Another man goes down. Steve uses his legs: He kicks the last man into the sea!
KICK!

George Takei (Lt. Sulu), Leonard Nimoy (Mr. Spock), and James Doohan (Chief Engineer Scott) at a Star Trek convention.

Wearing the cult regalia, as above at the 1976 Star Trek Convention, is a way of celebrating the Trekkie religion stimulated by contemporary media.

Charles Bronson adapts to the urban setting the mythic stance of the cool cowboy. He appears above in a "High Midnight" duel in *Death Wish*.

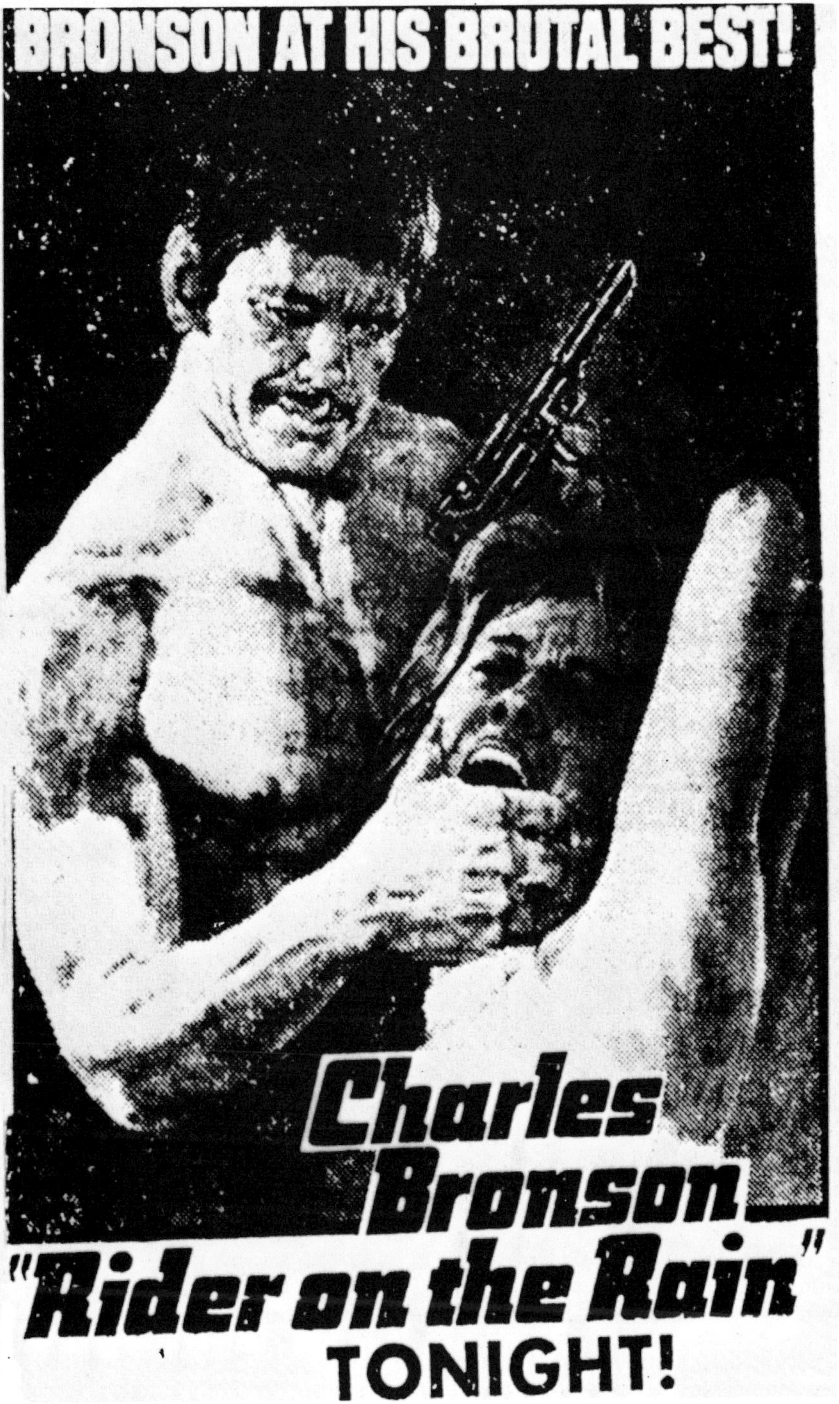

In *Rider on the Rain* he displays the typical pop renunciation of sexual union for the sake of redemptive brutality.

Classical heroes strained against agonizing limits. Here Laocoön is punished for breaking his priestly vow of celibacy to Apollo. His masculinity is intact, though a later generation provided fig-leaf modesty.

Superman's lack of the unmistakable signs of manhood in his torso provides the historical model for *Playboy* redeemers who always keep their cool. Here is the perfect mythical image of power without passion.

He could capture the Meanies of this world without risking his own blood or shedding any of theirs. If they were hurt, they had only themselves to blame.

However beguiling the invitation, true Supermen remain unmoved. Redeemers belong to everyone, and the Lois Lanes who get mixed up with them are left with the one problem Supermen cannot solve.

the cowboy tradition. The first time he fires an archaic weapon in the Tucson gun club, a muzzle-loading .45-caliber pistol, he hits the bull's-eye. This is clearly a mythical feat, wildly improbable with an untested, primitive weapon, particularly for a man who had not touched a gun since his youth. Kersey is portrayed as having sworn never to touch a gun after his father's death many years before. The pacifist who hates guns is elected by fate, by his incredible sharpshooter's eye. The unwilling vigilante, stoically accepting his duty, but taking no pleasure in the killing, reflects the traditional pattern. His duels with the bullying muggers also fit the paradigm of the Main Street shootout. Even though he faces virile adversaries three at a time, he guns them down with ridiculous ease. His bullets strike the mark, and only in the final duel is he wounded. Even then, the hero can be only superficially harmed.

Once these features are pointed out, most persons would agree that they are biased. But while the images flicker on the screen, not a ruffle of doubt is evoked. Pseudo-empiricism accounts in part for this remarkable credibility. The viewer has the illusion of actually seeing muggers in every alley; he witnesses the brutal rape scene as a real occurrence; his eyes convince him of the cowardice and incompetence of the muggers. When one considers how difficult it would be to sustain a similar credibility while reversing the patterns, making the bad guys shoot straight and the hero miss, one recognizes mythic forms at work. The selective details are accepted by the audience because they fit a mythic paradigm.

IV

Werther invitation is a process by which a myth system explicitly presents desirable models to be accepted by viewers. Some of those who participate vicariously in the mythic drama internalize the behavior patterns and subsequently follow them when they face analogous situations. In this way, Werther invitations are sometimes followed by Werther effects. In the case of *Death Wish* the archetypal model of the Old West Vigilante provides the invitation for responding to the modern urban situation. Kersey's modeling his behavior after a mythical paradigm constitutes a powerful inducement to the audience to do likewise—either to become a superhero vigilante or to remain passive while waiting for vigilante salvation. In the latter case the passive public in the film reinforces the inactive spectator stance of the audience.

The origin of mythical redemption in *Death Wish* is Edenic. It is not until Kersey travels to Tucson, far from the corruption of the modern urban Babylon, that the vigilante solution appears. It is advocated first by the Tucson developer, who considers self-reliance and six-gun self-defense as a law of nature, the powerful secret of western vitality and tranquillity. The Tucson advocate of these rural virtues is himself an embodiment of the paradoxical elements that comprise the traditional American sense of paradise. He unites love of nature and a fascination with the machines that domesticate nature; love of guns and yearning for law and order; disdain for profit and an obvious delight in the expensive pleasures of life; a love of unspoiled nature and pride in tract real-estate development. Apparently single, though seemingly well-integrated, he becomes for Kersey the source of redemptive wisdom. And it is he who provides the pearl-handled pistol that starts Kersey on his redemptive mission in the urban no-man's-land.

The visit to Old Tucson is the moment of recognition in which the invitation of the mythical Western paradigm strikes home to the grieving, liberal Kersey. The tourist crowd stands around while the sheriff shoots it out with the bad guys between the saloon and the jail. As six-gun and shotgun cut down the invaders with divine efficiency, the camera pans to Kersey's face to show that something has clicked to overcome his civilized reticence. The power of the mythical model is communicated by the total conviction on his face, and from this moment on, the audience is certain that he will take up the invitation to become a vigilante-redeemer in his own beleaguered city. The Werther effect is both immediate and compelling.

Once Kersey embarks upon the mythical path, his behavior becomes an invitation for others in the film. As details about each victim are reported, previously cowardly and demoralized citizens begin to take action for themselves, and their more passive neighbors applaud them. A stalwart old black woman is reported to have turned on a purse snatcher and driven him off with her hatpin. A crew of construction workers catch a criminal and give him a suitable beating before the authorities can arrive. The sensational publicity attracts newsmen from all over the world in quest of details about the unknown vigilante. It is as if the entire world were eagerly awaiting this modern appearance of the old-style redeemer. Everywhere heroes would now arise from the common people to pattern themselves after this example. The traditional idea of America as the redeemer nation echoes in this story, both for the hero and for a helpless world, yearning for the redemptive age to dawn.

One can only speculate about the actual impact of such invitations upon audiences. But it seems plausible that the presentation of Werther effects within the film itself provides a more powerful inducement than would the presentation of the Edenic paradigm alone. The tourists at Old Tucson in the film simply stand around in their sloppy clothes, stupidly gawking when the archaic drama is enacted. In their passive state, they are more easily moved to amusement than to actual emulation of the staged shootout. But when the capable, aggrieved Kersey takes up the mythical invitation and thereby gains popularity as a selfless redeemer, a Werther momentum begins. The film superhero's successful adaptation of the archaic myth for modern circumstances helps diminish the audience's reservations. The Werther momentum is sustained when members of the television audience in the film arise to adapt the model for themselves and their own neighborhoods. Even those who refuse to emulate the heroic model feel an admiration for those who do, and are thereby led to emulate the stance of the applauding, passive public in the film. In either case, *Death Wish* invites us to take a mythical path out of the modern urban hell.

V

Mythic massage is a process of assuring spectators that the gap between myth and reality can be bridged. In *Death Wish,* the vigilante actions of the modern superhero solve the knotty problem of urban crime. Mythical redemption works out in everyday life according to mythical expectation. Complex social problems are neatly solved with a single gesture; tangled human relations are sorted out and resolved; evil is eliminated with a single heroic stroke. In *Death Wish,* the elements of mythic massage touch the fate of villains and vigilantes, the achievement of justice for the community, and the redemptive impact on the world.

The fact that Kersey escapes with mere flesh wounds after the lethal series of duels with his assailants brings modern experience into conformity with the mythic plot of the Old Tucson shootout. The old woman and the hardhats who emulate this example likewise survive their encounters unharmed. The modern villains are so cowardly and dumb that one need not fear the weapons in their hands; fate will conspire with their weakness of character to render them impotent. At this point the process of mythic massage has elements of wish fulfillment that are strikingly similar to the Ghost Dances of the Sioux in the post-Civil War period.[11] By enacting the ritual dances celebrating the return of their fallen comrades, their lost buffalo, and their invulnerability to the white man's bullets, they gained assurance of invincibility. Then they embarked on the final series of battles that ended in the bloody snowdrifts of Wounded Knee. The process of mythic fantasy proved more effective in their minds than in reality. A dose of this kind of reality would have been fatal to the wish-fulfilling pattern of *Death Wish.* If Kersey had been killed in one of the early duels, and if the lady had been knocked aside in her attempt at hatpin self-defense against a powerful young mugger, the sense of assurance would have abruptly ended for the audience.

That justice can be achieved by the vigilante method is the assurance produced by the mythic massage of *Death Wish.* As the press accounts in the movie make clear, each of the victims of Kersey's executions has a prior criminal record. Each attacks the seemingly passive Kersey without provocation, thus fully earning the fate he receives. Moreover, a dramatic drop in violent crimes is reported and discussed repeatedly in the film. Law and order were therefore achieved for the community. If a more realistic picture of vigilante miscarriages of justice were presented, the sense of closure would dissipate. What would the impact on the audience be if one of the "muggers" turned out to be Kersey's peaceful neighbor on a midnight stroll? Or what would be the effect of revealing the reason why sensible police departments discourage vigilante practices, namely that it invariably increases rather than decreases violence? The film pictures the New York City Police Department as having merely political reasons for dissuading the vigilante, and embarrassed that Kersey alone could do more in the way against crime than their entire organization. Thus by technomythic artifice, the film skirts the objections that common sense would make against the mythic redemption scheme.

The most blatant proposition in *Death Wish*'s massage concerns world redemption. Reporters from all over the world are pictured as clamoring to get the message about the vigilante and his dramatic campaign against urban villains. Crime is a worldwide problem, and here is the means of redemption, not just for New York but also for the world. The traditional American sense of being a "City Set upon a Hill" as the moral example for the world is combined here with the naïve narcissism typical of the superhero cult. Public acclaim of the superhero's exploits, though usually shown to have no appeal to the hero himself, provides a powerful confirmation of the myth. Paul Kersey is shown several times devouring media reports about his vigilante exploit. He is too cool to need the assurance of such acclaim, but he takes a grim pleasure in receiving confirmation that the redemption he has wrought is efficacious for the entire world. America's restoration to moral leadership among the nations is explicit in the scenes with foreign reporters and newscasts. They speak many languages, but all praise the same redemptive achievement.

The power of mythic massage is enhanced by its unavailability in the real world. Most people experience life as an endless series of difficulties in which gratification is seldom more than temporary. In the arena of communal problems, where the requirements of order and justice are constantly in tension with individual needs and desires, final solutions are even more elusive. But when redemption from these limitations is offered in a powerful modern embodiment of a familiar and appealing myth, nostalgia combines with a yearning for easy solutions to bring off the massage. The presence of these mythic contrivances becomes even more evident when one examines the process by which the *Death Wish* scenario was adapted.

VI

The story of *Death Wish* was derived from a novel by Brian Garfield bearing the same title. Ironically, Garfield had intended that his novel exhibit the pathological roots of "golden violence" in the mythic fantasy patterns of American culture. He commented that ". . . this kind of thing could happen and it's a dangerous possibility. The movie suggests not only that it could happen, but that it *ought* to happen." Garfield was so disturbed by the movie's "vicious distortion" of his novel that he appealed to the Federal Communications Commission to ban its showing on CBS television, or at least to present a warning to the audience about its excessive violence.[12]

Even a casual reading of *Death Wish* reveals a profound transformation of viewpoint, content, and characterization. We would like to term this process *mythic alchemy*—the transformation of cultural materials to fit a mythical scheme. It is accomplished by editorial techniques such as omission, invention, rearrangement, and emphasis. Garfield's novel does not begin in a Hawaiian Eden, nor does it present Tucson as less afflicted by crime than New York. His protagonist muses about the situation in Arizona, "No place was immune any more. You thought of muggings and murders as dark city things—as if wide boulevards and low rooftops and a brass desert sun would inhibit them—but the crime rate was alarming here too. . . ." Rather than experiencing revelation in Old Tucson, the Paul Benjamin of the novel conceived his campaign of vengeance almost immediately after the death of his wife. In an argument with his son Jack, a lawyer who opposes the desire for vigilantism, Paul remarks, "Do you really think those savages deserve all that complicated fine print?"

His son replies, "Well then what would you suggest? . . . Catch them and string them up from the nearest rafter, is that the idea?"

Paul Benjamin answers, "It's better than they deserve. They ought to be hunted down like mad dogs and shot on sight."

Sensing his father's attraction for the mythical fantasy of six-gun justice, Jack retorts, "So you'd like to just strap on a pair of cowboy sixguns and go out there and gun them down, is that it?"

"Right now, that is exactly what I'd like to do."[13]

Frustrated by his son's refusal to help him get a gun permit, Paul goes to Tucson with the intent of purchasing a pistol there. There is no need to overcome his reluctance in using firearms, since he had served in the Army, unlike the Paul Kersey of the film, who was portrayed as a conscientious objector.

In the concluding pages of the novel, it becomes clear that Benjamin has become a crazed and vicious murderer. He rents a car in order to set a trap for anyone who might attempt to burglarize it. When a pair of teen-agers opens the hood, Benjamin steps out of hiding and guns them down. Just before their murder he mused, "Someone has to guard the city. Obviously the cops weren't doing it. . . . Then it's up to me, isn't it?" After these killings, Benjamin reads a magazine interview with a psychiatrist who discusses the New York vigilante:

> That's why a man like this captures our imagination so vividly—he's acting out fantasies we've all shared. . . . It's the lone wolf aspect that appeals to the American sensibility. One rugged individualist out there battling the forces of evil–it fits right into our mythology. . . .

The interview concludes with a harsh and disturbing judgment:

> . . . These killings of his are having about as much effect on the total crime picture as you'd get by administering two aspirin tablets to a rabid wolf. . . . It's no good condoning any of this man's actions, no good trying to put a high moral tone on them. The man's a murderer.

As Benjamin muses on these words, he asks, *"Have I done enough?,"* and answers himself, *"They* are still out there."[14]

The vigilante leaves his apartment to look for prey, finds a group of teen-agers dropping rocks on a passing train, and begins to gun them down. When one of the boys attacks with a knife to defend the others, Benjamin shoots him in the face. As the boy lies bleeding on the pavement, the vigilante shoots him twice more in the head lest he survive to identify him. Benjamin also wants to pursue and kill the girl who escaped, but it is too late. The campaign to guard the city has now degenerated into murdering simply to protect the vigilante's identity. Deciding that she probably hadn't seen his face, Paul walks past a nearby policeman. Even though the weapon hangs unconcealed in the vigilante's hand, the cop intentionally turns his head in the other direction. It is Garfield's final image of a society condoning vigilantism, wishing its own death.

Brian Garfield's literary treatment of mythical violence enjoyed only mediocre success in comparison to the film. The transmutation of the novel to match the golden elixir of monomythic redemption opened the door to mass acceptance. In addition to becoming a hit film in America, *Death Wish* was a leading box-office attraction in Latin America, France, Italy, and Japan. The film established Charles Bronson as a superstar in America, a status he had earlier achieved abroad. It inspired novels by Philip Rawls, *Bronson: Blind Rage; Bronson: Streets of Blood;* and *Bronson: Switchblade.*[15] In these stories Bronson lives, not as actor but as violent avenger, having placed an indelible stamp on the urban vigilante role that now becomes synonymous with his name. *Death Wish* also helped to crystallize an image of mythical violence and sexuality that was used in the rerelease of *Rider on the Rain* in 1975, capitalizing on the spectacular success of *Death Wish.*

In *Rider on the Rain,* Bronson plays a U. S. Army colonel attempting to track a psychopathic killer who has escaped from a German base with sixty thousand dollars from a cash box. The colonel comes to a French town where he discovers that a lovely young woman had been raped by the psychopath, whom she secretly killed and disposed of in the ocean. Mellie fears telling anyone about the incident, partly because her husband is an irrationally jealous Italian. Colonel Dobbs, without revealing his official identity, begins a campaign of harassment against the woman to force her to tell what she knows about the psychopath in order to retrieve the money. He tortures her brutally: In one scene, he spins her on a chair and forces excessive amounts of scotch down her throat; he holds a pistol to her head and pulls the trigger, hoping to coerce a confession. Dobbs divulges that her husband has had an affair with one of her friends. For a moment he has the opportunity to possess Mellie sexually, but he is uninterested. The colonel's sexual purity is further evident as he enters a brothel to rescue the woman he has been abusing. He brutally attacks the madame who stands in his way and beats up all her henchmen while retrieving Mellie. The movie ends happily when the woman discovers the cash and returns it to Dobbs, thus ending his campaign against her. Mellie is reconciled with her husband without his ever knowing about the rape or killing. She is also freed from a childhood trauma that resulted from witnessing her mother's indiscretion. As Steven Whitney puts it, "By the end of the film, Mellie has regained her identity, has grown from traumatized child to adult."[16] Torturing a helpless woman for money never turned out more redemptively.

The advertisement for the rereleased *Rider* contains an image that is archetypal for the violent superhero. Bronson is shown with his shirt removed, holding a raised pistol in his left hand while his right hand twists the terrified face of the slip-clad woman. The words "Bronson at his brutal best!" are overlaid. Sexual interest in this image is replaced with brutalities rationalized by the mission. Sexual arousal is displaced by a threatening pistol. While the scene did not actually occur in the film, it distills the symbolic significance of the role that Bronson popularized in *Death Wish.* In spite of its disturbingly pathological character, Bronson's role in *Rider on the Rain* was greeted with enthusiasm. Dan Knapp, the reviewer for the Los Angeles *Times,* commented, "It is Bronson's most memorable role. He plays a relentless, brash, but likeable, even loveable, undercover agent."[17] The appeal, we submit, lies largely in the psychic readiness of the American audience to welcome redemption as long as it is combined with a suitable measure of sexual renunciation. This chaste union, typical for the American monomyth, appears in the most unlikely places, as we shall soon discover.

IV
"Playboy's" Gospel: Better Wings than Horns

"It is better to have wings than horns."—George Herbert, *Jacula Prudentum* (1640)[1]

". . . There is an enemy out there. This country—indeed, the whole world—consists of two opposing forces: us, and those who would force their values and their attitudes on us. Totalitarianism has been the major evil in this world since the beginning of civilization. . . ."—from Hugh Hefner's "20th Anniversary *Playboy* Interview," January 1974[2]

A peculiar pattern of sexual renunciation surfaces in *Star Trek* and *Death Wish*. Paul Kersey's role of urban vigilante requires that he become a chaste and violent monastic who channels his creative energy through a pistol. In *Star Trek,* Spock and Captain Kirk are both unmarried, except to their duties on the *Enterprise.* Sexual relations are either instinctual, as in the case of Spock, or instrumental to the mission, as in the case of Kirk's escapades. Since sex cannot be integrated with the personality of one engaged in a redemptive mission, it must be segmented, placed in a separate compartment sealed off from the world of work, public affairs, and one's deepest personal commitments.

We find an embodiment of this monomythic sexual pattern in superhero comic books where the idealistic savior figure wants nothing to do with girls, "except to help them," as Jules Feiffer observes.[3] There is a deeply rooted preference to have the "wings" of angelic chastity rather than the "horns" of devilish lust. This is found even in materials like *Playboy* magazine, which has rarely been accused of advocating chastity, for the ideal "Playboy" is strikingly similar to Gary Cooper or Superman; all he wants to do is help needy Playmates and then gracefully move on. Segmentation ensures that his cool demeanor betrays not a single lustful thought.[4]

What mythical pattern unites the Playboy and Superman, Doc Savage and Norman Mailer? Why is it so appealing? How should we evaluate sexual segmentation? To put it another way, is it really better to have wings than horns?

I

The sexual segmentation pattern in America assumed its definitive shape in *Superman* comics. Jerry Siegel and Joe Shuster conceived the format in 1933 as seventeen-year-olds, and when first published in 1938, Superman became ". . . the most popular and powerful folk hero in American fiction." He was the infant survivor of Krypton who was raised by the kindly Kent family. After their death he ". . . decided he must turn his titanic strength into channels that would benefit mankind. And so was created . . . SUPERMAN, champion of the oppressed, the physical marvel who had sworn to devote his existence to helping those in need."[5]

A permanent romantic impasse is portrayed in the triangle of Clark Kent, Lois Lane, and Superman. Clark Kent, the clumsy, bespectacled alter ego of Superman, loves Lois Lane, but she despises him while eagerly chasing Superman. The handsome superhero, however, lacks the need to be sexually responsive. Jules Feiffer explains the pattern of segmentation:

> Clark Kent loved but felt abashed with Lois Lane; Superman saved Lois Lane when she was in trouble, found her a pest the rest of the time. Since Superman and Clark Kent were the same person, this behavior demands explanation. It can't be that Kent wanted Lois to respect him for himself, since himself was Superman. Then, it appears, he wanted Lois to respect him for his fake self, to love him when he acted the coward, to be there when he pretended to need her. She never was–so, of course, he loved her. A typical American romance. Superman never needed her, never needed anybody–in any event, Lois chased *him,* so, of

> course, he didn't love her. He had contempt for her. Another typical American romance.[6]

This fantasy appeals to comic book readers approaching puberty. Steranko's own reaction in his *History of Comics* suggests that the audience projects its real identity onto Superman. "Lois was too school-girlishly romantic to see beyond Kent's blue suit, red tie . . . and spectacles. She looked at him with adamant disdain, while we looked smugly at her. Superman's reaction was about equal to ours."[7] Readers knew they were no more attractive to beautiful females than Clark Kent, but the fantasy led them to imagine that under their drab exterior was a redeemer figure so virile that females would tremble with desire. But a self-contained superhero would not need such affections in the least. Result: a smug segmentation of one's relationship with females. The ideal is for partners like Superman and Lois Lane to be kept permanently apart.

A revealing episode from the 1940s dramatizes the pattern of segmentation.[8] Its opening caption explains that ". . . for years Clark Kent, in his identity as SUPERMAN, has been saving Lois Lane from peril after peril. And all this time Lois has always had to play the role of the damsel in distress. . . . Can you imagine what would happen if Lois were unexpectedly to find herself gifted with superhuman strength?" The "Lois Lane–Superwoman" story opens with the frustrated triangle. Clark Kent is pleading with a busy Lois Lane.

"Lois–I hate to be insistent. But won't you please tell me once and for all if you care for me?"

"I like you, Clark. But how could I really care for a man like you when I've associated with someone as confident, outspoken, and assertive as SUPERMAN! I'll care for you when you're like SUPERMAN . . . which will be NEVER."

She strides across the street and is struck down by a truck. The doctor reports she can be saved only if a certain brain surgeon can be found. Superman goes into action to solve the mysterious disappearance. While he is gone, Lois lapses into a dream state in which she pictures herself as having been turned into a superwoman by a blood transfusion from Superman. She gains incredible strength, and finds herself leaping through the air at tremendous speed.

Sewing herself a proper tricot uniform, she flies into the redemptive task. But her ultimate aim is to get her man. Superwoman Lois Lane begins in an area traditionally reserved for the female heroes, settling a family squabble. She persuades an angry couple to "bury the rolling pin and make up." Of course they do.

With her new X-ray vision Lois then sees some thugs kidnaping a helpless man. She flies to the rescue, beats off the thugs, and discovers that the victim is none other than Clark Kent. She forcibly carries him to dizzying heights to prevent him from revealing her new identity to the newspaper editor. But Dr. Skowl's aircraft catches the pair in a large net, mistaking her for Superman. The villain upbraids his bumbling accomplices and decides to destroy the strangely dressed woman. When Kent hears this vile resolve, he changes into his Superman attire and flies to her rescue, only to be stopped by Skowl's electric device. Superman is strung up for the *coup de grâce* when Lois, alias Superwoman, turns the machine against its inventor. The "archfiend" is destroyed by the "frightful beam of his own deadly ray." Then Lois lays her cards on the table to the man she adores.

"For five long years you've led me a dizzy chase on a romantic merry-go-round, my fine-feathered friend! Well, that's all changed. I've got some super-powers of my own now. And YOU'RE going to listen to ME!"

Superman mutters, "But–but . . ."

"I'm crazy, batty, dippy, and slap-happily in love with you, you great big wonderful man . . . and the point of all this romantic by-play is that I want a DEFINITE answer to one little question: WILL YOU MARRY ME?"

Superman responds, "I . . . er . . . that is . . ."

Lois clasps him to her ample bosom, plants a kiss on the side of his mouth, and responds with "I accept!!!" to the marriage proposal he has not really issued. He glances over to the comic book reader, his hands stretched out in a helpless shrug as she holds him against her lovely breasts, and says:

"ULP! What chance has a mere SUPERMAN got??"

At this climactic moment, Lois awakens from her dream, the brain operation having successfully been completed. Superman has saved her again, but there at the door of the hospital room stands the perpetually despised Clark Kent. He has waited for hours with his flowers.

From the point of view of males approaching puberty, this is a powerfully attractive fantasy. The fumbling advances of indecisive males like Clark Kent are compensated by the fantasy that beautiful women will throw themselves upon true supermen. And beneath Kent's clothing there *is* that *super* man. The blundering exterior merely disguises the true self, and since females cannot see below the surface, the reader should view them with Superman's tolerant contempt. Identifying with Superman, the reader can pretend that sexual yearnings are unimportant, or that such disturbing feelings simply do not even exist. Rude lust disappears, it is assumed, behind the angelic façade of indifference. A disciple of Superman desires only to help girls, to be their redeemer. Girls would lose themselves in admiration–if only they knew this true identity. With neat incision, the traditional masculine task of sexual initiation is projected onto the female. Why be a dummy like Clark Kent? Be cool like Superman!

This variant of the segmentation motif is reflected in the visible omission of sexual organs in the depiction of the Superman type of hero. As Reitberger and Fuchs observed, in all the hundreds of wide-stanced, aggressively masculine poses, their muscular bodies clad in tricot have no "roundish, protuberant anatomic structures," to use a dictionary phrase. As compensation for this absence, Superman bears the redeemer's cape, the wings of angels as it were, to consummate his duty to help girls in trouble. The abandonment of human sexual awareness and responsibility has never been more alluringly or idealistically portrayed. The realm of sexual conflict and pain, the acknowledgment of sexual desires and identity, and the ceaseless need for maturation are dismissed by a cool shrug. Sexual ambiguity is forsaken to permit quick and neat redemption. An incidental curiosity of comic book history was Superman's marriage in the daily newspaper strip, which was quickly squelched. Subsequent romantic involvements have taken place exclusively in dream settings.[9] Sensing that the powerful sexual fantasy could not be sustained amid the cares and tribulations of marriage, the editors exercised sound mythic logic. The permanent segmentation of a Superman remains always preferable to the ambivalent reality of a Clark Kent.

II

A similar pattern of segmentation is visible in most other popular superhero stories. Batman has a permanent relation to his male counterpart, Robin, but never forms an abiding liaison with a woman. Billy Batson is called to be Captain Marvel with the injunction, "You are pure in heart. You have been chosen." This purity prevents anything beyond a boyish crush on the well-endowed Beautia Sivana, who betrayed her own evil father for Captain Marvel. Her feelings for the superhero and his coolness toward her are similar to the Superman triangle.[10] Torch, Sub-Mariner, Green Lantern, and Spiderman rescue girls but never marry them. Their feminine counterparts like Wonder Woman and Lady Blackhawk remain single. It is somehow inconceivable that Mary Worth, Matt Dillon, Rex Morgan, or Marcus Welby would ever get married. And judging from the fates of the fiancées of Ben, Joe, and Hoss Cartright, and others, even planning to marry a fictional hero seems to be the most lethal enterprise in America.

Philip José Farmer's recent study of the pulp superhero Doc Savage reveals the rationale of this peculiar segmentation pattern. Farmer notes that in the 181 issues appearing from 1933 to 1949, the "Man of Bronze" was supported by a team of male associates in his fight against the forces of evil. With the exception of his curvaceous cousin, Patricia Savage, no females played a role in more than a few episodes. This "Lady Auxilliary and Bronze Knockout" was summoned only reluctantly by the Doc, and no romantic connection was hinted between the two. Farmer asks the key question, "Given Doc's unusual vigor and his undoubted desire for women, why did he remain chaste . . . ? His excuse was that his enemies would strike at him through any women he became involved with." The answer is that his role as benefactor of humanity, financier, management expert, and annihilator or rehabilitator of criminals simply could not be combined with home and family responsibilities. As Farmer explains, "He is the scientific savior. As saviors always must, he suffers loneliness and a sense of isolation from the people. He has to be ready for those who would daily crucify him."[11]

This is very close to the pattern observed in Superman. For the sake of redemption, sexual relations must be kept in a separate and usually empty compartment. The masculine ideal is to help women; their admiration is welcome, but not their attachment. Feiffer supplies an apt description of this segmentation pattern, which seems applicable to pop culture as a whole.

> Our cultural opposite of the man who didn't make out with women has never been the man who did—but rather the man who could if he wanted to, but still didn't. The ideal of masculine strength, whether Gary Cooper's, Lil Abner's, or Superman's, was for one to be virile and handsome, to be in such a position of strength, that he need never go near girls. Except to help them. And then get the hell out. Real rapport was not for women. It was for villains. That's why they got hit so hard.[12]

III

Though at first it may seem implausible, the superhero segmentation pattern is basic to *Playboy*. Superman and Doc Savage avoid even the thought of sexual liaisons, whereas the ideal Playboy would obviously feel embarrassed without one. But a curious series of discrepancies between the stated *Playboy* philosophy and the powerful pictorial icons in the magazine leads us to assert that mythical segmentation is an unacknowledged premise. We also suspect that the paradigm of the cool redeemer has shaped its vision of sexuality.

Mutuality, enjoyment, and consent are key principles in the *Playboy* philosophy. So long as intercourse is between consenting "Playboys" and "Playmates," publisher Hugh Hefner sees no compelling reasons for opposing it, even if the parties are not acquainted in the least. He is critical only when sex becomes irresponsible, exploitative, coercive or somehow hurtful to one of the partners concerned. At best the relationship should be a loving one, if for no other reason than the prospect of higher levels of pleasure; he suggests that "the best," most personally significant sex expresses the powerful emotions we associate with the term "love." *Playboy*'s philosophy holds that because of the greater emotional rewards, "personal sex" should take precedence over impersonal.[13]

These themes of personal involvement are missing in the beautifully engraved icons that make *Playboy* famous, the ten-by-twenty-three-inch Playmate foldouts, or the pictorial fantasy sequences. In most of these stirring photographs the women are alone; men, if present at all, are blurred and subordinate. These images possess an explicit autoeroticism, with a strong expression of female sexual passion, often accompanied by some form of self-stimulating or masturbatory activity. The Playmates rub their bodies against blankets, provocatively straddle pillows, allow cords to drape over their pubic areas, and spread their legs invitingly, presumably for any male who would care to drop in. While the Playmate photos project a symbolic invitation to Everyman, the icons of the pictorial fantasies tend to present featureless, anonymous males. Distinctive women are portrayed with lush, peachy bodies and an amazing variety of pubic hair tints. They loll in aroused consent, but their attention is not directed to male lovers. The icons portray undifferentiated sexual gratification in which the identity of the male is irrelevant. Iconic sex in this strictly impersonal form contravenes the value claims of the *Playboy* philosophy.

The ideal of sexual fun is also contradicted in a startling way by the icons. Hefner claims that the magazine strives to make sexual relations as attractive as possible. Yet the pictures consistently portray it as a purely female enjoyment. Never are men pictured in a state of sexual excitement or delight. The icons carefully mask any evidence of male arousal, while offering a surfeit of female ecstasy. The men in the pictures are remarkably cool about these encounters, even though their attractive partners are lyrically eager. In a magazine dedicated to male sexual pleasure, this is remarkable indeed. This contradiction is reflected in Harvey Cox's puzzling accusation that *Playboy* is "antisexual" in its emphasis on "recreational sex."[14] How could sex as pure fun turn into such a grim and dutiful drag?

The puzzle deepens when one observes that sexual encounters

in *Playboy* appear to be the product solely of female sensuality forcing itself upon inattentive males. Enthusiastic sexual aggression is assigned strictly to females. One of the spread-legged Vargas beauties gives a promiscuous note to Will Rogers' well-known statement that he never met a man he didn't like. Another Vargas woman in a revealing fragment of a British redcoat uniform expresses her grateful amazement to John Hancock that his is the largest she's seen.[15] In contrast, the males for whom the magazine is presumably published are seldom pictured as vigorously seeking sexual fulfillment. Men appear to be doing women a favor, giving them something they desperately need, rather than acting upon their own freely expressed impulses. It is puzzling that the quest for honest male pleasure should go so bafflingly astray in an era that has unshackled itself from the archaic notion that sex is sinful.

These icons of repressed male sexuality produce jarring discrepancies with the *Playboy* ideals of liberation, maturity, and frankness. The *Playboy* philosophy proclaims the good news of a new form of candid maturity, permitting harmony of body, soul, and mind.[16] Given such a lofty gospel, one could imagine that if Hefner were writing *Star Trek* stories, he would introduce stylish leisure and sexual gratification for Kirk, Spock, and their Playmates on board the *Enterprise*. He would redesign the bridge to resemble a yacht rented for a *Playboy* party. Yet when one turns to the pictorial icons in the magazine he controls, male images of integrating body, mind, and soul are entirely lacking. The icons deny the very existence of male sexual urges or pleasures. These "Playboys" are as impassive and cool as the superheroes on the ascetic bridge of the starship engaged in cosmic redemption.

These discrepancies become comprehensible if one views *Playboy* as an extension of the Superman pattern. The male role is to "help girls" and "get the hell out," as Feiffer so nicely puts it. One responds to the sexual call to redemptive duty, just as Superman does in nonsexual arenas, with efficiency, strength, and coolness. No matter how much the Lois Lanes say they love it, the supermen must remain impassive. In a world of supersex, the fulfillment of the male role has become a hard duty, and as with most redemptive obligations, pleasures become peripheral.[17]

The key to Hefner's extension of the fantasy world of *Superman Comics* was the creation of the Playmate icon. The Playmate is the ideal female because she has only one thing on her mind. She needs sexual gratification so badly that she will gladly receive help from anyone. Thus an insatiable sexual void is imagined so that Everyman can help a damsel in distress. In one of the *Playboy* cartoons, a cheerful satyr has to turn away a naked woman because of the pressing demands of the other lovelies he has already laid out on the turf. He politely excuses himself because he has already begun foreplay with six others.[18] This image is employed in a 1975 Playmate sequence in which a shapely woman has mounted a wooden dock post in ecstatic expectation. In a later pose she lies nude on a bed in readiness, a dreamy look in her eyes. The caption inquires what might lie in this Playmate's future. "Either modeling or acting would go a long way toward satisfying her need–which she's quite candid about–for a lot of attention. Whatever she does, she intends to give it her best." In the context of the seductive sequences, the "attention" this Playmate desires and the "need" she has are clearly sexual.

The Playmate icons picture the need for sexual redemption as so urgent that feminine self-control completely disappears. These models are helpless even to finish undressing themselves. They need a competent man. Now. In another touching autoerotic sequence, a Playmate beauty poses with panties partly down, caressing herself sexually, her eyes closed. Her need is desperate. In the next shot, she has her slip almost off, and stands with breast uncovered and mons displayed, a yearning look on her face. On the opposite page, she discusses her career and her need for a serviceable male with staying power.

> "I'm a strong-willed, ambitious person, and when it comes to my career, I know exactly what I want. But when it comes to romance, I'm open to suggestions. . . . I'm looking for a very bossy man, really. I never like to be the boss, but I always seem to wind up in that role–and I'm getting pretty sick of it."

Commenting on the type of man she needs, the Playmate reports,

> "It's important for a man to work at a good job and make good money–but that's not all. He should also be honest–and faith-

ful, because when I'm going with a guy, I want him just for myself."

In other words, beautiful Playmates like this will cling to their saviors. They want and need Playboys. Who will enlist for this cause of serving womankind? That is the unspoken altar call to the would-be supermen who hear *Playboy*'s gospel.

The image of women as helpless Playmates is dominant even in the seduction sequences of *Playboy*'s pictorial fantasy. In place of the more traditional image of male artifice gaining power over initially uninterested females, *Playboy* offers a redemption scheme in which males simply fill already existing needs. In the February 1975 pictorial fantasy, for instance, the "French Maid" in an exclusive party is not supposed to be in on the orgy. The women in expensive clothing are draped all over the living room in various states of undress, fingering their sexual organs, or waiting for their fully clad helpers to come through. The fetching maid is then shown fellating a champagne glass while inserting her hand into her drooping panties. The obliging but cool man of the house finds her in this desperate plight and calmly agrees to do his duty. The caption reads, "As the party starts to warm up, so does our French maid, who finds it difficult to remember her station. Monsieur can sense this. Wandering about the manse, below, he finds her and decides to get on at her station." The scenes that follow have her frantically undressing, while he looks off sleepily. "Would monsieur like me to make the bed?," she asks shyly. "No, monsieur would like her to make the monsieur."[19] At no time is the male in a state of sexual tension or readiness. He does nothing more than oblige the lovely maid, while she is in a state of sexual ecstasy. In the final scene she lies beside her cool savior with the parted lips of one who has just had her deepest need fulfilled. The male paradigm here is clearly the selfless superhero, the one who redeems helpless women from their suffering plights.

Playboy's fiction sometimes gives direct expression to this selfless savior motif. In a story by Al Capp, a female artist is painting Eros.[20] She requires the use of a male model, *in status erectus,* and thus works at her easel in a see-through negligee. The sexually naïve José attempts to fill this demand but collapses exhausted under physician's care before she gets very far. His friend Edgar, intrigued by the challenge, takes on this strange assignment. After less than three years as the Eros Erectus, he dies from heroic exertion. This story brings to symbolic clarity the motifs implicit in the *Playboy* icons. Woman here has the ravenous sexual appetite of the Playmate, and anyone courageous enough to attempt to fill it risks his life. It is a ridiculous scheme when stated bluntly, but it makes perfect sense within the framework of selfless superheroes who risk their all to "help girls" in their distressing need.

If *Playboy* males have no sexual desires and no aggressive traits, this proves they have an angelic purity. The obliging males of the *Playboy* icons are indifferent to any personal gratification. Like Superman, their zeal is only to help. This pose of selfless innocence and masculine reserve is consistent with the basic segmentation pattern we observed earlier as a concomitant of the redemption scheme. It is not a sign of degeneracy that Playboys engage in sexual intercourse while Superman refrains. Since they never do so for self-gratification, they remain true to the Superman ideal of rising only to fill the needs of others. The cool impassivity of their expressions despite close proximity to sexual idols is proof enough that they have wings instead of horns.

Playboy thus has a natural link to extend a final motif of the Superman fantasy, namely female admiration. Lois Lane admires Superman's heroism and finds his tricot uniform infinitely more attractive than the business suit of the staid Clark Kent. In the fashion feature sections of *Playboy,* the women respond to the men the way Lois Lane responds to the Superman uniform. Struggling to receive manicured attention, they cling to the well-dressed fellows. Yet the men in the fashion ads are unmoved by this admiration. Like Superman, their demeanor is indifferent or even contemptuous. The most friendly of the male models manage only a hint of a smile as the admiring Lois Lanes rub up against them.

The role of fashionable clothing as a tricot equivalent for men who play the cool superhero role is demonstrable in almost any issue of *Playboy.* In the July 1975 issue, there are ads about "suits to keep summer from burning into a sticky wicket." The first picture in the fashion sequence features a cool, scornfully indifferent male in a white suit blowing smoke into the air while a woman behind him sighs in a sexual straddle. The caption is "She's having a tropical heat wave, but he couldn't care less." In the next picture, the woman in the background is fanning herself with one hand while the other is buried in her pants. She sits on a block of ice cooling her passion, while the well-dressed man stares into the distance. On the following page, a scantily clad girl draws her long skirt tightly up to her pelvis, and eagerly downs a phallic beer while the man in the peach-colored suit drags gangsterishly on a cigarette holder, the symbol of ultimate detachment. The ad reads, "The pause that refreshes–at least for him, thanks to his one button gabardine suit. . . ." In the next photo, a cool man in a blue suit tolerates an impassioned kiss by a beautiful girl whose white smock gapes open in the front. She speaks as the sexual aggressor: " 'You're fan-tastic,' she says, and he readily agrees. . . ."[21]

The power of this tricot fantasy is evidenced by Hugh Hefner's report that the articles on male fashion consistently evoke the greatest response from readers, surpassing enthusiasm even for the monthly Playmates.[22] Fashion serves as the "how to" feature in the *Playboy* fantasy world. How can a reader get lovely Playmates to make themselves available for salvation? By wearing a uniform. Instead of fighting off thugs or saving nations from yellow hordes, the *Playboy* superhero qualifies for feminine admiration by purchasing the right costume and assuming the proper look of insouciance when females become too troublesome in their admiration.

Our view that mythic segmentation lies at the heart of the *Playboy* fantasy has been confirmed at each decisive point. We have discovered how it came about that St. Hugh, who has broken so many lances for Lady Pleasure, allowed his vision of liberation to be shaped by a formative encounter with the Superman triangle. His covert gospel offers gratification without penetration, seduction disguised as salvation, and helping hands without a heated brow.

IV

Playboy's gospel unites a host of discrepancies with commercial success, as we have seen. The more carefully one describes the logic of the gospel, the greater is the sense of mystery that it should ever have found its apostles. How does *Playboy* make its mythic content appealing and believable? What are the results of believing *Playboy*'s gospel? We believe that the techniques of mythic conveyance include crusading idealism, pseudo-intellectualism, and iconic photography.

Given the power and widespread dispersion of redemptive crusading in pop materials, it should not be surprising to find the same spirit in *Playboy*'s attack on America's sexual rigidities. The magazine presents itself as an idealistic crusade rather than degenerate voyeurism. Its goals are serious, in the oldest American sense of fighting battles against apocalyptic adversaries. The *Playboy* philosophy is at war against the misguided, Puritanical version of sex, whose "shackles" Hefner and *Playboy* are helping America to discard. It takes the side of the crusading younger generation against the crippling hypocrisy of its elders. The magazine loves to print reactionary letters from preachers who foolishly direct Puritanical sermons against *Playboy*'s degeneracy and irresponsibility. It prints frequent reports about book-burning campaigns and other repressive campaigns by the uptight counterreformers in conservative churches. Readers thereby derive confirmation that *Playboy* is the vanguard of a liberal crusade, a mortal enemy of those who conspire against the freedom of sexual expression. As Hugh Hefner remarked in the "20th Anniversary *Playboy* Interview," "This country–indeed, the whole world–consists of two opposing forces: us, and those who would force their own values and attitudes on us." Hefner clearly sees himself borne on white wings through this sexual revolution. "We live in a period of rapid sociological change," he stated, "and I am on the side of the angels."[23]

The aims of the *Playboy* crusade have a touch of the grandiose, reflecting a long American tradition of campaigning for millennial redemption. The magazine allegedly performs "a considerable service" by struggling for liberal sexual attitudes. By encouraging healthy sexual behavior on the part of unmarried adults, *Playboy* seeks to eliminate the pain, the broken hearts, and wasted years—the "bitter" legacies of sexual hangups. This will actually serve to stabilize marriage for the society as a whole, because readers will allegedly have the capability for durable marriages because they have achieved extra reserves of "maturity and stability" from the magazine. They will also be far more discriminating in choosing spouses with whom they can attain lifetime compatibility.[24] Judging from the most prominent material in the magazine, this noble purpose is to be achieved by indulging in fantasies about a world of sprawling Playmates; admiring them and living out the fantasies they arouse will, presumably, equip one to maintain stable relationships with real women. But the spurious benefits notwithstanding, the effectiveness of the stratagem has been undeniable. In a culture preoccupied with redemption, the profession of crusading ideals is perhaps necessary to make one's message believable.

A second means by which the mythic quality of *Playboy*'s fantasies gains disguise is its pseudo-intellectualism, a near relative of the pseudo-empiricism of *Star Trek*. The magazine regularly features the work and ideas of leading writers and statesmen as well as articulate celebrities. Even the fiercest critics of *Playboy* admit ". . . it has some of the most important interviews that are being published today. . . ." Jane Fonda went on to acknowledge, ". . . They also run some very important articles, and I recognize them as such." *Playboy* fiction includes works by some of the best-known writers in contemporary literature. The highest fees of any current magazine are reportedly paid for such works. Most articles deal with serious, nonsexual topics.[25] When sixty contributors attended the lavish *Playboy* International Writers' Convocation in 1971, notables such as Arthur Clarke, Arthur Schlesinger, Jr., Sean O'Faolain, Alberto Moravia, John Cheever, John Kenneth Galbraith, Tom Wicker, Garry Wills, Murray Kempton, Harvey Cox, and Art Buchwald were on hand. The editorial strategy in spending an estimated two hundred thousand dollars for this convocation is the same as naming Hefner's editorials from 1962 to 1965 "Playboy Philosophy"–to sustain the appearance of intellectual solidity.

The purpose of this intellectual bravura is to create the impression that reasonable and creative people approve of *Playboy*'s gospel. The inclusion of occasional articles and interviews that are critical of the magazine gives credence to the claim of enlightened open-mindedness. It is as if *Playboy* presents a reasonable, coherent world view with nothing to hide. The problem is that the crucial mythical structure of the *Playboy* fantasy world is never acknowledged. Morton Hunt's book *Sexual Behavior in the 1970's,* published by the Playboy Press and serialized in the magazine, symptomizes the function of intellectual camouflage. Hunt makes but one reference to *Playboy,* mentioning that it first showed female pubic hair in 1972.[26] *Playboy*'s fantasy patterns, which hold such fascination for contemporary males, are not even mentioned. Intellectualism here does not serve the unfettered quest for truth; it protects a mythical fantasy world from close examination. Intellect can disguise as well as illuminate reality.

Sophisticated pseudo-intellectualism diverts attention from a mythic paradigm that is embarrassing when explicitly stated. Some of the *Playboy* contributors have vaguely sensed the discrepancy between their intellectual talents and the visual icons. "How can anybody critique this magazine when nobody reads it?" asked Nicholas von Hoffman at the Writers' Convocation. "I couldn't read my own piece. I read the first page and then–boob alley!–I was lost in the boobs."[27] The juxtaposition is both distracting and disarming. One glances back and forth between the beautiful icons and the scholarly articles and ends up with superficial quibbles rather than fundamental critique. The meaning of Playmate flesh is rendered opaque by the flurry of stylish rhetoric.

Playboy's third technique of mythic conveyance, the most effective of all, is the use of visual images to produce "boob alley." The photographic skill is undeniable, but the power of these photos lies primarily in their mythical content. This is iconic photography in which an image is made into an object of uncritical devotion by shaping it according to a pre-existing mythic paradigm. The segmented world of Playmates and superhero redeemers is adapted and presented photographically, conveying a fantasy that overpowers one's normal sense of reality. To articulate the Playmate-redemption scheme verbally renders it laughable, but to do so iconically has proven effective beyond Hefner's expectations. He is conscious about the role of fantasy in the photographs. He complains that life would be oppressively dull without "dreams and aspirations"; therefore, the magazine consciously supplements its reports on the real world with fantasy material.[28] We are not critical of dreams as such nor of the creative interaction between dreams and reality. But the *Playboy* icons present fantasies *as* the real world, creating imaginary needs and then offering fulfillment by equally imaginary means.

Iconic photography gives readers the impression that Playmates really exist, that sexual redemption is yearned for not just in a dream but also in actual persons whose names are provided. One from 1975 reclines invitingly with a sultry look, struggling to get the last of her clothing off. In another icon she aggressively straddles a satin pillow. Her lush body waits expectantly in various moods of sexual conjugation, and her words are those of the projectively conceived Lois Lane: "She describes herself as perky, flirtatious, and occasionally aggressive ('When I know what I want, I go after it.'). Generally speaking, she's extremely active." Here is the gospel injunction that shakes one's very being: Give this Playmate the help she needs! Rescue the perishing, for her sake and for yours! She is knocking at heart's door; please let her in to sup with you!

But the truth is that iconic Playmates are not waiting for Everyman in poses like this. The realism of Playmate photographs is pure artifice, painstakingly achieved while thousands of ineffective poses had to be discarded. Who would ever suspect this while reading the captions about a Playmate's cold, her singing with a school band, her piano lessons, and her recent graduation from a theatrical institute? These all create the pseudo-empirical impression that the icon is real, that there actually are Playmates who sigh for salvation.

Iconic photography, pseudo-intellectualism, and crusading idealism serve to inoculate males against the nasty recognition that the fantasy of female aggressiveness is a winged projection of their own sexual desires. The Superman image of sexual purity and selflessness is retained by projecting the "active" role onto imaginary Playmates who pose commercially before Hefner's cameras. Angelic innocence is thus maintained to deny mythically the realities of male sexuality in twentieth-century America. It is quite a feat for a secular magazine like *Playboy* to replicate the efforts of medieval theologians in restoring to Eve the horns of lust.

Rollo May has diagnosed this trait and links it with a propensity toward both impotence and brutality in contemporary behavior.

The ". . . endeavor to love with the renunciation of power is a product of the tendency toward pseudo-innocence." The latter is May's term for the self-deceptive pretense of innocence about the power that one exercises. In the long run this pretense incapacitates a person. As May observes, "A person must have something to give in order not to be completely taken over or absorbed as a nonentity." He insists on the ". . . necessity of combining self-assertion (power) with tenderness (love) in the sex act." To deny male self-assertion and to exchange tenderness for dutiful redemption is finally to render Playboys incapable of sustaining relationships with real partners. It is impossible to believe that males achieve the "transition into maturity" that Hefner promises by occupying their minds with fantasies like the cartoon in the April 1975 *Playboy*. An eager female, clad in a revealing negligee, explains her scheme to one of the two innocents who sit in her room with a look of bewilderment. She *had* told him to bring a friend, she says, but she never promised she had a roommate.[29] Her void requires several men. Even the fantasy of this disguised form of gang rape is projected onto the female. Playmates will simply do anything to get selfless males to service them.–It is self-deceptive, though we have no inclination to rationalize male dominance. Even the "Last Tango" takes two. Yet *Playboy*'s mythic massage closes one off from the realities of human sexuality, in which power is exercised by both males and females, while neither really redeems the other.

V

The fantasy of innocence, in which males merely act on the wishes and needs of females, is a happy, nondialectical world. In a world lacking in conflicts of egos, an Edenic harmony is supposed to prevail. Hefner has followed a formula that we shall find central in "The Land of Disney": Eliminate the troubling, messy elements of sexual and biological existence in order to create a happy world in which frustration disappears. To live in such a world is not just the Playboy's goal; it is his right and his moral obligation. As Hefner describes him, he must not view life as a "vale of tears" but as "a happy time." He should take pleasure in work but prevent it from becoming the single purpose of his life. Alertness, awareness, taste, sensitivity to pleasure, the ability to absorb life's experiences "to the hilt"—these are the canonical virtues in *Playboy*'s gospel.[30]

What happens to such innocent self-deception when it encounters the real world of sexual conflict? What do Playboy redeemers do when their expectation of spread-legged readiness is not fulfilled? A Rowland Wilson cartoon poses this dilemma quite dramatically. A battered crusader has just withdrawn his bloody weapons from the body of the dragon and stands unbelieving before the beautiful princess he has just redeemed. She folds her arms defiantly and tauntingly addresses him as a "male chauvinist pig" who wants her to deliver now. Clearly, he hasn't got a chance.[31] The male frustration and rage expressed by this cartoon can easily boil over into brutality, which is designed to turn bitches into the bunnies they ought to be. At this point the fantasy world of *Playboy* makes a final logical U turn in violation of its principles of mutual consent and noncoercion.

In the May 1975 issue, *Playboy* broke the rape barrier by publishing Oakley Hall's story "The Spoils of Buenavista." The caption gives it all away by sending male sexual fantasies flying into orbit: "He whipped her again with the riding crop and she began to undress. 'Please,' she whispered, 'do not hit me anymore.'" The story concerns Robert MacBean, who is fighting with an *escuadrilla* unit during the Mexican revolution in 1914. As the unit innocently rides past a *hacienda,* a shot is fired, killing one of its members. The dead man's brother, ". . . the best man in the *escuadrilla;* the bravest, most competent and the humblest, who had never before this asked anything for himself," called out, "Roberto, I think we must take this evil place that would not let us pass in peace." They fought their way into the adobe courtyard and found the fat priest, the beautiful *patrona,* and her mother hiding in a concealed chapel. When the priest was dragged away for execution and the mother slipped out, MacBean was left alone with the imperious mistress of the evil *hacienda.*

> The girl stood motionless, tall as he was, full-breasted, full-hipped, wearing black boots, a black, full skirt, a black jacket

> with a profusion of white ruching at the throat . . . her right hand, holding the riding crop, fell to her side.
>
> "We are at your mercy, Señor Capitan," she said in a low voice. "Will you abuse us?"

MacBean silently decides to acquiesce in her request for safe passage, even though she had ordered the senseless attack on his men. But as he turns, she strikes his face with a riding crop and fires a revolver at him. He wards off the shot, deals her a staggering blow across the face, rips off her blouse, and slashes her folded arms with the riding crop.

"Holding the riding crop poised in his right hand, her blouse in his left, he slashed her yet again before she began to undress." He laid his weapons ". . . on a chair on the other side of the little chapel from the sobbing girl, the altar and the pillow before it."[32] The story leaves the reader to imagine the rest for himself.

The pattern here is similar to the dragon-slayer cartoon: an aggressive, bitchy female who must be put in her place. Her sexual attributes, described so provocatively by Hall, match her attack on the innocent column of guerrillas. Her every word and action are pictured as exuding the lust for power over men; the riding crop is the perfect symbol of her yearning for mastery. MacBean is as innocent an avenger in the final rape scene as the guerrillas were in attacking the "evil" *hacienda.* The church and its altar being in league with this evil, he has no choice but to violate them as he justly violates and punishes her. He has no intention of "abusing" the girl until she forces him into it. The story provides the logical answer to the question raised by the Rowland Wilson cartoon. If women refuse to be bunnies, they should be laid as bitches. It will do them good.

This rationalization for brutality is implicit in the sexual redeemer fantasy whenever women do not offer themselves with indiscriminate abandon. The mythical logic requires that men respond to such frustration either with autoeroticism or with brutality. The Playmate-redeemer scheme not only sets up expectations doomed to inevitable disappointment but also provides a moral justification for rape. If proudly aggressive women refuse to welcome their redeemers, they deserve the violent sexual punishment that will surely turn them into pliant Playmates.

Playboy would never admit the retributive logic implicit in the Oakley Hall story and the Rowland Wilson cartoon. If it cannot admit the redemption scheme buried in its own icons, it surely would not acknowledge the dark side of its Playmate myth. Yet the message radiating from the *Playboy* icons and the internal logic of the redeemer fantasy seem to take precedence over the urbane and witty remarks of the Playboy Advisor, who properly counsels against coercive sex. It is well for editors to advocate such prudence, but the fantasies they have sponsored are far more powerful than their advice. And as those who study primitive religions know, myths have a logic of their own. They impel forms of behavior that love and kindness would defy.

Norman Mailer has explored the brutal scheme of the innocent male as sexual redeemer in his short story "The Time of Her Time" and in his novel *An American Dream*. The extent to which the monomythic paradigm can invade even high-culture materials is visible in these stories featuring sexual retribution as a means of redeeming unwilling women. Sergius, the bullfighting instructor in "The Time of Her Time," is a sexual superman, ". . . a Village stickman who could muster enough of the divine It on the head of his will to call forth more than one becoming out of the womb of feminine Time, yes a good deal more than one from my fifty new girls a year. . . ." Although his reputation attracts women from all over Greenwich Village, Sergius has the cool, disinterested purity of the superman Playboy.

> When you screw too much and nothing is at stake, you begin to feel like a saint. . . . I always felt an obligation–some noblesse oblige of the kindly cocksman–to send my women away with no great wounds to their esteem, feeling at best a little better than when they came in. I wanted it to be friendly (what vanity of the saint!). I was the messiah of the one-night stand. . . .

After a night with one of his needy Playmates, the redeemer's overpowering desire the next morning was ". . . to kick the friendly ass out of bed . . . and get in again myself to the blessed isolations of the man alone."[33] Superman's yearning to "get the hell out" was never more colorfully stated.

When Sergius encountered Denise Gondelman, an aggressive intellectual from New York University, the redeemer urge turned into brutal rage. As they argued about T. S. Eliot at a Village party, Sergius recalls: "Her college-girl snobbery . . . so inflamed the avenger of my crotch, that I wanted to prong her then and there, right on the floor of the party. . . ." He yearned to ". . . lay waste to her little independence. . . ."[34]

The first time Sergius made love to Denise, she attempted to dominate him. He brutally slapped her in the midst of intercourse, breaking her arrogant rhythm, and ". . . for a moment she was making it." Then she slipped back into her greedy pattern: ". . . she had fled the domination which was liberty for her. . . ." She admitted she had never been brought to orgasm by normal means with her boyfriend: ". . . An aggressive female and a passive male—we complement one another, and that's no good." So in their final encounter Sergius is determined to redeem her forcibly. He turned her over, "wounded her," and when she was about to reach the climax whispered in her ear, "You dirty little Jew." This final humiliation and subordination ". . . whipped her over. A first wave kissed, a second spilled, and a third and a fourth and a fifth came breaking over, and finally she was away, she was loose in the water for the first time in her life. . . ." But Sergius, the suffering messiah to the end, is unable to gain satisfaction for his own aching body as she sobs, "Oh, Jesus, I made it, oh Jesus, I did." She leaves the studio transformed but ungrateful, the look of a bullfight killer in her eyes.[35]

Congressman Stephan Rojack in *An American Dream* is married to Deborah, ". . . a Great Bitch [who] delivers extermination to any bucko brave enough to take carnal knowledge of her." This treacherous, thoroughly evil woman confesses during one of their altercations to having had analingus with other men. Rojack strikes her, and as she attempts to mangle his "root," he strangles her. It is almost as if this murder cleansed the world of evil. "I was weary with a most honorable fatigue, and my flesh seemed new. I had not felt so nice since I was twelve." The triumph over a demonic adversary completed like the adolescent superhero fantasy, Rojack is drawn upstairs to the room of the German maid. Masturbating like a Playmate, she had left the door ajar in the hope of being rescued by the master of the house. He accepts the invitation but brutally shatters her rhythm, then follows his impulse for rapelike buggery. In the midst of her thrashing resistance he humiliates her even further with, "You're a Nazi." Soon ". . . she was becoming mine as no woman ever had, she wanted no more than to be a part of my will. . . ." This violation is pictured by Mailer as having transformed her womb:

> It was no graveyard now, no warehouse, no, more like a chapel now, a modest decent place, but its walls were snug, its odor was green, there was sweetness in the chapel, a muted reverential sweetness. . . .

Reduced to subordinate status, the maid expresses gratitude for her brutal redemption. "'Mr. Rojack,' . . . 'I do not know why you have trouble with your wife. You are absolutely a genius, Mr. Rojack.'" His heroic status exultantly confirmed, Rojack finds the courage to escape legal retribution for the murder of his dragon wife. He throws her body out of the skyscraper window. And true to the superhero success formula, the zealous murderer and buggerer triumphs over other corrupt enemies and escapes to the paradise of central America—an "American Dream" that has turned into a monomythic nightmare.[36]

VI

We do not believe that writers and editors need to be prisoners of sexual segmentation, despite a mythic heritage that impels them in that direction. Hefner and Mailer are trapped by their zeal against the flaws of past myths and blinded to the mythic paradigms implicit in their own work. To gain a broader perspective here, a constructive alternative is offered by Shakespeare, though we mention him a little reluctantly, for fear that readers will accuse us of a highbrow campaign against pop culture. Shakespeare was in fact a popular artist in his own time; the passage of history has elevated him to high-culture status. We have no nostalgic reverence for the Renaissance. The value of Shakespeare in this discussion lies in the fact that he too was interested in myths of sexual segmentation, and he attempted to shatter them for his audiences. His material drew the audience into sexual fantasies without allowing it to succumb to their spell. He dramatized myths so that their implications and consequences became apparent. He did not delude his audience into believing that perennial human dilemmas can be eliminated by attacking presumed bastions of evil such as "Puritanism." The responsibility to cope is left with Everyman, not with Superman. The substance of Shakespeare's morality looks archaic by modern standards, but as a thinker, he is much more radical than Hefner, in his ability to unveil for his audience destructive mythic paradigms.

Shakespeare exhibits his skill in dealing with sexual myths in *Love's Labour's Lost*. In this play, King Ferdinand and three of his lords have vowed to abstain from worldly pleasures for three years. They wished to pursue truth whole and unadorned. Their calling was to ". . . war against your own affections, And the huge army of the world's desires. . . ." In abstaining from dainty fare and the sight of womankind, ". . . the mind shall banquet, though the body pine." It takes the buffoon Armado to state clearly the traditional ideal of segmentation implicit in such an action:

> Love is a devil; there is no evil angel but Love. Yet was Samson so tempted, and he had an excellent strength; yet was Solomon so seduced, and he had a very good wit.[37]

Very soon after the oath is sworn, with some reluctance on the part of the shrewdest of the lords, the princess and her entourage arrive from France to conduct diplomatic business with the King. The ladies very quickly dash cold water on heroic resolve. The men fall madly in love and begin to break their vows, each attempting to disguise his state to his comrades. The façade of cool mastery crumbles before the power of love, for as Biron puts it, "By the Lord, this love is as mad as Ajax. It kills sheep; it kills me, I a sheep. . . ." The would-be scholars discover that only the acceptance and integration of sexual love can evoke the deepest sources of human creativity. Biron speaks for his royal colleagues:

> For when would you, my lord, or you, or you,
> Have found the ground of study's excellence
> Without the beauty of a woman's face?
> From women's eyes this doctrine I derive;
> They are the ground, the books, the academes

> From whence doth spring the true Promethean fire. . . .
> But love, first learned in a lady's eyes,
> Lives not alone immured in the brain;
> But, with the motion of all elements,
> Courses as swift as thought in every power,
> And gives to every power a double power,
> Above their functions and their offices.

Like it or not, the men are forced to admit that they simply cannot maintain the cool, ascetic life. They are human, and the impulses of love are stronger than the ideal of segmentation. "The sea will ebb and flow, heaven show his face, Young blood doth not obey an old decree. We cannot cross the cause why we were born. . . ."[38]

So the segmented ideal is set aside—they think. The men decide to act their aggressive parts, to follow their fantasies and love in a direct and forceful way. They give up their oaths and plan a warlike campaign to overpower the women. If love be given its reign, let no barriers stand in the way. Here is their martial resolve:

> KING: Saint Cupid, then! and, soldiers, to the field!
> BIRON: Advance your standards, and upon them, lords;
> Pell-mell, down with them! but be first advis'd,
> In conflict that you get the sun of them.[39]

But Shakespeare takes care that this yearning to snare women seductively from their blind side advances no farther than the silly oaths of continence. The witty women make fools of the partners they so fondly adore, puncturing the fantasy of male dominance by besting them at their own game.

The women turn out to be neither stupid bunnies nor provocative bitches. Transcending stereotypes of medieval submissiveness, they are mature and vigorous personalities, interested in something considerably more stable and satisfying than momentary affairs. The men cannot cope with them by segmenting sexual urges into a special, seductive compartment suitable for male pleasures alone. They discover that enjoyment is dependent upon mutual commitments that involve the whole being. The segmentation they thought they had overcome by renouncing the Puritanical oaths will take time and reflection to be outgrown. So the consummation of marriage now devoutly wished by the heroes must wait until fantasies have been tamed by mutual realities.

Shakespeare arranges for both the Puritan myth of ascetic coolness and the Renaissance myth of bold male seduction to crumble against the realities of human personality. With humor and a grasp of mythic function, he lets his audience discover that segmentation is unworkable, integration can only be achieved with fidelity, exploitation is inappropriate for humankind, and maturity requires the integration of love and creative self-control. Most of these values would be verbally assented to by Hefner, though they are obviously in conflict with his icons. But Shakespeare's means of conveying these perennial verities of the human condition are the deft depiction of mythic paradigms and the gentle puncturing of the fantasies they engender. Neither pedantry nor preaching could possibly work so well as this charming, brilliant play to dispel the mythic haze long enough for the human reality to show through. In the vivid dialogue between male and female, actual sexual partners replace projected fantasies. Human love replaces redemption ripoffs. And both sexes are rendered more capable of living in the real world of sexual conflict.

The mythic frankness of Shakespeare allows us to grasp with finality Hugh Hefner's technique of arousing the slumbering mythic fantasy that had long found American adherents. His crusade against destructive sexual fantasies and hangups has imprisoned him and his devotees in a new set of fantasies which, as we saw in the stories of Oakley Hall and Norman Mailer, can be lethal when mixed with irascible human reality. One discovers here the hazards of cultural reform, in that the attempt to reject a myth so easily becomes a novel way of being captured by it. It was Nietzsche who put this message in its most memorable form:

> Beware lest a statue slay you.[40]

V

Walking Tall with Buffalo Bill

Buffalo Bill was ". . . one of America's strange heroes who has loved the trackless wilds . . . and who has stood as a barrier between civilization and savagery, risking his own life to save the lives of others."—Prentiss Ingraham in a dime novel[1]

"There's nothing wrong with guns in the right hands."—Buford Pusser to his eight-year-old son in *Walking Tall*[2]

The imposing statues of popular heroes are not all the products of imagination alone. In the decisive periods when myths are born, certain historical figures come to assume heroic grandeur, capable of capturing the imagination of the public while the heroes are yet alive. The process of the mythical reshaping of contemporary figures has frequently been described, in arenas such as sports, film, music, politics, and military affairs. The fascinating process has no need of explanation here. But the shape of the mythical paradigm in American popular heroism deserves closer definition. And the extent to which it arises from denying the reality of the "six-gun mystique" needs clarification. In the story of Buffalo Bill there are some clues to the emergence of a monomythic hero-type, standing with a firearm between threatening savages and innocent damsels. Buford Pusser offers a contemporary example of such myth-making that follows the pattern of the western hero who struggles for law and order against the forces threatening civilization. Michael Straight's *Carrington* provides an imaginative sample of western history-making that does not fall prey to the monomythic paradigm. The task is to discover an approach to the

American past that offers hope for moving beyond the illusory ease of six-gun and hickory-stick justice.

I

The decisive formation of western heroic imagery took place when the daring and attractive William F. Cody began to style himself as "Buffalo Bill." Showman Cody convincingly played the redeemer role for the Wild West show audiences, thundering away victoriously on his horse to avenge civilization's claim against the outnumbering savages. In the self-portraits of the shows and the seventeen hundred novels and stories written about his exploits—many written with his collaboration—this heroic image was developed with brazen exaggerations that even Cody privately acknowledged as unrealistic. In brief stints as a scout in the Indian wars he participated in historical events that he then re-enacted in mythic form before the audiences of Europe and America. John Burke, one of Cody's many biographers, senses the oddity of this instant transfiguration:

> One of the most striking sidelights of the creation of our Western mythology is that it was being fabricated, recast, and enlarged upon almost immediately after the events upon which it was based were taking place. . . . The heroes . . . joined in the process by portraying themselves and reenacting their supposed deeds. Would Achilles, for instance, have abandoned the forces laying siege to Troy and hurried back to Athens to play himself before a crowded amphitheater? No matter, this was modern America, where a man had the right to cash in on his fame.[3]

This heroic image was developed out of materials and events whose true character required constant suppression of discordant elements.

Will Cody was born on an Iowa farm in 1846 and moved with his family to troubled Kansas seven years later. His abolitionist father died of wounds inflicted by adversaries after only three years in bloody Kansas. At eleven, the strapping boy began work to support his family. Cody recounts, perhaps with considerable exaggeration, the slaying of his first two Indians on a wagon expedition in his first year with a freighting firm. He returned home on foot the following year, after being captured by a Mormon militia company, and was promptly placed back in school. The ". . . swaggering twelve-year-old . . . resisted the educational process to the best of his abilities," slipping away for several more treks west before returning home long enough to learn to write. By the time he was a teen-ager, Will could speak Indian dialects and survive alone in the western mountains. After a stint as a Pony Express rider, as a participant in occasional Indian battles and frequent drinking bouts, he served for a while as scout for a Kansas cavalry unit. His exploits in a thieving Kansas bushwhacking unit during the opening days of the Civil War earned him the reputation as ". . . the most desperate outlaw, bandit and house-burner on the frontier."[4]

The fictional celebration of Cody's early life required that the negative implications of these escapades be suppressed in favor of a redemptive idealism. In his waning years Buffalo Bill adopted the line from Prentiss Ingraham's dime novel, "I stood between savagery and civilization most all my early days." Ingraham had described Cody as ". . . one of America's strange heroes who has loved the trackless wilds, rolling plains and mountain solitudes of our land, far more than the bustle and turmoil, the busy life and joys of our cities, and who has stood as a barrier between civilization and savagery, risking his own life to save the lives of others."[5]

The redemptive mission began after an uproarious celebration with a group of Kansas Volunteers, when Cody woke up the next morning to find himself enlisted in the U. S. Army. Despite heroic tales to the contrary, his major action in eight months of Civil War service was with Louisa Frederici, a spirited young woman who lived with her family in St. Louis. Accounts of how they met are romanticized in several accounts of Cody's life. He rescues her from a runaway horse in one tale. In another, Bill rescued Louisa from a drunken artilleryman and his cronies. The winged rescue scene prefigures the sexless, caped redeemers of twentieth-century comics:

> But before he [the drunk] could . . . bend his hot, sensual face toward her pure lips, a horse and rider came rushing down the street with the speed of a winged bird. . . . "Oh, sir, you are so

> brave and good! . . . I would have died before they should kiss me," said the lovely girl.

In fact, Private Cody saved Louisa from nothing more than the completion of an afternoon nap. He jerked the chair out from under her while she dozed in the parlor.[6]

After due apologies, the attractive pair fell in love, and a year later they married. Will Cody was twenty years of age when this occurred, a circumstance the dime novels all gladly suppress. In the mythical tales Cody remains as pure and unattached as a Christian angel. But the actual Cody alternatively endured, ran away from, and betrayed his impetuous wife for the next half century. A wildly jealous woman unsuited to a harum-scarum life in frontier shacks and hotels, she made Cody's life miserable in his brief stays at home. She fiercely criticized his heavy drinking, crude carousing, and sporadic support of the family. He came home long enough in 1876 to witness the sickness of his daughters and the death of his only son. By 1881, after Louisa surprised him at the end of a Wild West tour and found him ardently kissing his actresses good-bye, a permanent estrangement developed.

Louisa Cody gained final revenge after her husband's death in 1917 by arranging with Harry Tammen of the Denver *Post* for burial on Lookout Mountain. She reportedly received a fee of ten thousand dollars for disregarding Bill's desire for burial outside Cody, Wyoming, rather than the spot advocated by his hated former associate, Tammen. Her revenge for a lifetime of indignities was soured when six of Cody's former sweethearts showed up in places of honor at his funeral, ". . . now obese and sagging with memories . . . beside the grave of hewed-out granite," as Gene Fowler described the scene. "One of the old Camilles rose from her camp chair . . . walked to the casket and held her antique but dainty black parasol over the glass. She stood there throughout the service. . . . It was the gesture of a queen." This was the awkward reality denied in the dramatization of Buffalo Bill as the bachelor who saved girls but was never romantically attached to them.[7]

The transformation of Will Cody from a good-looking frontier roughneck and successful Army scout to a nationally known redeemer figure began in 1869. Ned Buntline, the prolific author of dime novels, came west to locate the 5th Cavalry, which had just subdued Chief Tall Bull's band. Buntline met Cody and used his name in the title of a dime novel series that attributed many of the legendary exploits of Wild Bill Hickock to him. Buntline's *Buffalo Bill: The King of the Border Men* was a daring piece of legend-making. It must have been surprising to Will Cody that his heroization included abstinence. In one of Cody's little sermons that Buntline wrote, the bibulous Bill declares, ". . . There is more fight, more headache–aye, more heartache in one rumbottle than there is in all the water that ever sparkled in God's bright sunlight. And I, for the sake of my dear brothers and sisters, and for the sweet, trusting heart that throbs alone for me, intend to let the rum go where it belongs, and that is not down my throat, at any rate." To Cody's integrity, it is conceded by his contemporaries that he never spoke or acted in this abstemious and sexually ascetic way outside of the novels. But the denial pattern nevertheless stamped the cowboy tradition with the image of a milk-drinking superhero who saves his kisses for his horse.[8]

Buntline's use of the nickname Buffalo Bill was apt. The year before meeting the author, Cody had worked as a buffalo hunter for the Kansas Pacific Railroad. In a single eighteen-month period he claimed to have killed some 4,280 of the beasts, on which Indian survival depended. Cody's autobiography describes the shooting contest in which he killed 69 buffalo in a single day, a vivid account of how the West was "redeemed."

> . . . I was using . . . a breech-loading Springfield rifle–caliber 50–it was my favorite old "Lucretia." . . . My great *forte* in killing buffaloes from horseback was to get them circling by riding my horse at the head of the herd, shooting the leaders, thus crowding their followers to the left, till they would finally circle round and round. On this morning the buffaloes were very accommodating, and I soon had them running in a beautiful circle, when I dropped them thick and fast. . . . I had "nursed" my buffaloes, as a billiard-player does the balls when he makes a big run.

This sport was suitable for eastern socialites, and Cody began escorting millionaires and European royalty. His gifts as raconteur, scout, and hunter, together with his ability to dress splendidly for the stylish expeditions, made him a popular figure. He was beginning to act the heroic role of the dime novels. Invited by his millionaire acquaintances, Cody made a grand tour of Chicago and New York in 1872, sitting through a performance of Buntline's play about the life of Buffalo Bill. Cody returned to lead a cavalry unit into a successful attack on a Sioux village near the South Fork of the Loup River. He earned the Congressional Medal of Honor for his dauntless charge into the camp and the killing of at least one Indian with his hunting rifle. He suffered a slight graze wound —the only one ever received in battle, according to Mrs. Cody, which varies from later newspaper accounts of 137 bullet, arrow, and tomahawk scars incurred in the defense of civilization.[9]

II

In Cody's dramatic duel with Chief Yellow Hand, the emerging heroic paradigm was permanently formed. Buffalo Bill was working with the 5th Cavalry to head off a band of Cheyennes who sought to join Sitting Bull in the wake of Custer's demise in 1876. In a skirmish between scouting forces, Cody claimed that young Chief Yellow Hand rode forward with a challenge to personal combat: "I know you, Pa-he-haska (Long Yellow Hair): if you want to fight, come ahead and fight me." This remark, if historical, implies an expectation of hand-to-hand combat, but when Buffalo Bill's horse stepped into a hole and fell, Lieutenant King reported that "Cody coolly knelt and, taking deliberate aim, sent his bullet through the chief's leg and into his [Yellow Hand's] horse's head. Down went the two, and before his friends could reach him, a second shot from Bill's rifle laid the redskin low." Despite a few flourishes in later accounts by Cody himself, it was about as chivalrous as shooting buffalo. His ruthless use of the .50-caliber buffalo gun allowed little doubt about the outcome of the "duel." Its mythical power derived from the dramatic setting, the cool efficiency of the hero, whose bowie knife "scientifically" scalped Yellow Hand, and the colorful outfit Bill had selected from his theatrical trunk. In Henry Nash Smith's words, "It consisted of a

Mexican suit of black velvet, slashed with scarlet, and trimmed with silver buttons and lace. . . . These costumes, fictional and actual, illustrate the blending of Cody with his theatrical role to the point where no one–least of all the man himself–could say where the actual left off and where dime novel fiction began."[10]

This incident became the model of countless duels in which cool and pacific superheroes always won. Elements of chivalry were inserted to fit the premise of "civilization" triumphing over "savagery" and to deny the actual aggression of Cody and his allies against the Indians. In some accounts the running skirmish became a formal duel reminiscent of the Wars of the Roses. As Cody re-enacted the incident in Wild West shows and told it repeatedly to audiences, he fired the first shot at Yellow Hand's horse while still on his own; then his horse stepped into a hole, and he fired from a standing position at the same moment as Yellow Hand sent his bullet whizzing past his head. Other eyewitnesses reported that Yellow Hand had no firearm, but this could not be allowed in the mythical re-enactment. It had to be made into a duel with a bad guy who fired first. The details about Yellow Hand's wearing an American flag as a breechcloth and flourishing the scalp of a blond woman, helped make it a fight against a perfect symbol of Indian aggression. In another fictional account Cody helped to create for a dime novel, the Yellow Hand paradigm of a chivalrous duel against an evil adversary is visible:

> Face to face, knee to knee, and hand to hand, Raven Feather and Buffalo Bill met. Twice the borderman parried the deadly thrusts of the wily chief–twice again the steel of the savage drank his blood, but weak from twenty wounds, the Indian's eyes were not sure, and soon the knife of the brave borderman reached his body with a fearful thrust. . . . Buffalo Bill, anxious as he was to hurry back to his loved ones, had to delay to have the blood staunched which poured from many a sad gash in his noble frame. . . .

Both the aggressive thrusts of the Indian and the pacific character of the redeemer figure are emphasized in this episode. The hero has no thought for himself, but he gladly risks his life for his mother and family.[11]

The theme of a hero whose gun saves civilization assumed central importance in the plays and Wild West shows Cody developed. Immediately upon returning from the Black Hills campaign, he toured with a melodrama entitled, *The Red Right Hand, or Buffalo Bill's First Scalp for Custer*. He re-enacted the chivalrous duel with Yellow Hand, his victory helping to take away the sting of the Custer "massacre." When the spectacular outdoor shows were developed in the 1880s, this violent ritual ". . . achieved an immeasurable impact on the national consciousness." Buffalo Bill toured England and the Continent, was feted by royalty and blessed by the Pope. Cody's tours helped place the stamp of monomythic redemption on the consciousness of the entire Western world. The show featured Cody and his scouts rescuing careening stagecoaches from howling Indian attacks, re-enactments of Custer's Last Stand, and the marksmanship of Annie Oakley. Cody always carried along the scalp of Yellow Hand and delighted in re-enacting the duel for fans. The highlights of the Wild West shows ". . . were the spectacles. An immigrant train, complete with oxen and mules, was attacked by whooping Indians. . . . A settler's cabin was attacked by savagely painted Indians."[12] It was a dramatic ritual of denial in which the reality of the invasion of Indian lands was transfigured into redemption.

A few critical voices were raised in Cody's time. Newspapers carried stories, editorials, and reviews that occasionally compared Cody's claims with historical facts or raised moral objections. The public display of Yellow Hand's scalp by Buffalo Bill elicited protests against ". . . the blood-stained trophies of his murderous and cowardly deeds." But this was distinctly a minority opinion. Even the sophisticated Mark Twain, who knew the West from personal experience and loved to debunk overinflated myths, wrote Cody that ". . . down to its smallest details the Show is genuine. . . . It is wholly free from sham and insincerity. . . ." General Sheridan, the commander of the Western Theater during the Indian wars, obviously placed more credence in the redemptive exaggerations than in his military reports when he ". . . proclaimed that Buffalo Bill had killed more Indians than any white man who ever lived." Theodore Roosevelt was well versed in western history, and surely recognized the enlargements of the Wild West shows, yet he applauded Buffalo Bill as

> . . . one of those men, steel-thewed and iron-nerved, whose daring progress opened the great West to settlement and civilization. His name, like that of Kit Carson, will always be associated with old adventure and pioneer days of hazard and hardship when the great plains and the Rocky Mountains were won for our race. . . . He embodied those traits of courage, strength and self-reliant hardihood which are vital to the well-being of our nation.[13]

The basis of popular credulity is visible in these statements about civilization's triumph through the exploits of its western scouts. Intelligent people believed in Buffalo Bill, despite the evidence to the contrary, because he dramatically embodied the Redeemer Nation concept. The Manifest Destiny of the nation to bear the burden of civilization against the irrational resistance of savages was so widely believed that accepting Buffalo Bill was virtually automatic. To question the deeds of the winner of a Congressional Medal of Honor was to cast the zealous ideals into doubt. It was downright un-American. Even for highly critical minds, Buffalo Bill's successful visualization of the western redeemer myth had a massaging effect. What they could no longer accept in the form of stated ideology, full of Manifest Destiny jargon, they readily believed when reduced to its visual basics. When Cody brought back real Indians from recent military engagements to stereotypically re-enact their defeat at the hands of Cody and the U.S. military, the critical impulse found it easy to surrender. Accepting the mythic stature of Buffalo Bill had an additional advantage of implicitly denying the sordid facts about western genocide. Thus those who might otherwise have argued about the means of western expansion were relieved to see that it was always the Indians who attacked the whites first and that Buffalo Bill was merely redeeming the innocent by killing the aggressive.[14]

The fact that the Wild West shows so perfectly embodied the emerging monomythic ideals lent credence to their advertising claim of educational value. The shows were not presented as mere entertainment, but as ritual evocations of the national ethos. When Buffalo Bill continued the shows rather than volunteering for the

Spanish-American War, his publicist Major Burke replied to charges of cowardice:

> Damn it all, what we are doing is educating you people! I am not afraid to say, sir, that the Wild West symposium of equestrian ability has done more for this country than the Declaration of Independence, the Constitution of the United States, or the life of General George Washington. Its mission is to teach manhood and common sense. We are not traveling to make money, sir, but only to do good.[15]

This denial of personal self-interest and the profit motive, ridiculous as it may sound, is congruent with the other denials we have noted. They are the incipient stages of an elaborate doctrine of selflessness that marks the fully developed monomyth.

Historian Kent Ladd Steckmesser has summarized the traits that surfaced in this development of the western hero: "genteel qualities" of Puritanical virtue; "clever traits" such as skill with weapons; "prowess" in the sense of always prevailing against numerous foes; and "epic significance"—the glorification of individual exploits.[16] These motifs are linked together in the definitive case of Buffalo Bill with a redemption scheme that Steckmesser overlooks, in which the hero relieves the community of its mortal threat from aggressive savages. The superior firepower of the white invaders is ritually denied by the chivalric code. The desire for profitable western lands is ritually repressed by the symbol of the redeemer who seeks nothing for himself. A more flattering version of current events could hardly be imagined.

Don Russell, the leading authority on Buffalo Bill, observes that the legendary West of his theatrical shows became the norm against which popular portrayals of the period measured themselves.

> It spawned many competitors and imitators, but the Cody show remained the biggest and best of the lot in its heyday—initiating an on-going process of illusion-making that has made its image of the West a part of our heritage. The Wild West show in its beginning was a representation of a historical era that was still contemporary. As time went on dramatization continued the illusion, as did the accompanying popular literature and its eventual translation to movies and television. The resultant legendary West derived in large part from the Wild West show.[17]

It should be added that the "illusion" involved a denial of aggression that was highly appealing to an expansionistic culture, and that out of this denial was emerging the American monomyth.

III

It is perhaps easy to smile condescendingly at the naïveté of Buffalo Bill's generation. Surely our contemporaries would not be so blind to the mythical recasting of current events. But the insight from the discussion of the myth of mythlessness should not be overlooked: It is the nature of myth not to reveal its presence to those it enthralls. A glance at the *Walking Tall* films may help to dispel any illusion of contemporary immunity. The films depict the legendary exploits of a sheriff named Buford Pusser, a selfless ascetic who risks his life to redeem the community from villainous spoilers. Pauline Kael notes the similarity between this film and the tradition established by Buffalo Bill: ". . . The Western cowboy hero hasn't disappeared: he's moved from the mythological purity of the wide-open spaces into the corrupt modern cities and towns."[18] The enormous success of these films at the box office indicates that the psychic resonance of the man standing between civilization and savagery is still sonorous.

The first film begins in the fashion of the full-blown American monomyth, with Pusser returning home through paradisal countryside. The lucrative wrestling profession is to be renounced because Buford cannot tolerate the "system" with its "organized dishonesty." The Pussers buy a farm with a lovely home, green fields, and fishing pond, but the idyll is broken when Buford unwillingly visits a local casino with a friend and intercedes when his friend is being cheated. Buford is savagely beaten, slashed, and left to die on a country road. The corrupt sheriff refuses to help him or to bring the culprits to justice. When the powerful wrestler recovers, he returns to the casino with a hickory club, fracturing the arms of the villains and coercing a financial settlement for earlier losses.

According to his "authorized biography," the real-life Pusser was seriously injured in a dice game fracas in 1957. He moved to Chicago and took up wrestling as preparation for the revenge he planned to take against the casino. Three years later Pusser returned with two friends, administered a beating to casino employees, using the now famous hickory club, and was indicted for assault, battery, and robbery. He and his friends got off with alibis in the form of doctored time cards from their Chicago jobs. There were no bare-chested pleas for law and order as in the film version of the trial (in which Pusser was acquitted). Pusser admitted to newsman Charles Thompson, "I beat hell out of the two bastards who cut me. . . . I hospitalized them something awful. Then I got in my car and drove back to Chicago, leaving them like they left me." In the mythical recasting of this uninspiring story, Pusser goes on to campaign for sheriff. His goal is to clean up the town. The corrupt incumbent tries to run him off a bridge to eliminate him from the race, but misjudges the speed and kills himself, despite Pusser's valiant effort to pull him from the wreckage. In actuality Buford Pusser's father had been Adamsville police chief and wanted his son to take over. "Son, my leg's been bothering me a lot lately. . . . I think you'd be the ideal man for the job."[19]

Later Buford won elections for constable and then county sheriff in 1964, using his position as chief to stage an illegal raid outside his jurisdiction to win votes. His father describes the action: "We didn't have any money," said Carl, "and we needed to attract attention. . . . We loaded up with guns and kerosene and hit the place. . . . We busted hell out of their operations. It was the first time around here that anybody ever touched those people, and voters knew we meant business." He won the election when his opponent died in an accident unrelated to Pusser and served as sheriff of McNairy County, Tennessee, from 1964 to 1970. The real Pauline Pusser ". . . encouraged her husband to run and was pleased when he won" though in the film version she opposes the idea. Political ambition touches even the families of superheroes, despite the mythical declarations against the system, and the mythical depiction of wives as posing temptations to betray the cause. Despite the crusading image in the movie, there are conflicting reports whether Pusser's tenure in office affected the state-line gambling and prostitution establishments. There is no disagreement that Pusser and his father clamped down on bootleggers, despite their stated sympathy with moonshining, in order ". . . to get the money they needed for equipment and men" through selling confiscated vehicles and liquor.[20]

The hero of *Walking Tall* appoints his fictional black friend Obra Eaker as his first deputy–in real life Pusser had appointed his father–and begins a dangerous campaign to clean up the town from the evil influence of the vice lords. The outsider status of the superhero is communicated by his refusal to wear a police uniform. In actuality Pusser wore the brown sheriff's uniform until the slaying of his wife, discarding it for ". . . tailored suits, colorful ties, and immaculate white shirts" in order to be "less noticeable" for assassins. Pusser apprehends those responsible for the deaths of civil rights workers from drinking toxic moonshine–another fictional incident–only to have the case dismissed on a technicality. Like the classical cowboy hero, Pusser repeatedly resists temptation to make illicit love to a seductive young widow. In the final Edenic scene before Pauline's death, Pusser embraces her tenderly, but the novelistic script released by Buford Pusser Enterprises makes it plain that no consummation occurs: "When he and Pauline went to bed, Buford fell asleep immediately, not out of exhaustion but out of peace and contentment." These elements of sexual renunciation seem invented to fit the monomythic scheme.[21]

In a statement from the Buffalo Bill tradition, Pusser tells his son in the film that he can have a rifle for his ninth birthday because "there's nothing wrong with guns in the right hands." As the sheriff recovers in the hospital after the ambush, the movie pictures this lad carrying his rifle bravely but tearfully down the corridor, the ". . . little prince taking up his fallen King's mission. . . ."[22] On the way back from Pauline's funeral, Pusser wreaks terrible vengeance on local vice lords. The townspeople respond to the invitation to vigilante justice, gathering around to burn up the shattered gambling equipment. The closing song, "Walking Tall," issues an explicit Werther invitation to the audience throughout this scene, urging it to take up the zealous crusade.

Despite its propagandistic power, this closing scene is fictional. Pusser witnessed no spontaneous burning of gambling equipment in the wake of Pauline's death. But the scene evoked standing ovations by theater audiences.

In contrast to the mythical world where good guys always win, the historical Buford, ineligible for office in 1970, lost the election of 1972 when charges of excessive brutality and other resentments were at issue. He boasted that he ". . . wore out more pistol barrels banging mean drunks over the head than the county would pay for." It was a more brutal means of retribution than the mythical film genre could accept, thus occasioning the adaptation of the photogenic hickory stick. Pusser collaborated with country singer Eddie Bond in writing and marketing "The Ballad of Buford Pusser." Like Buffalo Bill, Pusser authorized biographies to enhance his heroic image. He defended the film myths on talk shows and went into public-relations work, giving away hickory canes to purchasers of automobiles. He earned 7 per cent of the profits on the film, which grossed an estimated fifty million in its first fourteen months. Even in the enlightened current age, there are benefits in playing the Buffalo Bill role of ". . . a one-man lynch mob, but with the judgment of a god."[23]

The myth-making process accelerated after some seventy million persons viewed *Walking Tall* and Bing Crosby Productions decided to produce a sequel. With Buford Pusser collaborating in the production of the screen play and planning to play himself in the title role, the premise of *Part 2 Walking Tall* departed even more radically from reality. The filming was postponed for several months because Pusser died in the crash of his Corvette in August 1974. A careful investigation by the state patrol indicated no evidence of foul play. The indestructible superhero, who had survived numerous wrecks and beatings, succumbed at last. Bo Svenson was recruited to play the title role. The false premises of the plot are that the state-line thugs made attempts on Pusser's life down to the moment of his death, and that he used the concluding years in the sheriff's office to track down his wife's killers. The fact is that Pusser had been out of office since 1970, so no one had any reason to drive him out. And the implication in the epilogue of *Part 2 Walking Tall* that the crime bosses had finally succeeded in getting rid of Pusser is equally false in light of the evidence about his death. The mythic process thus transforms Pusser's private resolve on leaving office, ". . . to work on solving Pauline's murder case," into a public campaign against organized crime. Vigilante vengeance becomes selfless crusading for law and order by a dedicated sheriff.[24]

The most remarkable feature of this film is an explicit pattern of *mythic denial.* Essential components of a myth are verbally or symbolically denied in the context of a story in which they play a central role. This form of denial, akin to the neurotic defense mechanisms discovered by Freud, serves here to immunize the audience against the criticisms that had been leveled against the historical Pusser.

• The denial of vengeance is articulated when Buford returns to his office, having won re-election while recovering from his wounds. His deputies ask what they should do ". . . to get those bastards who shot you and your wife." He replies, "The only thing any of us gonna do is keep the law for the folks who pay us our salaries. I ain't about to use this office to get vengeance on the people I owe it to. . . ." Yet vengeance is clearly the single plot line of *Part 2 Walking Tall.* One by one Pauline's ambushers are tracked down in the course of the movie. The novelistic script of *Part 2 Walking Tall* concludes the prologue on this vengeance theme, indicating that the entire story is its enactment: "But Buford Pusser had sworn his oath to his dead wife: 'They'll pay for this, I promise.' *And this is how Buford Pusser kept his promise to Pauline. . . .*" This commitment to personal vengeance is congruent with many actions reported about Pusser's life.[25]

• The denial of Buford's violent tendencies is communicated by scenes of tenderness toward his children and employees. The film depicts him touching people affectionately on the cheek, and he always uses maximum restraint while making arrests, even at risk to his life. But the advertisements for *Part 2 Walking Tall* feature Buford's violence in the form of the demolition of Stud Pardee's Camaro in retribution for trying to kill him. The film showed an earlier racing scene in which Pardee had callously caused the death of an older driver, and revealed his connections with the bootlegging syndicate to justify the violent destruction of the car at a county fair. In a similar way positive results are contrived when Pusser uses physical duress to gain the names of the ambushers and their associates. But the violence of these scenes is counterbalanced by Pusser's tenderness to his mother, to his secretary, and to his black friend, Obra Eaker.

An interesting sidelight on the denial-of-violence theme is the account of the advertising campaign for the first *Walking Tall*. It stressed the "raw violence" in the film, with the result that audiences were very sparse in the opening weeks after its release. Charles Pratt, the president of the film company, conferred with Cinerama officials to develop a new ad campaign ". . . that played down the violence and depicted an embrace between the hero and his wife. . . . The result was a complete turnaround." Audiences began to pack the theaters.[26] They would accept and appreciate the violence only if it were denied. Later they were prepared to respond to the violent ads for *Part 2 Walking Tall* because Pusser's nonaggressive character was firmly established by the original *Walking Tall*. There is nothing wrong with a little violence so long as it stands between civilization and savagery.

• The denial of the conspiratorial premise that lies at the center of *Part 2 Walking Tall* is made when Buford Pusser decides to make the arrest at a black tavern. After Pusser calls an ambulance for the seven-foot Steamer Jackson, Pusser's deputies rush to the scene, certain that he had been caught in another ambush. One of them grabs the handcuffed giant by the neck, "Someone *pay* you, man, to set this thing up?" Pusser calms him down, "Now, Obra, we can't start seeing shadows behind every tree, can we?" Yet the premise of the film is paranoid, as the crooks make one attempt after another to kill the superhero. The conspiratorial premise is repeatedly stated in the script: "It was clear to the sheriff that the plots against him would continue in deadly earnest until one of them succeeded." The film repeatedly reveals that the crime chief in Nashville is ordering these attempts on Buford's life, and leaves the definite impression that he had finally succeeded in causing Pusser's fatal accident.[27]

The public adulation of Buford Pusser fits the pattern of Buffalo Bill in striking ways. The comparison with cowboy heroism was made by the Nashville *Banner:* "Wyatt Earp, Bat Masterson and Wild Bill Hickock tamed a lot of mean desperados. The name of Buford Pusser now joins the list of those fearless lawmen." He was named "outstanding young man of the year" by the Tennessee Jaycees, "Honorary Sergeant of Arms" by the Tennessee House of Representatives, and chosen "National Police Officer of the Month" by a detective magazine. Pusser received "reams of law-enforcement credentials" from governmental units around the country, including more than one hundred deputy sheriff commissions. He had acquired a kind of mythic license to attack offenders everywhere. Local religious leaders also applauded his battles in terms reminiscent of the ever-triumphant Buffalo Bill. The real life Reverend E. E. Thomas, who frequently held services in the county jail, told Pauline,

> The Lord is not going to let some criminal snuff out his life. . . . Remember, David, too, had a tough battle with Goliath, but he won because God was on his side. Sheriff Pusser is a lot like David. The only difference is that the sheriff has many Goliaths to fight while David had only one. The sheriff will win because God is with him!

The transposition of the 6-foot, 6-inch, 250-pound Pusser with a .357-magnum pistol and AR-15 automatic rifle for the diminutive David with his three smooth stones is proof of the power of monomythic denial.[28]

At Pusser's funeral, the Reverend Russell Gallimore compared the deceased to another man "who walked tall," Jesus Christ. The two men were equally nonviolent, he stated, taking up big sticks for the sake of peace. Like Pusser, Jesus ". . . took for his weapon a stick–a stick that was used against him–and in the final analysis, it took the form of a cross." Gallimore called on ". . . the Christ who walks tall on this earth to help us pass through this valley of grief." So powerful had been the technomythic presentation of Buford Pusser that his stick, transformed by the movie from a weapon of personal vengeance to an emblem of restraint in the enforcement of law, becomes symbolic not just for his life but also for the Christian religion itself. The crucified Christ himself is validated by comparison with the monomythic Pusser. It is a status to which even Bill Cody would not have aspired.[29]

IV

The lives of Buffalo Bill and Buford Pusser reveal the role of denial in providing a monomythic shape to current hero-making. In the glorification of weapons as the barrier between savagery and civilization, the elaborate pretense of restraint in their use, the denial of self-interest, and the renunciation of affections, these heroes attain redemptive powers matching those of legendary gods. Readers may object, however, that our analysis presupposes a simplistic distinction between myth and history that is merely a variant of the myth of mythlessness. Perhaps our selectivity in discovering facts at variance with monomythic images reveals nothing more than a different set of mythic sensibilities. If it is a truism that historical vision always reveals mythic expectations, how can one hope to provide any plausible alternative to the monomyth? Confronted with this dilemma, it is instructive to examine Michael Straight's attempt to cope with the legacy of Buffalo Bill in his historical novel of 1960, *Carrington.*[30]

Straight's subject was the Fetterman Massacre of 1866, which occurred near Fort Phil Kearny in Wyoming. A group of eighty-three soldiers led by Lieutenant Fetterman was slain near the Lodge Trail Ridge by a large group of Sioux warriors. The central figure of the novel, Colonel Carrington, was commanding officer at the fort. In Straight's vision, Carrington was a judicious and admirable man, but his occasional vacillation prevented his ever earning the respect of his men. As a former abolitionist, he lacked the sense of racial superiority that most of his men felt. He also realized what no one else cared to admit—that the seven hundred badly trained and ill-equipped soldiers at Fort Kearny were no match for thirty thousand braves. His refusal to fight and his attempts at conciliation with the aggrieved Indians helped to provoke the fatal mutiny.

Lieutenant Fetterman, an audacious officer sent to strengthen Carrington's deteriorating unit, became an attractive competitor for the loyalties of the men in the regiment. He shared their impatience with the indecisive, kindly, and militarily maddening actions of the colonel. Not grasping the military dilemma, despite his proven bravery in Civil War battles, Fetterman decided to play the heroic role that Buffalo Bill would have staged theatrically with greater success. Defeated Indians on the later Wild West shows were less menacing and motivated than those Fetterman envisioned slaughtering. Carrington had received intelligence from the Cheyenne that the Sioux planned to aggravate Fort Phil Kearny with minor but provocative guerrilla raids. They hoped to lure the soldiers beyond Lodge Trail Ridge, where an overpowering force could quickly annihilate them. Boasting that "with eighty men I will ride through the entire Sioux nation," Fetterman mutinously defied his orders not to move beyond the ridge. He led the entire company to death; his emasculated body was found at the bottom of the heap of his comrades.

Straight's picture of the men who went to their deaths was disturbing and complex. Some were drunkards, tortured by their war memories and aching wounds. Some were sympathetic with the Indians and disgusted by the genocidal hatred that flared so frequently among the other men of the regiment. Straight was conscious that he was defying the mythic conventions so decisively stamped upon popular tastes by cowboy Westerns. In Straight's tragic vision, there was no war between savagery and civilization, as in the tradition of Buffalo Bill or *Walking Tall*. It was rather the clash of two proud cultures, each possessing its own savagery. Straight moved beyond the popular stereotypes of good and evil, stating in an interview with John R. Milton, ". . . No one in this novel . . . is villainous, in the sense that he wills evil. Everyone in the book . . . tries to carry out his duty. . . . They brought about evil . . . because they could not understand the nature of their actions, or else, because they had no sense of good and evil."[31] This conclusion about the massacre was shaped by an unusual degree of historical discipline. Straight spent long days walking and photographing the landscape in the region of the battle, untangling the hidden military logic that had acted itself out in 1866. He camped at the site during the relevant seasons, and studied letters, military dispatches, diaries, and medical reports at the Old War Records Branch of the National Archives. He spent long hours with Indians, discussing their understanding of the events and observing their sign language as they re-enacted for him the dialogues he had reconstructed between the chieftains and the U.S. military. He spent time with mule skinners and did research on Irish speech. But in presenting his fictional story of the massacre, Straight recognized the role of his own imagination and selectivity. While making no claim to have discovered the final truth, he refrained from the mythic denials required by the Buffalo Bill tradition.

Straight's portrait struck mythic nerves, as he discovered during the early sixties, when the novel was considered as the subject for a Hollywood film. Since the royalties from the sale of *Carrington* had earned Straight a meager fifty cents per hour, the suggestion to make the novel into a film was appealing. But he found that the very historical accuracy he had attained made the novel unacceptable as Hollywood film material. Living comfortably in Buffalo Bill's historical shadow, with its morally stereotyped conflicts between white civilization and red savagery, filmmakers found *Carrington* too unyielding. Straight describes their reactions:

> The novel, they said, would make a very good movie; it was set in the right country; it had the requisite number of battles with Indians; and so on. Only, they had three very serious reservations. . . . The first was that the leading character in the novel was an intellectual; that was very bad, they said. I agreed, but I added that there wasn't much that I could do about it. . . . The second matter that bothered them was that the central character had a number of weaknesses. I said, that's right: he did. . . . So then they came out with the third reservation; and that was the gravest of all. The fact was, they said, that my novel had an unhappy ending. I said, that's right; but there's nothing very cheery, after all, in the deaths of eighty-three men. At that, they were very glum.[32]

The mythical expectations of the audience were such that they might not pay the price of admission. The novelist's fifty cents per hour seemed generous compared to the market value for historical realism in Hollywood. In subsequent years "new" Westerns such as *Little Big Man* and *Soldier Blue* were produced, reversing the stereotypes so that Indians assumed virtuous roles. But one wonders whether historical realism of Straight's caliber is marketable even yet.

The difficulties in separating the monomyth from western history are symbolized in the epilogue to Straight's novel. Ironically, it presages the rejection of the novel as film material. Retired General Carrington, who had been relieved of his command after Fetterman's foolhardy attack on the Sioux, returned to the scene decades later for official ceremonies sponsored by the city of Sheridan, Wyoming. A monument was to be dedicated on Massacre Hill. The old and unfairly treated Carrington seized the opportunity to relate what he knew about the mutiny and its subsequent coverup. "In a quavering voice he cried, 'Here is the place and this is the hour for justice to historical truth.'" It was a long and sordid tale, and like the events themselves, it did not lack its complexities.

> The General's voice dwindled, and when at last he stood rocking on his cane, no one was certain whether he had finished or given out. By then many of the spectators had moved away, for, interesting as the General's arguments were, he had spoken too long.

After a picnic lunch, ceremonial speeches by others reverted to the heroic imagery of the West. A congressman gazed at the monument to the dead soldiers and remarked that ". . . truth and justice prevail with the running of the years." Sergeant Sam Gibson, retired, told how ". . . he had come West as the youngest soldier in the Second Battalion–and stayed on to avenge the dead." As in the Buffalo Bill stories, the side of right is ever triumphant despite occasional reverses. Then ceremonies were cut short because the audience was hot and uncomfortable. Gibson found his way back into town and attempted to tell some of the patrons in a crowded saloon about how it was at the time of the mutiny. No one listened. He tried to order a drink, which had been a favorite at the old fort. "'Give me an Old Tom, just like we had up at Phil Kearny!' The bartender shook his head. 'Never heard of either one.'"[33]

Here is perhaps the most characteristic form of denial in monomythic culture. Certain that history conforms to mythic expectations and that civilization has subdued savagery, one has little interest in the details. The myth of Buffalo Bill's West is kept intact by denying the memories that would convey the manner of its enactment. In the year of the Bicentennial, a group of high school students in California proposed that the nation's capital be moved to the site of Buffalo Bill's ranch. Their teacher explained in an interview, "We feel the nation's capital should be in North Platte, but I think a name like Buffalo Bill or something like that would be more appropriate." Nebraska Secretary of State Allen Beerman applauded this campaign with a monomythic declaration about restoring paradise: If federal officials were moved to Buffalo Bill's town with its ". . . clean air, water and open spaces, perhaps they would end up with clean and open minds." Clinging to such hopes blinds one to the sobering message of western history. As Michael Straight suggests, the true heroes were the Carringtons, who sought to avert the fatal clash between the races, not the killers who were certain that civilization would be redeemed by buffalo guns. Straight maintains that "if Carrington had succeeded, in that winter of 1866, the whole course of the Indian Wars would have been altered."[34] Belief in the possibilities of conciliation and peace admittedly contains some mythical elements, but it may prevent us from following the next generation of Codys and Pussers. It is an admirable thing to walk tall, but Walking Tall with Buffalo Bill can lead us right over the Lodge Trail Ridge.

VI
Heidi Visits a "Little House on the Prairie"

> "Heidi is going to stay here and make you happy. We shall want to see the child again, but we will come to her. We shall come up to the Alm every year, for we have reason to offer thanks to the dear Lord in this place where such miracles have been wrought for *our* child."—the grandmother of the girl healed in *Heidi,* by Johanna Spyri[1]

Violence is not the only means of redemption in monomythic material. One finds problem solvers and miracle workers using less forceful means. But the transformations they accomplish are no less dramatic. In the most complex human dilemmas, against the barriers of sloth, jealousy, and hardness of heart, the domestic superheroes work their magic of happy endings. Like Heidi, they contrive to heal the sick and bring happiness to the lonely. A grateful world heaps upon them blessings and honor because their purity and cheerful helpfulness are the catalytic agency for modern miracles.

Popular figures such as Dorothy in *The Wizard of Oz,* Maria in *The Sound of Music,* Little Orphan Annie, and Laura of the *Little House on the Prairie* television series have literary predecessors in Little Nell, Florence Dombey, Little Dorrit, Elsie Dinsmore, Pollyanna, and Heidi. There are even male counterparts in current television fare, figures like Dr. Marcus Welby, and Charles Ingalls of the *Little House.* The traits of these domestic redeemer figures, both male and female, match the pattern of Mr. Spock and Buffalo Bill. Only the means of redemption change, while the pattern of sexual segmentation, selfless virtue, and extraordinary powers remains intact.

I

The origin of current domestic redeemers can be traced to the Protestant piety of the nineteenth century. In contrast to earlier Puritan piety, it concentrated on the domestic realm and the transformation of individuals. Issues of public justice and problems of managing a "commonwealth" receded from sight at the same time that the traditional doctrine of the depravity of man was being replaced by utopian dreams of the perfectibility of man. Early Puritans had accounted for human flaws in the commonwealth by meditating upon universal depravity, the presence of those elected for damnation, and the unfortunate sloth of the saints. The recession of these answers in the nineteenth century, visible both in Protestant liberalism and in the circles of secular Enlightenment, left an uncomfortable anomaly for believers in the perfectibility of man and society. If everyone is perfectible, why are there so many irascible and disruptive persons in one's family and community? If salvation is to be universal, why do so many seem to reject it? If the pursuit of happiness is blessed by Providence, why are so many people so unhappy?

An increasingly optimistic Protestantism answered these questions by emphasizing the need for both evangelism and loving works. Both would convert the unhappy and achieve the promised perfection of society. Wave after wave of revivals and reform movements spread the conviction that a selfless, loving act would melt the hardest heart and solve the thorniest problem. The exhortation "If everyone practiced love, these problems would disappear" replaced the jeremiads of an earlier generation. A self-reliant and optimistic public was thus granted the responsibility for societal redemption at the same time that the notion of miraculous divine intervention in human affairs was becoming old-fashioned. "God has no hands but our hands" was the newly popular refrain. But the knotty question still remained: What about those dilemmas that resist the application of well-intentioned love and admonition?

The classical Catholic tradition had possessed an idea which might have been usable here—that of the "saint" who through special divine gifts was a channel of miraculous redemption. But earlier Protestantism had fiercely rejected the concept of special saintliness declared efficacious by churchly authority. It was replaced by the "priesthood of all believers." Early Puritans applied the term "saint" to every believer who takes up the pilgrimage of faith, while rejecting the notion that any son or daughter of Adam could be redemptive for others. "Christian" in *The Pilgrim's Progress* could be exemplary for others but never redemptive. The best of the Puritan "saints" had forever to retain the introspective quest for secret sins. Thus only the "word of God" communicated by the spirit could redeem, said the Protestant divines of early America. But as the nineteenth century repeatedly demonstrated, the word alone did not suffice, either for incorrigible individuals or complex conflicts in society. There was a need for embodiments of redemptive love that would have a superhuman capacity to redeem, yet still remain democratically ordinary. A culture that had given up the belief in the Virgin Mary or guardian angels stood ready for their democratic replacement.

The popular literature of Protestant culture spawned a new redeemer figure, a superheroine who solves problems by selfless love and virtuous cheerfulness. She is a model of moral purity, seeking nothing for herself, while loving others in a generous but sexually segmented manner. Female redemptive power requires a soul and body uncontaminated by sexual passion. We can trace the emergence of this sexless heroine pattern in the novels of Charles Dickens, which were widely popular both in England and America during the nineteenth century. Scores of heroines were born in the minds of authors inspired by Dickens. He would surely have been astounded by such fertile propagations from his angelic virgins.

Little Nell in *The Old Curiosity Shop* was the first of Dickens' characters to embody the new scheme. With utter selflessness, this pretty fourteen-year-old spends her frail life to save her degenerate grandfather. Harassed and finally foreclosed by the villainous dwarf Quilp, the lonely pair escape London by night and begin a desperate pilgrimage. Like a pathetic Moses, Nell leads her confused grandfather out of danger. She hoped to regain a peaceful solitude where happiness would be possible, but in the end Nell gains only her own death. As the Dickens scholar Steven Marcus points out, "That 'fresh solitude' for which Nell prays is also her original state, her destination, that earliest home. The idyllic recollection of Eden, of life restored to its pristine harmony, has here developed clearly on the side of its tendency toward death." For the sake of this redemptive mission to recover Eden, Little Nell repeatedly forces her dissolute grandfather to flee temptation and vice. When, for example, she discovers that his companions have involved him in a planned robbery, she awakens him to insist on immediate flight:

> The old man rose from his bed, his forehead bedewed with the cold sweat of fear, and, bending before the child as if she had been an angel messenger sent to lead him where she would, made ready to follow her.

The angelic imagery is used throughout the book to refer to the purity of Little Nell. When her friend Kit finally locates Nell in her dying moment, he explains, "I have been used, you see . . . to talk and think of her almost as if she was an angel."[2] Sexual purity is combined with selfless renunciation of happiness, making this appellation appropriate.

While Nell remained the innocent suffering-servant, whose angelic virtues provided only temporary respite for her grandfather, later Dickens heroines are more effective. Florence Dombey's selfless love for her cruel and hardhearted father effects a miraculous moral transformation. It occurs after Paul Dombey had lost his fortune, having earlier driven his wife and unwanted daughter Florence from his mansion. He is embittered at the world for the death of his only male child, on whom the dynastic hopes of Dombey and Son rested. He unfairly blames his daughter for rivaling his dead son in health and vitality. Sunk in ruin, he was incapable of restoring relationships with Florence and others:

> . . . So proud he was in his ruin, or so reminiscent of her only as something that might have been his, but was lost beyond redemption–that, if he could have heard her voice in an adjoining room, he would not have gone to her.

In an amazing gesture of Christian charity, Florence seeks her fallen father, asking his forgiveness for having left home–he had cruelly driven her out in rage over her sympathy for his second wife, Edith. This breaks the hardened heart, and he responds, "Oh, my God, forgive me. . . ."[3]

The redeemed Paul Dombey returns with Florence to live out his life in her home, expressing to his grandchildren the affection he had withheld from his own daughter. Florence also redeems the alienated Edith, who replies thus to her selfless overtures: "Florence! . . . My better angel! . . . purest and best of natures,–whom I love . . . [you] who might have changed me long ago. . . ."[4] As a result of her encounter with Florence, she sends a message of reconciliation to her husband. So in the most irreconcilable domestic conflicts, the intervening love of selfless redeemers like Florence Dombey is effective in the end.

In *Bleak House* the wisdom and virtue of Esther Summerson triumph over a decadent world, redeeming all whom she touches. A. E. Dyson observes that "her intelligence is chiefly moral and intuitive. . . . She can 'smell out' people's moral natures by instinct. . . . She is also given a high degree of self-knowledge and unusual gifts of self-sacrifice . . . a convincing depiction of moral goodness. . . ." The same pattern holds for Little Dorrit, who as J. Hillis Miller suggests, is pictured by Dickens as ". . . a person who is altogether good. And this miraculous goodness is imagined as the persistence into adult life of the purity of childhood. . . . Little Dorrit derives all her power to help her father and others around her from her preservation of the simplicity, loving-kindness, and faithful perseverance of childhood." It is miraculous because Dorrit is an adult who ". . . understands the wickedness of the world, and is able to accept and love even that."[5]

Dickens' angelic redemption scheme is particularly prominent in *Hard Times,* where Rachel's selfless love for Stephen Blackpool and his alcoholic wife saves him from a desperate act of murder to free himself from an intolerable marriage. He falls on his knees before the lovely Rachel and says, "Thou art an Angel. . . . Thou changest me from bad to good. Thou mak'st me humbly wishfo' to be more like thee, and fearfo' to lose thee when this life is ower, a' the muddle cleared awa'. Thou'rt an Angel; it may be thou hast saved my soul alive!"[6]

This image of the ideal woman as an angelic redeemer figure, communicating divine love to a fallen world, became a crucial tenet for Victorian literature in the wake of Dickens. Tennyson expressed the ideal in his description of The Princess:

> No angel, but a dearer being, all dipt
> In angel instincts, breathing Paradise,
> Interpreter between the gods and men.

It is an image of selfless love devoid of sexual connotations, combined with a perfect conformity to the post-Puritan virtues of cooperativeness, cheerfulness, and submissiveness. Redemption here takes the form of the transformation rather than the annihilation of incorrigibles. The suffering servant replaces the horseman with the avenging weapon. Except for the seemingly instinctive need of these Victorian heroines to submit to male authority, they betray no sense of female sexual identity. As H. R. Hays wittily puts it, this literature makes women into "the bell-shaped angel" who, given the "conspiracy of silence" concerning sexual relations, presumably "produced young by parthenogenesis."[7]

II

A series of female writers took up the presentation of the superheroine in the wake of Dickens. Harriet Beecher Stowe modeled her depiction of "Little Eva" in *Uncle Tom's Cabin* after Little Nell. Martha Farquarson developed the female redeemer figure in the *Elsie Dinsmore* series beginning in 1868. Elsie was the pious heroine who would redeem others by bursting into tears at hardness of heart. She brought her irreligious father to repentance by fainting at the piano when he tried to force her to play secular music on Sunday.[8]

For current Americans perhaps the best known of such heroines is Heidi in Johanna Spyri's book by that title, which was translated in 1884. This perpetual favorite has been repeatedly printed, filmed, and recorded in America. Its appeal to the American audience seems to reveal an appetite for tales of redemption not shared by every culture. The orphan Heidi is brought to the Alps to live with her old grandfather, a recluse at odds with religion and society. Her cheerfulness and redemptive manipulations turn the forbidding mountains above Dorfli into a veritable Eden. After rescuing Peter and his goat from a precipice, Heidi offers her lunch in exchange for his promise not to punish the errant animal. "You may have it all. . . . But then you must never, never beat Distelfinck, or Schneehopli, or any of the goats." This manipulative strategy succeeds in permanently altering Peter's treatment of the goats; bribing was never more redemptive. Heidi also keeps Peter's blind grandmother company, giving her something to live for once again. After Heidi's very first visit, the old woman went to bed saying, "If she will only come again! Now there is something still left in the world to give me pleasure!"[9] Heidi talks her previously antisocial grandfather into repairing the shutters on the primitive house where the old woman lives, to the amazement of all. As Heidi humbly manipulates the older males, one by one, the process of redemptive transformation is well on its way.

The Alm-Uncle's resistance against sending his eight-year-old granddaughter to school or church brings about a fall from Paradise. Heidi is taken to Frankfurt, where she becomes the companion of the crippled Klara. Heidi is desperately homesick in the lowlands, feeling ". . . as if she were in a cage behind the long curtains. . . . Like a little bird placed for the first time in a handsome cage, she flew from one window to another. . . . She felt that she must see the green grass and the last melting snows on the cliffs." Heidi selflessly becomes Klara's friend and brings joy to her life but constantly runs afoul of the rigid disciplines of the governess. The governess becomes convinced Heidi is mad because she lashes out against the crowded city, which seems so antithetical to life when compared with the Alps: "If the robber-bird should fly over Frankfurt he would scream still louder, because so many people live together and make each other wicked, and do not go up on the cliffs where it would be good for them." Convinced that she would never see her beloved mountains again, and fearing she would appear ungrateful if she complained, the child who has begun to bring such remarkable changes in her companion falls into despondency. "Heidi dared tell no one that she was homesick.

But in her heart the burden grew heavier and heavier. She could no longer eat, and every day she grew a little paler. At night she often lay awake for a long time thinking of the Alm."[10]

In terms conventional for both European and American pietism, Heidi is told by Klara's grandmother that religious submission would provide a happy solution to her desperate loneliness. "You see, Heidi, the reason you are so sad is because you know no one who can help you. . . . If you pray every day and trust Him, everything will be made right for you, and you will soon have a happy heart again." The child replies, "I will go now, right away, and ask God to forgive me . . . and I will never forget Him again."[11] Shortly thereafter Heidi begins sleepwalking and betrays to the summoned doctor that she dreams of being on the Alm with her beloved grandfather. The good doctor prescribes the Alpen meadows.

Upon her return to the Alps, Heidi's role as a selfless redeemer develops rapidly. She uses the money Herr Sesemann sent along to buy white rolls for the blind grandmother, who has trouble eating the hard, black bread. After Heidi tells her grandfather how the "dear Lord" must have planned for her to return with money for the rolls and the ability to read to the blind woman, a miraculous change comes over him. He climbs up to her loft that night, and finds her lying there with folded hands, having thanked God as she had promised. "Then he, too, folded his hands and bowed his head. 'Father,' he prayed, 'I have sinned against Heaven and before Thee and am no more worthy to be called Thy son!' And great tears rolled down his cheeks." The next morning he puts on his coat with the silver buttons for the first time in years and takes Heidi to church, to the amazement of all. The community welcomes him back as if the years of hostility and alienation had somehow disappeared. The old man confesses, "The dear Lord was indeed good to me when He sent you up on the Alm."[12] The simple faith that God uses her to achieve the happiness of others keeps Heidi from reflecting on her own role in this miraculous melting of a hardened heart. She remains as pure and selfless as the first day she skipped up the Alm to her grandfather's hut.

The next phase in the redemption tale concerns Klara's doctor, who visits Heidi because the crippled girl is too weak for the promised visit. He is still mourning the loss of a family member, but Heidi cheers him with the promise that there is no sadness in the Alpen paradise. "'Oh, oh!' exclaimed Heidi quite gaily. 'Nobody ever has a sad heart here–only in Frankfurt.'" She goes on to assure him that ". . . the dear Lord knows some joy which is to come out of this by and by." He ultimately moves up to Dorfli to live with Heidi and her grandfather. For both the doctor and the grandfather, ". . . their chief joy in the house is that they will be together with their happy child. 'My dear uncle,' said the doctor one day, 'I feel as if, next to you, I am the one to whom she belongs, and I want her to share in my property like my own child.'"[13] This is indeed a happy world in which all sadness is relieved and the selfless redeemers are made rich. Heidi makes the Alp into a shrine with her healing for all.

Since Heidi cannot read to Peter's bedridden grandmother when winter storms isolate their hut, she teaches the obdurate boy to read. He says he does not want to learn and has no desire to read hymns to his grandmother. "This obstinacy made Heidi angry. With flashing eyes she placed herself in front of the boy and said threateningly, 'Do you know what will happen if you never learn anything?'" She goes on to describe what would happen to him if he were sent to Frankfurt to the boys' school. "'I'll learn to read,' said Peter quickly." This threat from our redemptive manipulator makes an eager schoolboy who learns the alphabet and ". . . followed Heidi's orders strictly, and every afternoon studied the other letters eagerly." Soon he delights his grandmother by reading hymns and astonishes the schoolmaster. When Peter's turn comes to read at school, the teacher says,

> "Peter, must I pass by you as usual, or will you try once more? –I will not say to read. Will you try to stammer through a line?"
>
> Peter read three lines, one after another without stopping. The teacher looked at him in astonishment.
>
> "Why, you could never even grasp the alphabet, though I tried hard enough to teach you," he said at last. "Now you can read quite easily and clearly. Who was able to work such a miracle, Peter?"
>
> "Heidi," was the reply.
>
> The teacher looked at Heidi in surprise.
>
> "I have noticed other changes in you, Peter," he went on.

> "You used to be absent from school a whole week—yes, several weeks together. But lately you have not stayed away a day. Who can have caused such a change for the better?"[14]

Who but Heidi? The schoolmaster rushes to the pastor after school to relate this modern miracle. It seems essential in this genre of redemption tale that the community recognize and applaud the powers of the redeemer, while the latter remains completely unaffected by praise. Selflessness must survive the elaborate ritual of adulation, deeply appealing to the fantasies of the audience.

The climactic miracle in the redemption story is the healing of Klara. She is carried up to the Alm the spring after the doctor's visit, along with her wheelchair and other paraphernalia. The bright sunshine and goats' milk begin a process of natural healing, which Heidi and the old man encourage. One day he carries Klara up to the meadow and leaves her with Heidi and Peter, not knowing that Peter had spitefully pushed the wheelchair over the cliff. When Klara wants to see the flowers higher up, Heidi's moment arrived. Ordering Peter to help, she commands Klara to take her first steps. "Klara did so . . . and suddenly she cried out excitedly, 'I can do it, Heidi! Oh, I can! See! I can take steps, one after another.'" Later, when Klara's grandmother comes to witness the unexpected miracle, she explains to Peter how this sin in destroying the wheelchair had been turned into good.

> Klara no longer had a chair to be carried in, and when she wanted to see the flowers she made a great effort to walk. . . . When one wishes to do a wicked thing, the dear Lord can take it quickly into His own hands and turn it into good for the one who was to be harmed.

The requirement for this miraculous transformation of evil into good is the selfless redeemer. The natural healing processes and providential coincidence are galvanized by the selfless good works of Heidi and her associates. Hence the Sesemann family resolves not to take the beloved Heidi back to Frankfurt, but to leave her where they can visit on seasonal pilgrimages. Frau Sesemann assures the blind old grandmother:

> Do not worry. . . . Heidi is going to stay here and make you happy. We shall want to see the child again, but we will come to her. We shall come up to the Alm every year, for we have reason

to offer thanks to the dear Lord in this place where such a miracle has been wrought for *our* child.[15]

The redemptive score of our innocent superheroine is thus a perfect one. She conveys the redemptive powers of the Alpine Eden to everyone she encounters: her bitter old grandfather, the lonely doctor, the illiterate Peter, his lonely grandmother, and now the crippled Klara. This redemptive paradigm matches the monomythic outline at every point. The selfless redeemer, lacking in any sexual consciousness, achieves marvelous solutions by which Edenic happiness is restored, and everyone lives happily ever after. This mythical plot varies from *Star Trek, Death Wish,* or *Walking Tall* only in the means of redemption, which are psychologically and religiously manipulative rather than violent. Whereas the masculine superheroes achieve sexual segmentation by renunciation, heroines like Heidi simply remain in the prepuberty state forever.

A surprisingly large number of figures in American children's literature and popular culture fit the Heidi model. Pollyanna is a sort of Yankee Heidi, who redeems an entire town and brings frustrated lovers together by teaching and living the "Glad Game." Little Orphan Annie fits the same pattern of permanent prepuberty arrest, playing the role of a thoroughly secularized Heidi whose miracles are sometimes wrought by her superhuman associates like Daddy Warbucks. The Nancy Drew and Cherry Ames series feature grown-up Heidis who never marry because they have so many mysteries to unravel and hostages to save. Dorothy in *The Wizard of Oz* transforms the Scarecrow, the Tin Man, and the Cowardly Lion before returning to Kansas without having grown perceptively toward feminine maturity. Mary Worth is a postmenopausal variant of the selfless redeemer guided by fate from crisis to domestic crisis to effect the miracle of happy endings.

III

One of the most striking developments in current pop culture is the emergence of male Heidi figures who redeem by nonviolent manipulations. It is possible that Santa Claus, shaped by the Victorian yearning for bringing domestic happiness, is something of a precedent in this regard. But figures like Lucas Tanner and Pete Dixon in recent television series about teaching in public schools seem to fit the Heidi paradigm rather closely. They are unattached sexually, possessing complete unselfishness and superhuman capacities to solve personal problems. Dr. Marcus Welby regularly effects psychological conversions of patients and relatives who deny the presence of illness or connive to escape treatment. Dr. Joe Gannon similarly performs difficult operations only to find the healing process thwarted by psychological barriers he alone can dismantle. At the crisis point, the superdoctors intervene in the private affairs of their patients, evoking confessions and resultant healings of body and soul.

In the *Little House on the Prairie,* Charles Ingalls shares the redeemer role with other members of the family. In the television series, in contrast to the novels by Laura Ingalls Wilder, Pa spends the bulk of his time and creative energy solving the problems of the community. The long, monotonous days and years behind the plow and building with primitive tools recede from view while a series of domestic crises find neat resolution within the miraculous space of sixty minutes. In one program Ingalls almost single-handedly relieves Walnut Grove of a typhoid fever epidemic after the doctor and minister prove incapable of coping with the deadly threat. He finds that the source of the infection is the cut-rate grain being sold in the community. Ingalls' taste for a different type of flour had protected him and his family from the epidemic. Once this exemption from the plight of other mortals in Walnut Grove is established, Ingalls leads the campaign to heal the community, using the church as a hospital. His issuing orders symbolizes the status of the domestic redeemer above the traditional redemptive agencies of society: "Reverend, bring shovels. We will have to bury the dead right away." The episode concludes with a touch of Heidi pietism after the plague subsides. "God lets it happen to strengthen us," remarks the minister.[16]

In another program Ingalls' coolness and moral sense keep the community from an unjust lynching. The man entrusted to buy seed corn from a distant town was accidentally pinned under the wagon, but the ever-stupid citizens of Walnut Grove immediately conclude he made off with their money. They scorn Ingalls and discuss violent retribution while he retraces the route and finds the injured man in the forest, saving both him and the community. Like Dickens' Esther Summerson, Ingalls has an unerring ability to tell "good guys" from "bad guys," and thus assures perfect solutions to moral dilemmas.[17]

The monomythic structure of these domestic redeemer tales can be traced in detail when one analyzes a *Little House on the Prairie* episode like "Ebenezer Sprague,"[18] which opens with the typical Edenic scene of the Ingalls children romping over the unspoiled prairie. Arriving from the wicked city like a hardhearted capitalist, Scrooge-like Ebenezer Sprague begins spoiling paradise by demanding a penalty payment because the completion of the new bank building is forty-eight minutes late. In a coldly hostile manner, he turns down Ingalls' friendly invitation to dinner.

The next day the women of Walnut Grove gather to consider how to remedy the lack of school texts for the poorer children of the community. They resolve, after the intervention of selfless Mrs. Ingalls, to take up a community collection. She volunteers to approach the difficult banker, but when she does, Sprague immediately accuses her of attempting to use "the wiles of a woman" to get a loan Pa Ingalls had applied for and rudely been refused. "My only duty is to run an honest bank and make a fair profit for myself . . . children will grow up without books." And thus a domestic impasse arises in the innocent town: The banker hinders the progress of farmers like Ingalls, and his refusal to contribute dooms the effort to provide books for needy children. What could possibly alter this Scroogish impediment to paradise?

The monomythic plot calls at this point for the emergence of a superhero. Sure enough, Laura unwittingly strikes up a friendship with the newcomer to Walnut Grove and innocently sets about the task of miraculous transformation. She has taken up fishing, which is Sprague's only hobby. Her first encounter with the unknown man at the pond is inauspicious but eventually she persuades him to use some of her doughballs for bait, so he can catch as many fish as she has. They end up riding back together in the buggy and she reports to her family at supper that the unknown man is now her best friend.

The next day Laura discovers the identity of her fisherman

friend, with whom she had innocently discussed the problem of the mean banker who would not contribute to the book fund. She returns to the fishing hole to confront Mr. Sprague with his deception. Rather than admitting it, Sprague accuses her of feigning friendship to get Pa's loan. She replies with perfect integrity, "All I wanted to have was a good friend." Ingalls strides into the bank the next morning as the cool avenger to administer a proper verbal beating.

"You broke that little girl's heart. She went down to that pond every day to see her best friend. . . . My little girl gave something to you. Friendship. You took it and threw it right back in her face."

Sprague replied, "I don't need friends."

"Well, that's good for you, Mr. Sprague, because you don't have any. You know, I feel sorry for you. You can't take anything, and you can't give anything except money. And as far as I am concerned, that means you don't have anything at all."

This denunciation recalls Heidi's harsh verbal punishment of Peter. The banker spends a sleepless night in his barren room, much as Scrooge dreams of his empty life without friend and family. In a miraculous conversion indebted far more to Dickens and Spyri than to Wilder, the television program depicts Sprague secretly sending a crateload of books to a surprised school. Laura is reconciled with the banker, and the program ends with Ebenezer Sprague in the bosom of his newly adopted family, like Dickens' Scrooge in the house of Cratchit. The formerly hard-hearted bachelor is hugging little Carey, who replaces Tiny Tim in the festive scene. The camera fades back through the window, showing the Christmas-like celebration in the Ingalls home, with a lovely cake at the center of the scene. Laura's reprise confirms the restoration of paradise through psychological manipulation: "I kept Mr. Sprague's secret about the books. And Pa got his loan and bought the forty acres. Mr. Sprague said I sure didn't lie about Ma's cooking. It was the best in the whole world." Johanna Spyri would have blushed to find so many Heidis around a single cake.

IV

Perhaps the most remarkable facet of the domestic redemption scheme in the *Little House on the Prairie* is its departure from the starkly realistic novels of Laura Ingalls Wilder. Her chronicles of the pioneer experience in the Midwest encompassed a great variety of topics that children have found interesting: Ma's wonderful cooking, Pa's fiddling for family singing in the evening, the many journeys to different homestead locations, the experiences of struggling with adverse weather, the encounters with insects and animals, and the struggles of survival as a farm family in the perpetual throes of bankruptcy. The opening lines of *On the Way Home* convey the somber and realistic material characteristic of these Wilder chronicles.

> For seven years there had been too little rain. The prairies were dust. Day after day, summer after summer, the scorching winds blew the dust and the sun was brassy in a yellow sky. Crop after crop failed. Again and again the barren land must be mortgaged, for taxes and food and next year's seed. The agony of hope ended when there was no harvest and no more credit, no money to pay interest and taxes; the banker took the land. Then the bank failed.
>
> In the seventh year a mysterious catastrophe was world wide. All banks failed. From coast to coast the factories shut down, and business ceased. This was a Panic.[19]

These lines from Laura's diary convey the blunt, courageous, unsentimental spirit that is characteristic of the entire series of children's books. The social order does not escape criticism, though the tone is never ideological. There are moments of comfort, security, and joy in the stories, but the predominant tone is of hardships, some self-imposed by the failure of family schemes to live well on the adverse prairie, and there are no miraculous redemptions of bankers.

When one compares these stories with the television episodes, it is clear that a process of *mythic alchemy* has occurred. By "alchemy" we refer to the purging of elements that do not fit monomythic premises. The novels are cleansed of their realistic compo-

Above,
the town that refused to re-elect Pusser immortalizes itself by association with the fictional super-sheriff of the films.

Right,
the figure who "Walked Tall" in films achieves here a permanent mythic identity: Death, as well as life, imitates art.

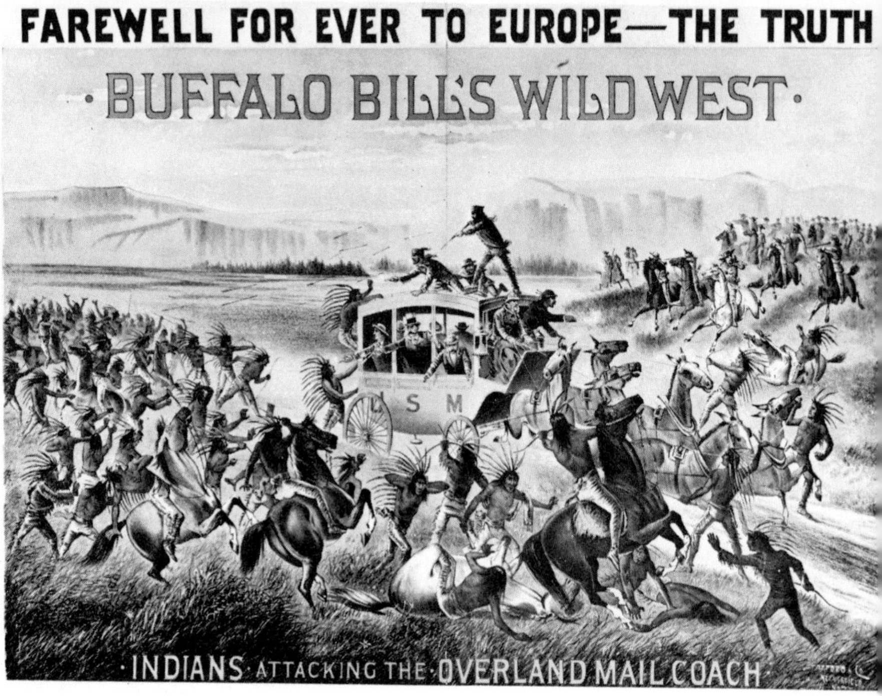
FAREWELL FOR EVER TO EUROPE—THE TRUTH
·BUFFALO BILL'S WILD WEST·
·INDIANS· ATTACKING THE ·OVERLAND MAIL COACH·

These pop redeemers of the nineteenth century provide the precedents for modern American varieties. In his European tour poster, Buffalo Bill "stands between civilization and savagery." Dickens exalts the dying Little Nell who lit the path to redemption with feminine goodness—"So shall we know the angels in their majesty after death." In *Heidi* the redeemer and her friend miraculously lead Klara in her first steps.

ABOVE, DON RUSSELL COLLECTION

The towns were bleak and often deep in mud, and on winter mornings Pa had to shovel the snow off the children's bed in Laura Ingalls Wilder's stories of pioneer life. The mythic sanitation of such scenes in the television version helps sustain faith in miracles of domestic redemption.

Disney extended the myth of the domestic redeemer in creating his Mary Poppins and Snow White. They are graceful, lovely, and tidy, performing more miracles than Heidi.

BOTH PICTURES, © WALT DISNEY PRODUCTIONS

Here is the wind-blown Mary Poppins whom Disney transformed into a titillating redeemer who floats down with miraculous grace. Below, the angry dwarfs in a nineteenth-century German woodcut arouse Snow White from her tipsy nap. Her adult body required considerable straightening and flattening by Disney before it acquired Heidi proportions.

Disney's film *Victory Through Air Power* offered world redemption through violence, symbolized by the eagle attacking the Axis octopus. This animation technique disguised the destructive effects of aerial bombing.

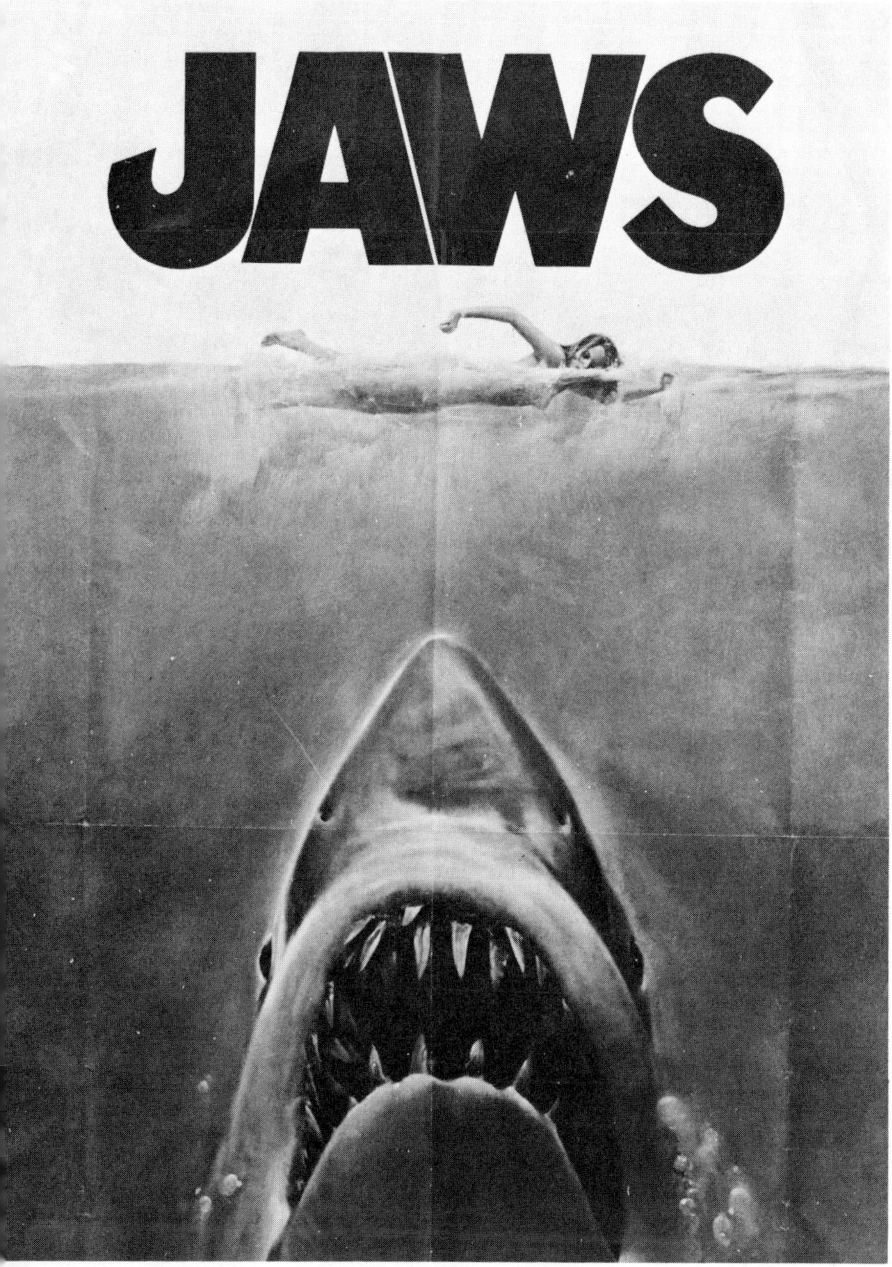

In this poster for *Jaws* the shark functions like the eagle in carrying out redemptive punishment. Like other disaster films, it suggests sexual retribution, instantly punishing the girl's provocative behavior with a rapish attack.

Is *Jaws'* Chief Brody really
a ripoff from Spiderman Comics?

nents and transformed from tragic saga to happy melodrama. When desperate circumstances arise, they are always neatly eliminated at the end of an hour program by miraculous redemption. Elements that might prevent an audience from being intoxicated by the mythic brew are filtered out.

In the novel *By the Shores of Silver Lake,* for example, Laura's older sister barely survives scarlet fever and suffers permanent blindness. The family tenderly cares for her with its limited means, saving pennies for years before Mary can be sent to a school for the blind. She learns to do housework without her sight, while Laura takes over chores and becomes "her eyes" by describing events, weather, and scenery. It is a courageous, ennobling story of coping with harsh reality. In September 1975, Lewis K. Parker described his interview with producer-actor Michael Landon and his cast on the *Little House* set in California. He asked whether the TV Mary would go through the ordeal of blindness. "No, but Mary will get glasses. . . . That'll happen in a show about her grades mysteriously dropping—all because she can't see the blackboard and doesn't want to tell anyone."[20] Sure enough, the next month the episode appeared. In the wake of Mary's bad report card, Pa finds her studying late at night. He writes the answer to the problem on her slate and says, "See that?" She looks puzzled, and must step closer to the slate to read what it says. Pa then devises an experiment to test her sight, subsequently taking her to Mankato to be fitted with glasses. Mary's schoolmates tease her as "four eyes," so she hides the glasses in a hollow log. Her chief tormenter, naughty Nellie Olsen, begins to boast about winning the forthcoming history contest. But Mary retrieves her glasses at the last minute and wins the highest grade. To make the neat resolution complete, Mary only has to wear the glasses for a month or so until her strained eye muscles are eased. The permanent affliction of blindness is thus distilled into a temporary, minor problem solved by the ingenuity of superdad. And everyone lives happily ever after.

For children who have read the realistic novels for the past two generations, the *Little House* television series must rank as one of the most flagrant violations of historical consciousness in current popular culture. The large viewing audience is assured it is seeing historical reality. As Michael Landon explains,

> So we take incidents from the books and build stories around them. We've pretty much shown how the real Ingalls family lived. . . . I got together with the art director and we researched more than fifty books on frontier life in Minnesota in the 1870's. . . . As a result, our show is probably the most visually authentic of any ever made about the Old West.[21]

Thus pseudo-empiricism is part of the believability strategy of the program. But even here the alchemy process is apparent. In place of mud and drought, there are clean streets and barnyards, and green fields. Instead of frequent tornadoes, grasshoppers, and blizzards, there are occasional bouts with adverse weather that always end happily. But the cumulative result of the transmutation is that the raw, threatening prairie and the ugly, raucous towns become Edenic. Natural evils that strike everyone without discrimination in the novels are distilled so that the Ingalls family is either spared or quickly retrieved by its virtue, hard work, and redemptive skills. The Pa Ingalls of the novels, the foolish, loving, bearded man plagued with mortgages, disasters, and crop failures is distilled in the television series into the handsome, smooth-skinned redeemer who devotes most of his time to rescuing the community. Historical details like Pa's stealing food for his family in *The Long Winter* and his fist fight at the land claim office in *By the Shores of Silver Lake* are omitted. The historical Ingalls family left behind a succession of abject failures. They miscalculated, lost their land, and had to move on. But the process of mythic alchemy makes them always triumphant in adversity, abiding in a stable paradise where children grow up romping over green meadows. The television orchestra always comes in on cue to sweep the audience into a nostalgia for paradise.

V

The most serious question to be raised about the scheme of domestic redemption concerns its efficacy in helping mere mortals cope with reality. What is its likely impact on persons facing the irremediable conditions of disability, accident, natural catastrophe, and death? What is its message to the poor, the defeated, the frustrated, and the disappointed?

Materials like Heidi and the *Little House* television series imply that if superheroes were present, a vast array of problems would be solved quickly and painlessly. But since there seem to be no such figures outside of popdom, there is really little that can be done. Passivity in face of adverse circumstances becomes linked with a tranquilizing nostalgia for Eden. The message is that all good people deserve happy endings, no matter what their limitations; however, since such happiness is not available in real life for most people, the natural conclusion is that something must have gone dreadfully wrong. A selective presentation of the past thus erodes the ability to live in the present and awakens the yearning for total solutions offered by modern propagandists of redemption.

The impact of the domestic redemption scheme on communal and familial leaders may be equally problematic. Those who identify with the redeemer figures and seek to emulate their feats in real life will find that targets of redemption are not as easy to change as one might expect. Nor is adversity so easy to alter. Without overlooking the need and potential of benevolence, it is nevertheless clear that cheerful Heidis do not generally succeed in reconciling alienated oldsters to church and community. Innocent Lauras usually fare no better by using fishbait to soften the lonely hearts of bankers. The manipulative techniques of pious abnegation and well-devised tongue lashings rarely evoke the miraculous transformations promised by the myth. They are more frequently the source of additional alienation. But since an illusion of perfect selflessness is essential to the redemptive scheme, one denies the personal motivations in order to mask manipulative campaigns. The myth teaches those seeking to emulate superheroes not to place their cards on the table, not to admit their own emotional needs, and hence always to assume the attitude of the injured servant when thwarted. When the stance of the innocent savior proves futile, explosions of indignation are imminent. Frustrating reality can turn domestic manipulators into male and female bitches. Massaged by the myth to believe that they require no growth or adjustment to adversity, would-be superheroes and heroines have a disconcerting tendency to withdraw from sustained encounters with reality.

The Laura Ingalls Wilder novels are a more reliable resource than their television distillations for coping with twentieth-century adversity. As popular and charming children's novels, they remain deeply grounded in human reality because they assume a tragic rather than a melodramatic stance. Tragedies treat limitations both in the worst and best of humans, bringing them face to face with their flaws. Sartre's line from *No Exit* is suggestive as we consider the limitations of the domestic redemption scheme: "Hell is other people." There is a limit to our ability to change others to suit our standards, and those who strive hardest at this task make the most perfect hells for themselves and their victims. While pop redeemer tales disguise this by the illusion of selflessness, tragic materials open us to reality and give us strength to endure without happy endings. Tragic heroes like Socrates and Paul suffer death as a consequence of actions they have freely chosen. In an orbit far beyond happy endings and miraculous escapes, their heroism consists in the disciplined acceptance of defeat and the firm hold to the truth as they saw it. The simple perfections of the pop redeemers are unattainable in this classic tradition. Heroes of the Greek tragedies, for example, fall because of their pride or because of a fate intimately linked to the virtues they possess. Their glory is the capacity to rise to moments of truth, to acknowledge their flaws and sins, and to live with the consequences.

These resources of tragic realism are required to cope with twentieth-century adversity. That they can be embodied even in popular materials suited for children is evidenced by the Wilder novels. There can be no facile assignment of tragedy to high culture and melodrama to popular culture. The Ingalls family of the novels deserves to stand in the company of Sisyphus and the Loman family in *The Death of a Salesman*. Such materials may provide the vision needed to live with domestic circumstances broken in part by our own flawed efforts to redeem. They reveal that life can be deeply satisfying without monomythic Glad Games, happy endings, and bountiful rewards bestowed on virtuous Heidis.

VII

Disney's Land: Saints and Sanitary Animals

> Disney's art ". . . reaches greatness, a degree of perfection in its field which surpasses our best critical capacity to analyze and . . . succeeds . . . in pleasing children and simple folk." —Mortimer Adler in *Art and Prudence*[1]

> "I'll stack 'Mary Poppins' against any cheap and depraved movie ever made."—Walt Disney[2]

After years of studying exotic foreign cultures, the distinguished anthropologist Hortense Powdermaker returned to Hollywood to live among the people of the film colony. During the period from 1947 to 1948 she examined their mores and artifacts and found strange taboos against "all biological aspects of the human species." Her informants helped trace this to "the Code," a voluntary scheme of self-censorship adopted by the Motion Picture Association of America. "The showing of toilets is rigidly prohibited. They are always missing in any bathroom scene. Even the sound of an out-of-scene toilet being flushed is deleted." This ban alone could hardly have retarded the development of screen art, but there were more serious prohibitions, including the nearly total suppression of sexual love. This remarkable colony, called "Sodom by the Sea" in its periods of greatest sexual scandal, forbade the depiction of the activities that presumably afforded the greatest pleasures for the actor-natives. "All suggestions of intimacy in and out of marriage are taboo. . . . In one film, the MPAA asked for the deletion of dialogue that indicated that a husband wanted to sleep with his wife. Even gestures of affection between a man and wife are taboo. The MPAA asked for omission of a scene in which a man was buttoning his wife's dress and kissed the back of her neck. . . ." According to Powdermaker, the taboos were hypocritical because they did not ". . . represent the actual beliefs, values or behavior of the people practicing them." It was an unusual situation for an anthropologist, since among primitive peoples ". . . taboos are an integral part of behavior and values. . . ."[3]

The filmmaker Powdermaker overlooked in her assessment was Walt Disney. He was exceptional in that he accepted the taboos with the sincerity observed in primitive cultures. Walt Disney needed no censor because he had internalized the values of the American public that had given the code its distinctive shape. He operated happily within the limits of "the Code" because it expressed his own sense of decency and artistic merit. Disney thereby became America's greatest pop creator, an international pop institution in himself whose work is considered uniquely suitable for children. One can hardly understand the American taste for the monomyth without a comprehension of Disney's land.

I

Like the Ten Commandments of the Old Testament, the Motion Picture Production Code was largely negative. The "nots" and "forbids" generously season every section. "No picture shall be produced which will lower the moral standards of those who see it." "Lustful and open-mouth kissing, lustful embraces, suggestive posture and gestures are not to be shown. . . . Blasphemy is forbidden. Reference to the Deity, God, Lord, Jesus, Christ, shall not be irreverent." But mere conformity with negative prohibitions is as incapable of inspiring art as it is of life. A key to Disney's creativity is that he did not feel restricted by these negative limits. He understood how the revulsive feelings that lay behind the code could be used to create characters with mythic appeal. But above all, Disney displayed unsurpassed gifts of story telling and developed complex innovations for presenting visual images. His genius was recognized by some of the most serious artists of his day. Leopold Stokowski and Deems Taylor respected his work enough to collaborate with him in the creation of *Fantasia,* a remarkable experiment in using abstract forms to illustrate musical ideas. Composer Jerome Kern remarked, "Cartoonist Walt Disney has made the 20th Century's only important contribution to music. In the synchronization of humorous episodes with humorous music, he has unquestionably given us the outstanding contribution of our time."[4]

Mickey Mouse was Disney's first great creative achievement, demonstrating the potential of the animated cartoon genre. Sergei Eisenstein, the great Russian film director, asserted that Mickey Mouse was America's most original contribution to culture. In 1935 the mouse was described by L. H. Robbins as ". . . the best known and most popular international figure of his day." It was a figure remarkable in part for its lack of sexual differentiation. Mickey's pants and lack of shirt are the only clues to his masculinity. His speech, provided by Walt Disney himself, was similarly sexless. Fritz Mollenhoef noted that "The larynx contains a most peculiar voice. It is crowing, thin, without modulation and we are unable to tell whether the character is a man, woman or child. . . ." Mickey lacked both whiskers and beastly paws. Instead he was given four-fingered hands, always neatly clothed in a pair of white gloves. Mickey's romantic partner, Minnie, was equally sexless in appearance. Though consciously modeled upon the human being in her upright stance and skirt, her upper torso was as devoid of mammary development as Mickey's lower torso was in genital protuberances. None of Disney's funny animals has embarrassing and potentially dirty orifices or appendages.[5]

Richard Schickel connects this peculiar sanitizing approach with animal life to a revealing episode in James Agee's novel *A Death in the Family,* in which a mother expresses her disgust for Charlie Chaplin: ". . . that horrid little man . . . he's so *nasty* . . . so *vulgar!* With his nasty little cane; hooking up skirts and things, and that nasty little walk!"[6] Here is the revulsive feeling behind the censor's code that Disney avoided in his mythical animal creations. The elimination of the human body, with its unavoidable sexual features, made Disney's animal comedy less intimate, less objectionable than Chaplin's films. By eliminating biological realities, Disney was able to present a version of sexuality that was highly entertaining for squeamish audiences.

In *Steamboat Willie,* Disney's first great mouse cartoon, Minnie and Mickey exhibit this peculiar version of sexuality after the steamboat has loaded its freight and puffs off down the river. Minnie arrives too late to board, so Mickey swings a crane with a hook on it alongside the bank where she is running. As the iron hook reaches Minnie's body, it suddenly assumes an anatomical, digital character. The hook reaches underneath Minnie's skirt to lift her body by the panties to the deck of the boat. The hook then slides out of her panties and elegantly places her skirt back in place, patting her bottom restrainedly in conclusion. An action that would have appeared "nasty" in a Chaplin film is rendered innocuous because the intimate touching is assigned to a mechanical finger and the motivation is helpful rather than lewd. Moreover, the sexual play has been displaced into the anal region.

In the cartoons that succeeded *Steamboat Willie,* one repeatedly observes anal sexual play. In *Moving Day,* Donald Duck gets his rear end repeatedly stuck in a goldfish bowl and struggles mightily to release himself. He gets a toilet plunger stuck on his rear which he thumps, tugs at, and twists in a long episode. This anal preoccupation of Disney was so strong that Richard Schickel was prompted to observe evidences of a fetish in which sexuality is transferred to infantile buttocks. He mentions the concluding imagery in *Fantasia.* "The sequence ends with the most explicit statement of anality ever made by the studio, which found in the human backside not only the height of humor but the height of sexuality as well. Two of the little cupids who scamper incessantly through the sequence finally–and blessedly–draw a curtain over the scene. When they come together, their shiny little behinds form, for an instant, a heart."[7] This form of sexuality was more innocent and wholesome than anything that humans could ever expect to experience. Sex had become sufficiently innocent, trivial, and enjoyable that every family knew it could trust itself to go to the movies.

Disney's discovery of sex without sex inspired some of his outstanding technical achievements in the field of animation. In 1932 Disney released his first color cartoon, *Trees*. It received an Academy Award as Best Cartoon for its ingenious presentation of a romance in the woods between two trees. Beautiful flowers and animals celebrated the courtship while a wicked, gnarled old tree became jealous and started a fire, which threatened to destroy the forest. The ugly tree is burned by the fire it started, and a timely rainstorm, triggered by birds flying through a cloud, rescues everyone else. The two trees are united in loving joy, hugging and kissing each other. The entwinement of the woody, anatomically undifferentiated bodies at the conclusion was a satisfying embodiment of antiseptic sexuality. The pulsing glowworm that had volunteered to serve as nuptial ring was the only sign of warmth.

It was in 1938 that Disney's sanitization effort achieved its first definitive expression. *Snow White and the Seven Dwarfs* appeared, receiving an Academy Award in the following year. The mythic transmutation of Grimm's fairy tale clearly indicates the interest in both cleanliness and sexual purity. The Grimm Brothers describe the dwarves' house as immaculate, ". . . small but indescribably neat and clean." Snow White in fact angered the fastidious little men by messing up their house, drinking up their wine, and dropping off to sleep in one of their beds. It was they who suggested that she could earn her board and room if she would promise to keep ". . . everything orderly and clean in our household. . . ." In Disney's film Snow White finds the little house a pigsty: ". . . The sink was piled high with cups and saucers and plates which looked as though they had never been washed. Dirty little shirts and wrinkled little trousers hung over chairs, and everything was blanketed with dust." She resolves to clean up the mess because they ". . . need someone to take care of them. Let's clean their house and surprise them." She and her "forest friends" become a veritable Heidi team, quickly solving the household crisis of the hapless dwarves. When they return from the mine, Snow White is asleep, worn out from her household miracles. Disney's princess then awakens, miraculously names the little men, and then insists that they wash and change their clothes before supper. After the miracles of sanitation and the baptism into cleanliness, the dwarves dance about their princess with utter delight. Like the males in *Heidi,* they achieve fulfillment by mere proximity to their sweet reformer. The final detail in the sanitizing campaign was to erase any possible doubt about the sexual implications of a young lady living with seven dirty old men. Whereas the Grimms allowed the lucky dwarves to sleep in their beds adjacent to the princess, Disney sends them all downstairs to sleep on the floor. It is as if Walt had stood before the fabulous dwelling of the Brothers Grimm with Snow White's words on his lips, "Let's clean their house and surprise them."[8]

Another triumph of Disney's, the perpetually successful *Bambi,* was billed as "A Great Love Story." Here Disney moved beyond anal humor, tree romance, and White Magic Cleanser to the subject of mating, but without the distracting and presumably unwholesome motif of masculine desire. In the de-eroticized love story, Bambi's first love is stirred by Felice's sexually aggressive approach. She nuzzles the passive buck as the colorful symbols of cartoon love radiate around them. Then the selfless and impassive Bambi is thrust into competition with another stag. In one of the most dramatic scenes of the film, the competing stag steps between Bambi and Felice and the hero is ". . . forced to battle against his will with the other deer." In the duel, which plays itself out like a scene in *High Noon,* the reluctant but powerful Bambi pushes the aggressor over a cliff. The fate of death is here assigned to the stag possessing normal animal instincts for mating and dominance. The pacific Bambi, lacking either sexual passion or the instinct to rule, thus becomes a father and Prince of the Forest at the happy ending of the film.[9]

The sexual paradigm in *Bambi* is virtually identical with that in the *Playboy* fantasy. The male is neither the aggressor nor the initiator of sexual relations. He waits to respond obligingly to female sexual needs. But in neither male nor female does there seem to be an expression of ego needs. Sexual union is the result of Felice's sexual void being joined with Bambi's sense of duty to help those in need. Conflict is thus inconceivable except when a bad stag slips into the scene. Sexual fears are eliminated, jealousy is rendered obsolete, and passion is permanently out of style.

The comfortable myth of Bambi-sex points to a recurring paradox in such material. Disney strove mightily after realism in the development of the technical aspects of his films. He made careful photographic studies of forest areas in Maine, working with live fawns as models for the cartoon illustrators. So exacting was the animation that the film was delayed several years in its release. But on the point central to the love story, Disney could not resist mythic alchemy. Sanitized of nasty animal characteristics, Bambi became a redeemer figure who could join the company of Superman.

Disney's nature films present the same paradox of painstaking photographic realism and mythic story line. Thousands and thousands of feet of film would be shot in order to construct a story in which animals act out human dramas. In the *Legend of Lobo,* Disney presents a young wolf whose mother has been killed and father trapped. Lobo joins a different pack and, after proving himself, becomes its leader. Lobo's mate is captured by a hunter who uses her to lure Lobo to a trap. Lobo leads his entire pack of wolves in a raid on the rustler's hideout and rescues his mate. Similarly in *The Moon Spinners,* Nikki and Mark seek refuge in an ancient Greek temple as they flee from the wicked Uncle Strato. The vicious cats living there leave them unharmed, but when the wicked Strato comes, they fall on him, scratch him, and drive him away. These are schemes that transform animal species into something they can never be. It is anything but realistic to depict animals with redemptive instincts. But the final irony in Disney's work is that fantasy life itself is sanitized, as evidenced by such things as the mermaid without nipples in the "Small World" section of Disneyland. Such a world is truly small, but its popularity is undeniable.

II

In a rhetorical manner, L. H. Robbins raised the question of Disney's remarkable popularity as early as the thirties:

> Why is it that university presidents praise him, the League of Nations recommends him, Who's Who and the Encyclopaedia Britannica give him paragraphs, learned academies hang medals on him, art galleries turn from Picasso and Epstein to hold exhibitions over his monkey shines, and the King of England won't go to the movies unless Mickey is on the bill?

Part of the answer is that Disney created a charming and novel means of film presentation whose animated motion and color had great appeal. Disney also displayed editorial genius in relating humorous episodes without wasting a single frame of imagery. But beyond these visual considerations, Mickey seems to embody what Robbins called the ". . . release from the tyranny of things. . . . He declares a nine minute moratorium on the debt that we owe to the iron facts of life. He suspends the rules of common sense and correct deportment and the other carping, conventional laws, including the law of gravity, that hold us down and cramp our style." During this same period, Burne Hogarth was creating a comic-book Tarzan with a similar function: ". . . He is the incarnation of our secret desire to be free from every form of insignificance, frustration, degradation."[10] Hogarth gave Tarzan hyperbolic powers of movement and struggle that could be plausibly attributed to his education in the jungle among higher apes.

Mickey Mouse, hardly a match for an ape, surpasses Tarzan and King Kong in the ability to do anything. His normal screen life is one of leaping, climbing, and manipulating as no human being ever could. Like a diminutive David, he always overcame his adversaries, regardless of their stature. Robert D. Feild wrote a moving account of Mickey's genesis and miraculous powers in 1942, after the first decade of cartoon life. He describes how Disney concocted the mouse as he worked in Kansas City:

> The original mouse, the spiritual ancestor of Mickey, is reported to have made friends with Walt years before in the garage that served him as workshop. He came to offer consolation during periods of despondency. Some say, even, that he trespassed on the master's drawing board, cleaning his whiskers with unconcern or hitching up his imaginary pants. The impression he left upon Walt's mind was such that it needed only a crisis for him to reappear in the form of a savior. Be this as it may, Walt had accepted a challenge, and he needed help. It was at this moment, on the train for Hollywood, that Mickey appeared. . . . Straightway he stretched out his gauntleted hand and said, "Put it there, pal," and a friendship was cemented for good and all.[11]

This momentous apparition of a mouse sounds more laden with significance than the encounters between St. Francis and his animal friends. Disney's faith in the mouse allowed him to move mountains of capital and to thrill a worldwide audience with screen miracles. Feild pays extravagant tribute to the cultural effect of Mickey, referring to his genesis years as ". . . a period of history in which civilization is going through pangs of rebirth while mankind struggles in a strange darkness, uncertain of its destiny." Disney's mouse played a virtually redemptive role in leading the world out of this "strange darkness":

> During those few short years between 1928 and the present [1942] it will be found that Mickey played no mean part. Not only did he give us courage when we most needed it, forcing us to laugh to hide our tears, but also he opened up new worlds of experience and contributed to the refashioning of our ideals. Without precedent, this imaginative little symbol frisked his way into the hearts of all. There is no corner of the earth into which he has not penetrated; there is no type of man from crowned head to primitive savage, that has not been won over.[12]

The age-old dream of a single, universal religious image seems, according to this account, to have been achieved by the frisky mouse. Icons bearing Mickey's sacred image multiplied by millions: dolls, toothbrushes, pencils, sweatshirts, beany caps, toys, and tableware all bore the licensed imprimatur.

Mickey Mouse was not, however, the greatest financial success for Walt Disney. Live-action films proved even more profitable. Disney achieved a perfect synthesis of film miracle and sanitized sexuality in *Mary Poppins*. It was his most successful creation, critically and financially, embodying many of the values of his earlier, animated films. Emboldened by his reductive experiments with sexuality, Disney has taken the charwomanish Mary Poppins from the Travers novels and has assigned the role to Julie Andrews. The often bad-tempered and unpredictable Travers figure underwent a mythic alchemy to acquire Heidi's angelic sweetness. Rather than being blown to the door of the Bankses' house by a gusty wind, Disney's Mary Poppins descends from the heavens on her umbrella, coming on the clouds in biblical style to set things right. A redemptive story line absent in the Travers novels is created. Whereas the Travers Mary Poppins creates chaotic situations with her erratic comings and goings, Disney's heroine causes a confrontation with the wicked, calculating bankers and precipitates the dismissal of Mr. Banks, who then renounces his mean-spirited, pecuniary outlook and becomes a father to his children. Disney's Mary Poppins, despite her physical charms and the availability of Bert, played by the handsome Dick Van Dyke, shows absolutely no romantic inclination. She remains, in her own words, "practically perfect." It is the perfection of a Heidi, manifest in a figure no one would mistake for a child. At the film's conclusion, this paragon angelically ascends, her redemptive task completed, in a scene that replaces her inexplicable departures at the conclusion of the Travers novels.[13]

Audiences and critics have been utterly disarmed by the sense of the miraculous with which Disney has so richly invested the film. Critics referred to "the technical wizardry of the film," to Disney's "vast magic-making machinery," and to the "magical moments" in the film. One critic lavishly suggested that *Mary Poppins* "showed why movies were invented." The film re-created the sense of the miraculous that has disappeared from most modern religion, invading an allegedly secularized nature by cinematic manipulation. When the untidy nursery is to be cleaned up, Mary assures the Banks children: "In every job that must be done . . . we find an element of fun. We find the fun and *snap!* the job's a game!" Straightaway the toys and clothes move magically to their appointed places, accompanied by the opening and shutting of drawers. It is a miracle more automatic and charming than anything Johanna Spyri could have imagined. It has also been more rewarding: By 1972, *Mary Poppins* had earned $45 million from its worldwide distribution, not to mention the secondary income from the sale of records, music, and other items licensed through the film.[14]

III

An aspect of Disney's work that perhaps deserves intense critical evaluation is his treatment of violence. It is closely related to what Glenn Gray noted in his book *The Warriors*. There is in human nature, according to Gray, a positive aesthetic delight in the experience of destruction:

> While it is undeniable that the disorder and distortion and the violation of nature that conflict brings are ugly beyond compare,

> there are also color and movement, variety, panoramic sweep, and sometimes even momentary proportion and harmony. If we think of beauty and combat without their usual moral overtones, there is often a weird but genuine beauty in the sight of massed men and weapons in combat.[15]

Disney understood this fascination with destruction, and many of his early animated films, particularly *Bambi, Snow White,* and *Fantasia,* show scenes of apocalyptic terror. Many children shudder at seeing the murder of Bambi's mother and the great forest fire. But Disney also understood those "usual moral overtones" of revulsion that audiences might bring to scenes of destruction, and mitigated them by happy endings.

The technique of animated drawing allowed Disney to retain a satisfying level of violence while removing the elements that might make his audiences squeamish. Given the freedom to make funny animals behave without following the laws of nature, he was able to immunize them against the effects of violence. Heads could be bashed in and bodies rolled flat, only to bounce back alive in the next instant. Destructive actions against the bodies of others became the stock device of cartoon humor. For instance, in *Steamboat Willie,* a goat eats some sheet music, and Minnie cranks the tail to produce a calliope version of "Turkey in the Straw." Other animals are then converted to musical instruments as Mickey squeezes them, bangs on them, and twists them. Music was never produced by more cheerfully sadistic means. In *Moving Day,* Goofy is smashed flat by a piano, and later his head and legs are crushed through a refrigerator door by the same malicious instrument. The cartoon ends when the hideous Sheriff Pete lights a cigar in front of an open gas vent, having maliciously struck the match on Donald Duck's beak. Everything is destroyed, including Pete's hide. He is shown suspended nude in a bathtub above a thoroughly wrecked house from which he had just dispossessed the innocent Goofy, Donald, and Mickey. These extreme varieties of bodily violence, which would obviously be fatal for human foreclosers, are defused by animation to permit the audience to have the good, clean fun they have come reverently to expect from Disney.

An important principle was discovered in these reductive experiments with animated violence: Never confront an audience with the uglier aspects of conflict that might cause feelings of unhappiness or ambiguity. Disney resolved to keep happiness as the cardinal value in his universe. Even in the films where stereotyped forces of good and evil confronted one another, unhappiness was banned, and cheerful endings were required. When he created Disneyland late in his career, he was fond of calling it "The Happiest Place in the World." The liberal use of this claim in advertisements indicates the appeal of a land populated by figures associated with defused violence that can be enjoyed without aftereffect. It is indeed happier than anything in the real world.

IV

The discovery of the limitless plasticity of the animated cartoon gave Disney an unsurpassed ability to depict moral judgments in his artifacts. Physical characteristics could be altered and stylized so as to convey simplified moralizations. In fact, Disney seems to have had little interest in moral gradations. For instance, Robert Feild relates Disney's comment about the little town at the foot of menacing Bald Mountain in *Fantasia*. "It sort of symbolizes something. The forces of good on one side and of evil on the other is what I'm trying to see in the thing. What other reason can there be for it?"[16] Disney's cartoons convey stereotypical messages by having trees, plants, and animals sway or sing sympathetically when virtuous characters appear. They shrink in revulsion or fly away on cue when a wicked wolf or witch appears. The appearance of good and of evil characters could be so completely stylized as to embody the moral judgment Disney wished to have his audience pass on them. The stereotypical potential is much greater than is possible for melodrama, for example, because the latter is limited by the fact that human beings must play the roles.

Disney's skill in visual moralization is evident in the creation of the witch in *Sleeping Beauty*. Bob Thomas relates the process of the artist working on Maleficent: "Because she was to turn into a dragon later, he gave her a horned headdress with a collar that resembled bat wings. Her cold, but beautiful face was encircled by black cloth, giving her a masklike look. Continuing her evil appearance, her robe was black with folds of purple revealed. The lines of the robe carried out the vertical motif, and the train curved with a snaky feeling." The animation process helped Disney reaffirm his hostility toward adult sexuality. The story outline he wrote for *Snow White* specifies: "THE QUEEN: A mixture of Lady Macbeth and the Big Bad Wolf–Her beauty is sinister, mature, plenty of curves–She becomes ugly and menacing when scheming and mixing her poisons–Magic fluids transform her into a witchlike hag." The "curves" of the wicked Queen are played off visually against the pure, straight lines of Snow White. A similar effort to associate curvaceous femininity with evil is made in *Night on Bald Mountain,* where demonic hags are presented with bare breasts and extended nipples–the only occasion in Disney's film-making career for unveiling these menacing anatomic structures. With every detail controllable, Disney's animation allows a transcendence of the subjectivity and ambiguity that usually afflict moral vision. Stereotypes that would be laughable when presented with live actors and actresses assume a strange, mythic power and believability.[17]

The surpassing of burdensome subjectivity through technical manipulation is particularly evident in Disney's propaganda film *Victory Through Air Power.* Disney was an early proponent of strategic bombing in the Second World War. He felt that the American Government was insufficiently alert to its potential for winning the war. Consequently, he collaborated with Major Alexander Seversky in making a film about strategic bombing, taking the career and ideas of Billy Mitchell as the point of focus. The film opens with a message that casts General Mitchell in the role of the redeemer: "Our country in the past has struggled through many storms of anguish, difficulty and doubt. But we have always been saved by men of vision and courage who opened our minds and showed us the way out of confusion." The narrator goes on to show how Mitchell was "ignored and ridiculed" and concludes with a dedication to the memory of Billy Mitchell and other gallant airmen. The film develops an extended and often animated argument for strategic bombing. Comic presentations of Axis stereotypes are employed. Seversky's scheme of a single united air command encompassing the entire globe and guaranteeing victory is graphically portrayed. Film historian Leonard Maltin summarizes the concluding scene:

> The final animated sequence shows Seversky's idealized air force in action, taking off for Japan, bombing the cities and factories and crippling their power. Then a giant eagle soars through the air, aiming for an octopus on the ground below: the eagle jabs at the head of the octopus, again and again, until it retreats and loses its grip on the map under it. The eagle triumphantly perches on top of the globe, and a zoom backward shows it to be the top of a flagpole flying the American flag in victory.

Maltin makes this insightful comment about the character of this "powerful" and "crystal clear" propaganda: "When Seversky refers to a shield of air power, we see an actual shield atop a relief map of Europe and see just how it works. When he talks about Hitler's wheel-like stronghold, the wheel is shown and the metaphor made real. The film is perfect propaganda because it leaves no room for argument; it *shows* you that what it says is true." Disney further strengthened his propaganda by sanitizing the violence he advocated. By drawing his argument to give it concreteness, he is able to eliminate elements that might arouse objections from his audience. James Agee noticed, for example, ". . . that there were no suffering and dying enemy civilians under all those proud promises of bombs; no civilians at all, in fact." Disney's animated leap from military metaphor to visual "reality" thus was able to serve whatever goals its creator wished to espouse, leaving the horrible human wreckage out of sight.[18]

Victory Through Air Power may have been a significant factor in shaping the attitudes of its audience, whose leaders had early in the war declared themselves morally opposed to the Fascist atrocity of strategic bombing. On the first day of American participation in World War II, President Roosevelt had called for each warring nation "publicly to affirm its determination that its armed forces shall in no event, and in no circumstances, undertake the bombardment from the air of civilian populations or of unfortified cities." In the following year he reiterated, "The bombing of the helpless and unprotected civilians is a tragedy which has aroused the horror of all mankind. I recall with pride that the United States consistently has taken the lead in urging that this inhuman practice be prohibited." H. C. Potter, one of Disney's film directors, reports the following anecdote as told by Disney:

> The British Air Force thought this [film] was the greatest thing that ever came down the pike, and the picture was much better known in England than it was here, in official circles, and early in the game Walt told me this story, and swore this was what happened. When Churchill came over to the Quebec conference, they were trying to get Roosevelt interested in this long-range bombing idea, and Roosevelt didn't know what the hell they were talking about. Churchill said, "Well, of course, you've seen *Victory Through Air Power*. . . ." And Roosevelt said, "No, what's that?" Air Marshall [sic] Tedder and Churchill worked on Roosevelt until Roosevelt put through an order to the Air Corps to fly a print of *Victory Through Air Power* up to Quebec. Churchill ran it for him, and that was the beginning of the U. S. Air Corps Long Range Bombing.

It is the kind of claim Leni Riefenstal could have made about her skillful and powerful *Triumph of the Will* on the theme of Nazi rallies ". . . which channelled the psychic energies of hundreds of thousands of people . . ." in Hitler's Germany. In both instances the most sophisticated film techniques were used to serve idealistic causes, resulting in needless death for thousands of innocent people.[19]

This reveals an ominous side to the allegedly harmless violence in Disney's cartoons, a subject that deserves more careful scrutiny than it ordinarily receives.[20] Entertainment in the form of violence without consequences works out more happily in the animated films than in history.

When Disney turned to live-action films, he transferred the techniques and mythic patterns developed through animation. The technical wizardry that had allowed Disney to reinstate the credibility of miracles allowed him to completely moralize the world of his films. With special-effects photography, skillful stunts, and ingenious gadgets, the entire universe could be made to comply with Disney's mythic vision. This effort has been faithfully continued since his death by the Disney Studio. In *The Love Bug,* the Studio created a redemptive Volkswagen possessing the human tendency to protect the weak. In *The Return of Herbie,* the heroic car leads a whole pack of driverless Volkswagens in thwarting the greedy ambitions of a real-estate developer, Alonzo Hawk, who wishes to deprive a poor, sweet widow of her charming firehouse home. Herbie even brings together a young pair for marriage, even though they wholesomely lack sexual passion. These moralized Volkswagens even attend the wedding at the end of the film, rearing on their hind wheels to pay tribute to the pair united by the heroic Herbie. In these films technology has been moralized as thoroughly as nature was in the earlier Disney films. These mythic treatments of nature, animal life, and technology have a profound kinship to the antihistorical spirit displayed in the *Little House* material. Every element of human experience must be transformed to suit the requirements of the monomyth.

V

Disney's efforts to create a sanitary form of happiness were regarded as the finest examples of educational entertainment. The hundreds of accolades he received prompted the question posed by his promotional literature: "What kind of man is this who has won the Medal of Freedom–highest civilian award in the United States –29 motion picture Academy Awards; four TV Emmys; scores of citations from many nations; and some 700 other awards, who has been decorated by the French Foreign Legion of Honor and again by the Art Workers Guild of London; has received honorary degrees from Harvard, Yale and the University of Southern California. . . ." The piece provides the answer to its question. Disney's mission was ". . . to bring happiness to millions. It first became evident in the twenties, when this lean son of the Mid-West came unheralded to Hollywood [and] began to animate his dreams. . . ."[21] That mission has seemingly been accomplished, as witnessed by the millions who have watched Disney's movies, television programs, and cartoons and who visit his amusement parks every year. They comment frequently on the remarkable feats of sanitation that keep Disneyland spotless despite hordes of littering tourists.

Far be it from us to carp at cleanliness, but the sanitizing urge is central to the power of Disney's mythic artifacts, and even the most sophisticated are willing to surrender themselves to its power.

Mark Van Doren wrote that Disney's ". . . techniques, about which I know little, must of course be wonderful, but the main thing is that he lives somewhere near the human center and knows innumerable truths that cannot be taught. That is why his ideas look like inspirations and why he can be goodhearted without being sentimental, can be ridiculous without being fatuous. With him, as with any first rate artist, we feel that we are in good hands; we can trust him with our hearts and wits."[22] When minds of this critical caliber are eager to accept the massage, we know that we are confronting artifacts of wondrous power.

Because Disney credibly reinstated the sense of the miraculous, it would not be surprising if a proper shrine is erected in the future. Like other monuments to the saints, it should have a wonder-working reliquary—a place where the instruments making screen miracles are on display. Universal Studios in Hollywood presently offers daily tours in which screen devotees on pilgrimage can experience "the miraculous parting of the Red Sea." A similar shrine for Disney might celebrate his contribution to the goal of the Motion Picture Production Code: "Entertainment which tends to improve the race, or at least to re-create and rebuild human beings exhausted with the realities of life. . . ."[23] But even the large-scale happiness that Disney manufactured is not able to entirely restore those exhausted with reality. As we shall see in the next chapter, the sense of dread and the urge to visualize the catastrophic side of contemporary life seem to be growing despite the happiness of monomythic endings.

VIII
Apocalyptic Jaws and Retributive Ecstasy

"The sight of hell-torments will exalt the happiness of the saints forever."—Jonathan Edwards, *The Eternity of Hell Torments* (1739)[1]

"Stupidity is an elemental force for which no earthquake is a match."—Karl Kraus, "The Earthquake"[2]

During the past four decades Americans have acquired a strange sense of anxiety and dread. A daily spectacle of appalling events compels us to recognize the fragility of our social existence: airplane crashes, bombings, kidnapings, air piracies, political assassinations, drought, starvation, muggings, pollution, overpopulation, mass murders, and cultic slayings have become part of everyday consciousness. These are bitter realities for Americans, who as recently as the nineteenth century still nourished millennial hopes. Bronson Alcott proclaimed, "Our freer . . . land is the asylum, if asylum there be, for the hope of man; and there, if anywhere, is the second Eden to be planted in which the divine seed is to bruise the head of evil and restore Man to his rightful communion with God in the Paradise of Good." The catastrophe films of our time have moved far beyond such optimism. *Earthquake, The Towering Inferno,* and above all *Jaws* have achieved staggering box-office success with their pessimistic images of corrupt civilization and its punishment. A somber mythic consciousness seems here to be at work, shaping a grisly image of the future as strangely attractive to fantasy as the mythically reshaped past. To an extent unparalleled by any other pop genre, the technomythic miracles of catastrophe films create believable images of destruction and redemption. Describing the psychic significance of these miracles of punishment takes us into a disturbing region of the American mind.[3]

I

The catastrophe films range through the spectrum of the natural and social crises with encyclopedic thoroughness, alert always to potential messages about civilization's failure. *Airport 75* takes us into the heavens, *Towering Inferno* into a modern Tower of Babel. *Tidal Wave* explores the raging crust under the ocean, while *Jaws* conjures up the primeval animal forces of the depths. *Earthquake* projects a destruction of the Los Angeles basin with explicitly mythic formulas and technomythic manipulations. The latter is particularly suited to analysis because its writer, George Fox, explains the way the earthquake's punishment of decadence is made "believable."

The story line of *Earthquake* features a series of personal vignettes framed by a cataclysmic event that defines their significance. As the film opens, we learn that seismological scientists have developed new predictive techniques through which they prophesy the destruction of Los Angeles in the near future. Working independently from the scientists, a talented architectural engineer, Graff, leads an unsuccessful one-man crusade against buildings with insufficient resistance to earthquake damage. He even refuses to carry out a project until its specifications are upgraded, a financially distressing piece of personal integrity in the eyes of his company. Graff's bitchy wife, Remy, is destroying their marriage through deception and self-imposed childlessness. Slade, a good but bitter cop, has been suspended from the force for damaging Zsa Zsa Gabor's hedge while chasing criminals. Denise is an attractive young widow taking up a career as an actress. Her sexual readiness proves to be important for the seismic activity of the Los Angeles basin. Miles Quade is an Evel Knievel-style motorcycle performer. His sister Rosa has a lovely body that stimulates male interest. A sinister character, Jody, is a supermarket clerk and National Guardsman who wears a blond wig and inspires taunts about his masculinity from the men who know him.

In the plot of *Earthquake,* the actions of these characters symbolically trigger the destruction of Los Angeles. Discovering his wife had aborted her pregnancy, Graff angrily leaves her and makes love with Denise for the first time. The screenwriter candidly describes his intent to establish a relationship between such personal events and the natural forces that destroy Los Angeles:

> An earthquake is a release of seismic energy. Our people ought to be as pent-up and ready for release as the ground under their feet. Without slamming them over the head with the fact, we ought to make the audience feel–unconsciously, in their nerve ends–that the quake is somehow generated by the characters they're watching, not the San Andreas fault alone.

Precisely what Fox intends is illustrated by the lovemaking of Graff and Denise the day their orgasms trigger the earthquake. "They have made love with a desperate urgency, giving way to a need neither had acknowledged until today." Nature's own urgency for release is similarly described by the screenwriter, Fox. "*For years, in these areas, the land has been compressed and warped, storing energy like a colossal spring.*"[4]

A similar connection between catastrophe and the behavior of the characters is visible in the Evel Knievel episode. The earthquake strikes at the precise moment Miles Quade is prepared to perform his motorcycle stunt. The timing is more than coincidental, because Fox admits that as he studied Los Angeles, he ". . . gradually developed the impression of a community unconsciously dedicated to a state of endless peril." The death of Miles Quade is a symbolic comment on the power of foolhardy entertainment to precipitate catastrophes. Such moralistic "causes" of the natural disaster are strewn throughout the script. In Slade's outrage that Zsa Zsa Gabor's hedge should be the cause of his suspension, there is a clear sense that society has become totally corrupt and thus worthy of destruction. In an episode at the supermarket, when Rosa discovers that she has forgotten her wallet, her ability to use her attractiveness as a pledge reveals the extent to which stated societal values have been corrupted:

> Dark and voluptuous, she radiates an almost childlike pride in her own beauty. All around the store signs further proclaim CREDIT IS DEAD–DON'T ASK FOR IT. Nevertheless, Jody tells Rosa that she can drop off the money the next time she

> comes in. The checkout girl glances at him in astonishment. Jody's gaze, full of suppressed desire, trails Rosa as she carries her groceries from the store.[5]

The moralistic scheme of *Earthquake* suggests that such causes precipitate an apocalyptic punishment of the offenders.

All the sinful characters in *Earthquake* receive physical punishment. Charlton Heston, who plays the role of Graff, suffers a rare screen death. Despite his efforts to rescue others, his infidelity with Denise apparently seals his fate. His dragonlike wife, who precipitated Graff's infidelity and caused her father's heart attack by meddling in company affairs, drowns along with him. Miles Quade dies during his stunt performance. Jody is killed by Slade after threatening Rosa with rape to prove his masculinity. Since Slade had earlier suppressed his desire for Rosa, he was able to play the redeemer role and gets her as compensation at the end of the film. Among the moral offenders in *Earthquake,* Denise is spared, but she has a son to take care of and is likewise chastened by the loss of Graff. Nature is pictured as responding in a neatly retributive fashion to the community's need for moral cleansing.

The correlation between violation of sexual mores and punishment by the forces of nature is characteristic for the catastrophe film genre. In *Towering Inferno,* a publicist for the building and his beautiful secretary have a fling in the bedroom adjoining his office; both die in the flames as the camera lingers over their agony. At the same time the faithful mayor and his unattractive wife are spared. In *Tidal Wave,* the first volcanic eruptions are stimulated by the lovemaking of an unmarried couple at the beach. They are permanently separated by the tidal wave in spite of the young man's heroism in saving others. As was evident in the death of the motorcycle performer, Quade, the moralized forces of nature take special displeasure in frivolity or revelry. *The Poseidon Adventure* begins its deathly upside-down voyage during a ballroom party. *Tidal Wave* opens with scenes of huge crowds amusing themselves at the beach. *Towering Inferno* begins with a party celebrating the opening of the building, and the fire develops while the celebration progresses.

These contemporary images of disaster are obviously parallel to biblical stories in which the pattern of retribution for sexual infidelity and frivolity is deeply embedded. The flood story in Genesis is placed immediately after the so-called "Second Fall" account in which the angels fall from heaven to take pleasures with the seductive daughters of Eve. The dismayed and angry Lord resolves to flood the earth after seeing ". . . that the wickedness of man was great in the earth, and that every imagination of the thoughts of his heart was evil continually" (Gn. 6:5). The announcement of the catastrophe to Noah is expressed in terms that supported the view that "flesh" in its sensual manifestations was punished: "And God said to Noah, 'I have determined to make an end of all flesh; for the earth is filled with violence through them . . ." (Gn. 6:13). In the Sodom and Gomorrah account, which features earthquake, brimstone, and fire, it was the lewd demand of riotous homosexuals to violate the angelic guests of Lot that provoked the retribution. As in the flood account, the only ones who escaped were Lot and his family, who heeded the demand: "Flee for your life; do not look back or stop anywhere in the valley; flee to the hills lest you be consumed" (Gn. 19:17). The paradigm was thus established for posterity: Sexual improprieties provoke natural disasters, from which only the pure and faithful will escape. The retributive principle is Deuteronomic: Sin brings disaster, while virtue brings success and escape from disaster.[6]

It is paradoxical that the disaster film genre struggles so hard for the modern illusion of visual realism while retaining the archaic conventions of retribution. George Fox tells with pride how accurately his film *Earthquake* depicts disaster. "Every moment of fictional destruction was checked out for what someone—I forget who—called 'the reality quotient.'" He argues that ". . . today's sophisticated audience wouldn't accept the scene if process photography and other obvious special effect tricks were used. It would look incredibly phony." To avoid this, Fox studied earthquakes of the past, interviewed earthquake victims, studied the San Andreas fault system, and interviewed seismologists. The "scientific accuracy" was further enhanced by the use of Sensurround, a sound system that created tremor sensations in the audience. The system ". . . has been refined to the point where, at will, it can affect specific parts of the human body." The film producers also considered but rejected ". . . bouncing huge chunks of styrofoam debris off the audience's head during the tremor scenes." They made rocking platforms for the sets and cameras to simulate earthquake motions. Thousands of special garments were used to simulate the deterioration of clothing during the progress of an earthquake. One hundred forty-one stuntmen were employed in the filming, some of whom were seriously injured.[7]

While the technological contrivances provide the believability of the modern catastrophe film, the archaic biblical plot with its fantasy of selective and moralistic destruction remains as the central dramatic convention. In point of historical fact, this sort of plot was almost required by the now defunct Motion Picture Production Code, whose moral strictures for films are so precisely satisfied by the catastrophe genre. Geoffrey Shurlock, administrator of the Code, stated that ". . . details of sin have to be balanced against details of compensation. There would be no sense in too much retribution for too little sin. This, of course, is not our problem. Ours is the other extreme of too much sin and too little retribution."[8] In 1966 the Production Code was replaced by the Motion Picture Rating System, but the catastrophe filmmakers retained the retributive scheme. This type of film provides the ideal fulfillment of the censor's yearning for sinners to be destroyed.

II

Untangling the way the punishment scheme gains credibility is crucial to understanding the attractions of catastrophe films. We suggest that such materials feature a kind of *mythic cuing*. The visual cues convey the message symbolically without the verbal articulation of religion or ideology. The technique juxtaposes visual fragments with conversational fragments as the story progresses. The selective focus of the camera forces the eye of the audience into stereotypical judgments essential to the development of the retribution scheme. Traditional evidences of depravity are rapidly flashed before one's eyes so that one is mythically prepared for the punishment that inevitably follows. Having "seen the evidence" of the sin, the sight of the punishment moves viewers to the acceptance of an archaic idea that would likely arouse jeers if articulated verbally as a biblical threat against sinners. Just as Mark Twain uncritically accepted a mythic presentation of western history in the Buffalo Bill shows that he would have scorned if stated verbally, so the modern audience is swayed by mythic cuing.[9]

The context for mythic cuing in the catastrophe genre is the sense of dread about the forthcoming suffering. Unlike historical catastrophes, which usually come when least expected, the horror of the film is anticipated with a combination of yearning and dread. From the safe distance of the theater seat, the audience undergoes vicariously the experience of escaping a horrible fate. The dread of being caught up in the cycle of annihilation is relieved by a double identification pattern: the personal identification with the superhero, who will inevitably escape death if he remains true to the faith; and the marking of those fated for destruction. To use the commonly accepted sense of the term, it is as if the "mark of Cain" were placed upon sinners so the audience can be sure of their annihilation and thus not identify positively with them during the viewing of the film. Mythic cuing relieves the audience of its sense of dread to the extent that it helps to eliminate painful elements of sympathy and identification with the doomed. It also offers a moral confirmation of the audience's righteousness, since only the virtuous survive.

III

Both in its novelistic and film versions, *Jaws* has been one of the great commercial successes of our time. It has been praised as "taut adventure" and "superb entertainment." So successful is its use of mythic cuing, which operates at times with subliminal subtlety, that it has thoroughly disarmed critics. For instance, Hollis Alpert of *The Saturday Review* concluded that the story content of *Jaws* is insignificant. "Does the film have any real meaning, other than a warning about where to swim? Probably not. It's a tale designed to thrill, and this is what it does."[10] *The New Yorker,* famed for its reviews of even trashy movies when they possess social significance, allowed a timid and condescending "Don't bite" to stand beside *Jaws* for months in its weekly movie listing.

In contrast to these nonchalant denials of meaning, we suggest that *Jaws* is an extremely skillful embodiment of the American monomyth. So rapid is its pacing and so subliminal its cuing that visual exegesis requires more than a single viewing to bring the monomythic details to conscious awareness. The film offers an excellent opportunity to apply technomythic critical theory.

• The American monomyth begins and ends in an Edenic setting. In *Jaws* the very name of the setting, Amity Island, suggests paradisal qualities. Just as Heidi left the evil Frankfurt to return to her Edenic Alps, Martin Brody has escaped from Manhattan, where there are ". . . so many problems you never feel you're accomplishing anything. Violence, ripoffs, muggings, kids can't leave the house–you gotta walk 'em to school. But in Amity one man can make a difference. In twenty-five years there's never been a shooting, or a murder in this town." The movie pictures the island as an unproblematic arena for children's play–until the malevolent shark arrives. And it is the one man, Martin Brody, who indeed makes the difference for the community in saving it from this threat. In the final scene, Brody swims back to a broad, deserted, paradisal beach on Amity Island whence evil has been expelled.

• The monomyth always features a disruption of paradise by evil. In the case of Amity Island, evil comes in many forms, but it arrives most conspicuously in the form of the great shark. The shark's arrival is precipitated by a provocative display of female sexual license. The movie begins on a beach with a party of young people smoking and drinking around a campfire. One of the girls sits at the edge of the group, clearly differentiated as an outsider. Approached by one of the young men, she proposes a swim, tossing off her clothing with abandon as she runs toward the water. Her shouts to come in are followed by the collapse of the drunken companion on the beach. She swims alone with voluptuous yearning, symbolically reminiscent of the eager Playmates in *Playboy*. Her companion having proved incapable of fulfilling her need, the males in the audience are cued to a *Playboy* fantasy, reinforced when the camera allows them to see her lovely, undulating form from the perspective of the shark below. This erotic display is provocative; and the censor's Deuteronomic Code, demanding the punishment of sexual depravity, lives on in the present by rationalizing the fate of the beautiful temptress. She is attacked by the shark. Although the Code stated that "adultery and illicit sex . . . shall not be explicitly treated . . . nor . . . justified or made to seem right and permissible,"[11] the movie dishes out more punishment than anyone would defend. Since impersonal nature enacts the decree, the scale of punishment is not tempered by the counterclaims of mercy.

The advertising for *Jaws* employed–without conscious intent, according to the film's producers–the phallic symbol of the shark streaking up toward the naked woman. Both visually and aurally, the attack scene carries out the sexual theme implicit in the ads. The music throbs to a climax as the shark approaches, and the initial rhythmic gasps of the woman after being nudged by the shark are orgiastic. This striking detail provides a subliminal reinforcement to the sexual power of the scene. The woman then clings to the phallic-shaped buoy in the water to protect herself until she is attacked and torn away. In later scenes displaying the remaining portion of her body, the audience sees long and red-polished fingernails and multiple rings–seductive symbols of former conquests. Although the filmmakers may not have consciously intended to create this impression, these details suggest a retributive justification of the shark's fatally rapish attack. The stereotyped temptress is thus the first to be punished for having aroused the appetite of the shark. But once symbolically corrupted by the woman, the shark continues its campaign against the island.

Just as in the Garden of Eden story, the corruption of Amity's inhabitants justifies the shark's disruption. The mayor and city selectmen are pictured as fatally corrupt, refusing to call for help or close the beaches for business reasons. The predatory campaign of the shark thus lasts so long that it shatters the safe reputation of the island and reduces the mayor to babbling. There is even an effort to incorporate the death of the Kintner child in the retributive scheme by providing a snatch of conversation in which his mother lets him back into the water for "just ten more minutes" after saying his fingers are "beginning to prune." Mrs. Kintner is stereotyped as overly mannish, too old to have so young a child, and unaccompanied by a husband. Despite the audience's natural sympathy for her loss, the subtle cues of the camera suggest she deserves the punishment of losing her child. This provides the ambivalence in the scene in which she slaps Chief Brody for not having closed the beach the week before; the audience has already been cued to recognize the unfair element in her accusation that Brody rather than the mayor is responsible, while she has been negligent in letting the boy swim too long. It is hard to avoid the conclusion that the producers of *Jaws* are unusually adept in finding reasons to punish the women whose faults have presumably contributed to the corruption of the modern paradise.

• In monomythic materials, citizens are unwilling to face evil and thus unable to act intelligently in its presence. Amity is Eden compared to New York, but its inhabitants and summer guests are bent upon the festivals and entertainments that catastrophe films love to punish. In the various scenes of the film, they are represented as utterly stupid and pleasure-bent. When Chief Brody experiences his first sense of urgency about the shark attack, he must force his way through the preparations for a silly parade. The citizens seem dumbly intent on pursuing their routines and ignoring the danger. When a big reward for catching the shark is posted, floods of incompetent fishermen descend upon the island, overloading their boats and menacing everyone's safety. When someone catches a large shark, the public assumes the danger is past and crowds onto the island by every conveyance. The camera cues the audience to view the public as lambs dumbly led to slaughter, a stock mythic background for the emergence of the redeemer figure.

• The democratic institutions in monomythic stories are invariably pictured as incapable of coping with evil. They are as helpless as the dumb public before the appalling threat from the mythic deeps. The Board of Selectmen is in the mayor's pocket, agreeing with his statement about the overriding need to keep the tourist trade. "I'm only trying to say that Amity is a summer town. We need summer dollars. If people can't swim here, they'll be glad to swim at Cape Cod. . . ." The mayor forces the coroner to falsify his report on the cause of the first death from "shark attack" to "boating accident." Later the mayor coerces one of the selectmen to lead his family into the water as the crowd of bathers clings fearfully to the beach. The crowd immediately follows them into the risky waters, and true to the quick-draw justice of the catastrophe genre, the selectman is trampled by the retreating crowd when a prankster shark fin is sighted.

Thus far the plot of *Jaws* correlates very closely with the American monomyth. The need of redemption by a superhero is clearly developed. But at this point the film seems to break out of the paradigm. There is redemption through violence, but where is the superhero? Surely the ineffectual police chief of Amity Island, who fires the shot that blows up the shark, is far from Superman! This question is intriguing enough to demand careful exploration.

IV

Some might insist that Martin Brody fits the antiheroic tradition of high culture rather than the superhero tradition of American pop culture. For instance, he is so fearful that the very thought of a boat ride throws him into panic: "On the water? But not drunk enough to go out in the boat! I can't do that!" Carl Gottlieb describes the producer's aim of creating such a flawed, indecisive protagonist. Chief Brody ". . . would have to begin as a man who lets others shape his decisions, even to the point where those decisions cost people their lives; he would have to discover his flaw, struggle to correct it, and emerge at the end of the picture as a man who has faced up to the demons inside him and conquered them while at the same time subjecting himself to the gruesomest sort of physical danger."[12] If such features were consistently developed in a story with a tragic structure, one would surely place Brody in the tradition of realism. But the story of *Jaws,* as we have seen, is monomythic down to the happy restoration of paradise at the end. Within the context of this story Brody clearly carries out the function of the violent redeemer. Other distinguishing traits correlate closely with the redemption formulas.

• The monomythic superhero usually is sexually segmented; redemptive obligations cannot be integrated with normal sexual responsibilities. Although Chief Brody is married, his lovely and understanding wife poses the typical barriers to his redemptive task. So in pop heroic fashion, Brody achieves sexual renunciation within marriage. In an early scene of the movie, she lies temptingly in their bed as he rises to perform his police work, then chats with her about trivia. As he leaves the room, her beautiful body is framed through the door. But he renounces temptation to resume his duties. In subsequent scenes Brody is repeatedly indifferent to his wife, who clearly loves him and desires more intimacy than he grants. At one point she hands him a drink while he studies the shark books. "Want to get drunk and fool around?" He responds with indifference, but when he sees his son playing on the sailboat, he shouts a harsh warning. The need to clear the beach of its threat to innocent children seems to eliminate the possibility of sexual gratification.

There is a scene in *Jaws* in which Brody's wife explicitly tempts him to forsake the redemptive task. On the day when their son is taken to the hospital for shock treatment after a close escape from the shark, Brody tells his wife, "You go on back home now." She replies, "Do you mean–New York?" Her inclination is clearly to return to Babylon and take Martin away from the dangerous island where ". . . one man can make a difference." In a final comment on sexual renunciation, the film closes with Brody and Hooper paddling back together in camaraderie toward an empty beach. It is as if a reunion with Brody's loving wife were subordinate to the lonely mastery of superheroes over evil. One cannot avoid the impression that Brody has gained his redemptive power through a renunciation of sexuality.

• The monomythic superhero is frequently aided by fate as he carries out his task. The fate-directed violence arrives in the nick of time. The incredible destruction of the shark by Chief Brody conveys a sense that the powers of destiny are at work. Up until the moment when Quint, the monomaniacal Ahab of a fisherman, has been devoured by the shark, Brody had been a bumbling crew member. He could not learn to tie a proper knot or keep from stumbling over the equipment. He was constantly afraid and eager for the help of other governmental agencies.

In the decisive duel with the shark, however, Brody's character gradually changes. He straps on his gun belt and begins to fire at the shark. In one dramatic image his gun-holstered silhouette is flared against the horizon in the style of a cowboy superhero. And strangely, as if he were Clark Kent, his glasses are no longer present as he takes up the superhero role. Yet he is able to shoot accurately the tank of oxygen that he had kicked into the shark's mouth in a moment of fate-controlled bumbling. One is reminded of the last-minute precision of the white-hat gun fighters, which allows them to kill black-hatted marauders who have drawn their weapons first.

• The hero in a monomythic story rarely originates in the community he is called to redeem. He is an outsider, either in fact or in attitude. Thus it is established early in *Jaws* that Brody is a newcomer who cannot be fully integrated in Amity. His wife, more eager to establish community than her isolate husband, says, "I just wanna know one simple thing. . . . When do I get to become an islander?" Her neighbor answers, "Ellen . . . never . . . never . . . You're not born here, you're not an islander, and that's it." This does not seem to bother Chief Brody in the least, his redemptive task being a sufficient *raison d'être*. Just as he does not join his wife in glad reunion at the end of the movie, there is no hint that he returns to a community that acclaims his membership. He returns in monomythic fashion to the uninhabited beach with his fellow outsider, Hooper, privately celebrating their victory over a fearful adversary.

• Given the congruity of Brody's actions with the monomythic paradigm, one looks about in pop culture for a figure who might provide a suitable model for this antihero who plays the superhero role. Although Brody is far from Superman or Buffalo Bill, he fits so neatly in the mold of Spiderman that one suspects a little cribbing.

Spiderman was "the first superhero to wear his neuroses on his sleeve." He is currently a leading comic superhero, selling around half a million copies per month. Stan Lee, who created the Spiderman figure, wanted a new type of ". . . strip in which the main character would lose out as often as he'd win—in fact, more often." He wanted Spiderman to be ". . . an ordinary guy . . . not too handsome, not too graceful, not too muscular. . . ."[13] Spiderman's alter ego, Peter Parker, is a striking match for Roy Scheider, who played Brody. Both have narrow shoulders, wire-rimmed glasses, worried expressions on faces with relatively small mouths, chins, and noses, and slender builds. Even the hair color and style of Parker is similar to that of the modest police chief of Amity Island.

The genesis episode of Spiderman exhibits plot and character parallels to Chief Brody. Peter Parker is bitten by a radioactively exposed spider, thereby gaining miraculous powers of climbing, reminiscent of Brody's climb along the precarious ship's mast in the final scene with the shark. Having discovered his powers, Parker uses them at first for public performances and private profit. In a pivotal episode he declines to pursue a crook who later kills his own beloved Uncle Ben. When Spiderman catches the murderer, he makes the chastening discovery: "That–that face! It's–oh no, it can't be. . . . It's the fugitive who ran past me! The one I didn't stop when I had the chance!" This provokes soul-searching and grief in Spiderman, reminiscent of the *Jaws* incident in which Mrs. Kintner slaps Brody and accuses him of responsibility for the death of her son. Spiderman says, "My fault–all my fault! If only I had stopped him when I could have! But I didn't–and now–Uncle Ben is dead!" [14] Similarly, when Mrs. Kintner asserts Brody's guilt for the death of her son, the mayor says, "I'm sorry, Martin, she's wrong." Brody replies, "No, she's not." Brody here takes up the role of the suffering servant, similar to Peter Parker at the *Daily Bugle,* where the editor is always raging about the crimes of Spiderman. He constantly berates the reporter for not producing an article or picture to expose Spiderman's fraud.

Spiderman's alias also plays the suffering servant role with Flash Thompson, his aggressive high school acquaintance who constantly bullies him and competes for the affections of Gwen. For instance, when Flash returns from the Army to visit Gwen, Peter Parker tries to defend his position and is rebuffed by the girl he admires: "For a boy who's always missing when there's any trouble . . . it's strange how hostile you can be to someone who's been in combat."[15] In a similar way, Brody is bullied by Hooper and Quint, both of whom are more virile than he. When the two toughies compare their battle and fishing wounds, all Chief Brody can offer is a little appendectomy scar. He has to tolerate their snide remarks about his uselessness on the fishing boat, just as he had earlier faced Quint's vulgar insults and sexual insinuations in his wife's presence while boarding the craft.

Who can say whether the creators of *Jaws* were actually influenced by Spiderman? The sources of the creative process are notoriously elusive. It suffices here to suggest that Brody is indeed cut from the same pattern as a highly popular current comic-book hero. Probably the same preferences that grant Spidey his preeminence among comic-book readers are at work among the huge audiences enthralled by *Jaws*. The hunger for redemption from evil and the suspicion about traditionally masculine redeemer figures is evident in both comic book and film.

At each decisive point, *Jaws* fits the pattern of the American monomyth. As a redemption drama with a sexually segmented redeemer, whose miraculous action is performed against a background of communal stupidity and institutional impotence, *Jaws* is at home with *Death Wish, Walking Tall,* and other popular artifacts. In addition, however, *Jaws* and other catastrophe films emphasize blood, suffering, and sacrifice in ways that take us to even deeper mythical roots. When exposed, they raise extremely disturbing questions about the state of mind that enjoys moralized destruction as entertainment and pretends to be unaffected by it.

V

Jaws drips with blood. Pools of blood spread ominously in the water after each attack by the horrendous shark. The fishermen constantly throw blood into the water to lure the shark, and after Quint has been devoured, Brody must walk through his blood on the deck of the sinking fishing boat. Bloody water drips from Brody's face after he destroys the shark, and when the oxygen tank explodes, a sea of blood showers downward into the sea. The camera cues the audience to the decisive significance of this scene. The point was caught by an eleven-year-old who, like many other children, saw the film repeatedly: "The best part was when there was blood in the water at the end." His friend responded, "Yeah, that was neat."

The precedents for redemption through blood reach back to the archaic ceremonies of atonement. As one passage of the Bible summarizes the matter, ". . . Without the shedding of blood there is no remission of sins." In an ancient myth that sounds like the plot of *Jaws,* the Babylonian god Marduk conquers the sea monster Tiamat. He forces "evil wind" into the dragon's mouth and then shoots her with his arrows.

> They marched to war, they drew near to give battle.
> The Lord [Marduk] spread out his net and caught her in it.
> The evil wind which followed him, he loosed it in her face.
> She opened her mouth, Tiamat, to swallow him.
> He drove in the evil wind so that she could not close her
>   lips. . . .
> He let fly an arrow, it pierced her belly.
> Her inner parts he clove, he split her heart
> He rendered her powerless and destroyed her life.

This episode plays a decisive role in the Babylonian myth of the creation of paradise by Marduk. Its premise is that chaotic sources of evil must be ripped apart for the sake of an orderly Eden. The writers of Genesis demythologized such material by having the monsters of the deep created on the fourth day of creation rather than sacrificially offering their bodies as the raw material of creation.[16]

In effect, the producers of *Jaws* remythologize this material, reverting back to the bloody and archaic myths of the ancient Near East. This is not to suggest that Hollywood spends its valuable time poring over books about ancient religion. Popular creative processes are seldom so deliberate. But the fact remains that they enlarge the shark by a third over the size of any known shark, thereby making it into a chaotic and mythic source of malevolence. As one of the film previews puts it, "It is as if nature had concentrated all of its forces of evil in a single being." The film pictures the battle against the shark as transforming Brody into a superhero and Amity Island back into the paradise it was intended to be. After Brody straps on his pistol and takes off his glasses for the mythic duel, and fires the shot that forces wind into the mouth of the monster, he swims back toward shore and asks Hooper, "Is the tide with us?" The scientist replies in the affirmative, and the formerly fearful chief says, "I used to hate the water." Hooper replies, "I can't imagine why." The blood of the supernatural shark has restored nature for human purposes and re-created Martin Brody in the process, while freeing the community from the threat of chaos. The priests of the Marduk cult could scarcely have done better in creating an artifact that embodied their archaic view that creation requires bloody destruction.

It is not so much the use of this bloody material but its appeal to the current audience that is intriguing and alarming. The appeal seems similar to certain religious materials that delight in picturing the bloody destruction of evildoers. Psalm 58 proclaims:

> The righteous will rejoice when he sees the vengeance;
> he will bathe his feet in the blood of the wicked.
> Men will say, "Surely there is a reward for the righteous;
> surely there is a God who judges on earth."

A similar audience appeal in moralized destruction is implicit in the biblical tale of the wicked Queen Jezebel seeking to dissuade Jehu from vengeance by sitting in the upper window at Jezreel with her beautiful makeup and ornate coiffeur. He demands that she be thrown to the ground, where her blood spatters the building and the trampling horses. Just as the crabs come to pick at the remainder of the temptress's body in *Jaws,* the dogs of Jezreel feast on Jezebel's bloody remains. In a parallel incident, wicked King Ahab is slain and brought to Samaria, where the prostitutes of the city wash themselves in the blood flushed from his chariot, while the stray dogs lap up the rest.[17]

What does the retelling of such tales of violent and bloody cleansings reveal about the state of a culture? What are the outlooks and motivations of persons who enjoy moralized suffering and bloody redemption? What is the relationship of such themes to the discomfort with the facts of human sexuality that thread through these artifacts?

In reflecting on these elusive questions, our attention fell upon the early church father Tertullian. In a well-known passage, he argued that the spectator pleasures offered by the Christian faith are immeasurably superior to popular Roman diversions. The faithful are promised the opportunity to witness the eternal suffering of sinful pagans. When the day of judgment comes, the Roman poets, tragedians, philosophers, charioteers, and wrestlers would be seen with flames billowing around their agonized bodies. Tertullian poses the following to his readers:

> What quaestor or priest in his munificence will bestow on you the favor of seeing and exulting in such things as these? And yet even now we in a measure have them by faith in the picturings of imagination . . . they are nobler, I believe, than circus, and . . . theaters, and every race course.

Tertullian's argument was repeated centuries later by the American divine Jonathan Edwards, who promised that "The sight of hell-torments will exalt the happiness of the saints forever."[18]

In these citations from Edwards and Tertullian, there is a strange exultation in the painful punishment of others. It is particularly striking in thinkers who harbor profound suspicions of ecstasy, especially sexual ecstasy, as they did. It is as if sexual ecstasy were replaced with *Tertullian ecstasy*–the enjoyment in seeing the punishment of the wicked. This at any event is what seems to be involved in the audience response to catastrophe films. Unlike sexual ecstasy, which is potentially communal and creative, involving love and mutual respect at its best, Tertullian ecstasy can be achieved privately. It demands no creative effort, only that someone suffer for the pleasure of others. Tertullian ecstasy works toward its climactic visceral gratification by a kind of inverted foreplay. Whereas sexual love begins with attraction, the preparation for retributive ecstasy requires revulsion triggered by negative stereotypes. The camera cues the audience to recognize targets of retribution by scenes of evil behavior and exclusion from the community. This de-identification of interest, an inversion of mutual respect and attraction, blocks any sympathetic response that the audience might have when the wicked suffer their punishment.

At the moment the evil of the marked ones becomes unbearable, and the desire for punishment reaches its climax, the moralized forces of catastrophe provide a kind of retributive coitus with an ecstatic release. The cheering of audiences in such scenes is evidence of a ritual release from tension. Tertullian ecstasy therefore provides one of the few publicly acceptable forms of visceral gratification or ecstatic release in American popular culture. The reward for the audience conforms to a Deuteronomic pattern of compensating every virtue and punishing every vice. The ecstasy of violent punishment is thus provided to those who identify with the pure superhero and his renunciation of sexual gratification. In the subtlest version of this tradeoff, we are allowed a faint and vicarious taste of sexual excitement in the almost subliminal orgiastic cries of the temptress in *Jaws,* acknowledging the need for sexual release at the very moment a symbol of yearning for it is destroyed.

A somewhat cruder celebration of ecstatic, sexually displaced retribution occurs in Mickey Spillane's *One Lonely Night*. In this novel, Mike Hammer is granted the opportunity to punish a socialite, Ethel, who had helped the Communist Party. He forces her to remove her clothes and then takes off his belt:

> A naked woman and a leather belt. I looked at her, so bare and so pretty, hands pressing for support against the paneling, legs spread apart to hold a precarious balance, a flat stomach hollowed under a fear that burned her body a faint pink, lovely smooth breasts, firm with terrible excitement, rising and falling with every gasping breath. A gorgeous woman who had been touched by the hand of the devil.
>
> I raised the belt and heard the sharp crack of the leather against her thighs and her scream. . . .

There is a deliberate effort in this passage to build sexual tension, while at the same time constructing a rationale for its denial. In spite of the spread legs and sensuous breasts, Hammer resists sexual temptation. With the judgment of her devilish evil pronounced, prepared in the reader's mind by the inverted foreplay of details about her traitorous actions, the release of "orgiastic sadism"[19] is provided by the blows directed toward the center of her sexuality.

It is difficult to avoid the impression that this monomythic retribution scheme is profoundly pathological. In its suppression of sexual energy and its diversion to retributive enterprises, often taking an explicitly antisexual and antifeminine form, the catastrophe films inspire memory of the most deranged sexual criminals of the past. In his book *Murder and Madness,* Donald Lunde describes the strange career of Peter Kürten of Dusseldorf, Germany, who committed thirteen murders and numerous assaults during his lifetime:

> Kürten began torturing and killing animals for pleasure at age nine. When he was 14 he attempted intercourse with a girl but

> was unsuccessful. Soon after, however, he strangled a squirrel and experienced the first of many orgasms achieved in conjunction with a sadistic act. . . . During his prison term he perfected the ability to achieve orgasm by fantasizing about sadistic acts. . . . Following his release, he began a career of killing that included strangling, beating and stabbing. The wide variation in the number of stab wounds or blows on his victims was readily explained by Kürten: he stabbed or struck his victims as many times as it required for him to achieve orgasm. . . . He viewed his victims as objects for his pleasure rather than fellow human beings.[20]

In a similar way, the victims of catastrophe films seem to be objects for audience pleasure whose destruction provides ecstatic release. The unlimited and impersonal scale of punishment in this genre serves to heighten the sense of audience release.

In an exploratory study like this it is not possible to do more than suggest the possibility that normal sexual fulfillment is being displaced by Tertullian ecstasy in catastrophe films. A wide range of detailed research projects would be required to investigate this properly. A worthy enterprise for social scientists, or for erotometric specialists like Masters and Johnson, would be to investigate the latent sexual content of monomythic materials. It would be interesting to see what they might discover by wiring up an audience for the opening scene of *Jaws,* where the temptress is rapishly devoured.

VI

Our readers are likely to retain a healthy skepticism about the speculative turn in this analysis of the catastrophe films. It may appear that we have exaggerated the significance of the details suggesting that *Jaws* contains the monomythic redemption scheme, the Edenic context, the moralized nature, the impotent institutions of democracy, the stupid community, the sexual renunciation, and Tertullian ecstasy. We are disturbed enough by our own conclusions to wish for a less sinister interpretation. But there is a final body of evidence that drives us toward our conclusion: Peter Benchley's novel *Jaws*. Benchley's story only superficially resembles the full-blown monomythic statement of the film. At several points the cinematic adaptation of this novel shifts the material in monomythic directions. It is a revealing demonstration of mythic alchemy.

The Brody of the novel is strikingly different from the Spider-man superhero of the film. In place of the thin Peter Parker physique with the virile head of hair, the novel describes a thickening two-hundred-pounder with a bald spot. In place of the recent arrival to Amity Island, the Brody of the novel had been a policeman for six years after growing up on the island. Rather than renouncing sexual gratification, Brody in the novel craves his beautiful wife and is enraged at her sexual indifference. "I'm not very big on screwing corpses," he remarks after a halfhearted invitation from Ellen. In place of the bashful, unassuming Brody of the film, the novelistic chief becomes drunk and rather uncontrolled at a party when he feels his wife is being attracted to Hooper. He can easily keep up with Quint in masculine vulgarity, as evidenced by his comment during one of the novel's voyages of the *Orca:* "I'll tell you what, Hooper. At this point, if someone came in here and said he was superman and he could piss that shark away from here, I'd say fine and dandy. I'd even hold his dick for him." The novel does not stereotype the selectmen as bearing the sole blame for communal irresponsibility, but notes minor elements of corruption in Brody's administration, including a cloudy record in dealing with drug rings.[21] In sum, the Brody of the novel is much more complex and realistic than the renunciatory redeemer of the film.

The chief's actions in the novel indicate his development and self-recognition rather than redemptive transfiguration. He does not resolve to take up the hunt after his own child is endangered—an episode missing in the novel. He acts in part out of a self-destructive frustration over the alienation of his wife's affections and in part out of guilt over his record as police chief. The novel describes his relationship to the shark: "Most of all, Brody needed it dead, for the death of the fish would be a catharsis for him." The element of selfless devotion to the redemptive responsibility characteristic of the film is missing entirely in the novel. A moment of self-recognition comes late in the novel when Brody speaks with Ellen after their reconciliation. She questions his motive for continuing the hunt:

> "Then *why go?*" She was pleading with him, begging. "Can't you ever think of anybody but yourself?"
>
> Brody was shocked at the suggestion of selfishness. It had never occurred to him that he was being selfish, indulging a personal need for expiation.[22]

Chief Brody embarks on the *Orca* despite his wife's resistance, but he does not succeed in killing the shark. After the fish has destroyed the boat and killed Quint, the chief lies helpless in the water, and the shark inexplicably swims away. Only luck saves Brody in the novel. And in place of the redemption of a stupid community by superhuman violence, the novel pictures the newspaper giving Brody a "vote of thanks" for struggling to keep the beaches closed until the shark left the area.

Other monomythic transmutations are equally significant. Quint is changed in the movie into a monomaniacal zealot who kills sharks for revenge and sings "Going swimming with bowlegged women" after having had three wives. He demands ten thousand dollars plus two hundred dollars per day for killing the shark; in the novel he charged a more normal charter price of four hundred dollars per day. This detail serves to contrast him to the selfless redeemer, Brody, who goes out on the *Orca* for redemptive reasons alone. Hooper is sexually aggressive in the novel, having an affair with Ellen Brody, but the film makes him into a Daddy Warbucks figure who selflessly uses his wealth in the pursuit of icthyological wisdom. For these benevolent interests the film allows Hooper to survive the battle. At one point in the novel the fundamentalist postmistress is cited advocating the retributive scheme typical of the movie, to explain why the shark selects Amity instead of East Hampton or Southampton. "She says it's God's will, or something like that. We're being punished for our sins," to which Brody contemptuously replies, "Balls."[23] Nowhere does the novel present the punishment and reward scheme typical of the film.

In particular, the novel does not connect frivolity, sexual temptation, and communal punishment in a magical manner. Christine, the shark's first victim, is not presented as a sexual temptress with rings and polished fingernails. Rather than the temptress luring an impotent Playboy from a beach party into the lethal swim, two young people, Tom and Chrissie, come from their cottage to make love on the beach. The novel refrains from projecting the film's stereotype of female aggressiveness with a total stranger. Also missing is the elaborate series of sexual renunciations on the part of the heroic chief of police. Brody's motivations for stalking the shark are somewhat neurotic, deriving in part from sexual failures with his wife.

All the changes enumerated here function to create a fantasy more satisfying to a mass audience than the novel's realism could provide. Peter Benchley complained about the drastic alteration of his material in the New York *Times* magazine while the final polishing of the screenplay was in process. "A finer hand than mine is at work on it now, someone who is doing what they call a dialogue polish, which is like referring to gang rape as heavy necking." The other screenwriter, Carl Gottlieb, reports that he would have liked to respond, "But it's not just me doing the gang rape. . . . Steven [Spielberg] held her down, and Dick [Zanuck] and David [Brown] gagged her, I was just, you know. . . ."[24] Given the subliminal material in the film version of *Jaws,* the reference to mythic distillation as rape seems apt. The "impurities" extracted in this distillation process were the novel's realistic presentation of sexual interests, the disparity between fault and punishment, virtue and reward, the recognition of evil within oneself rather than the destruction of evil in a demonic figment of sharkish imagination, and the element of final mystery in nature as embodied by the fish's sudden departure from Amity's waters. But the results of the distillation are financially intoxicating. There are rumors that the commercially successful film will be followed by *Jaws II,* with a ninety-foot supershark. One is tempted to speculate that it will begin with an attack on a *Playboy* yacht party and end with some new Spiderman defending an ocean liner sailing toward another island paradise in the South Seas.

VII

The American public's mood of anxiety and dread about the future, so faithfully expressed in the catastrophe films, cannot be dismissed. Their attempt to predict the consequences of present lifestyles, and the quest for the moral structure of human experience stand in the best traditions of social responsibility. Yet monomythic materials are so preoccupied with moral stereotypes and repressed sexuality that attention is diverted from aspects of social life and current behavior that are truly latent with catastrophe. Karl Kraus' *The Last Days of Mankind* may help us understand the impact of catastrophes and the role of human responsibility in causing them.

Karl Kraus was a Viennese social critic and writer who spent the greater part of his life pondering the nature of the disasters that fell upon the Austro-Hungarian Empire. He felt that his fellow Viennese unduly magnified the significance of sexual irregularities at the expense of ignoring practices possessing a more ominous social character. "Corruption is worse than prostitution," he wrote; "the latter might endanger the morals of an individual; the former invariably endangers the morals of an entire community."[25] Kraus traced this corruption with shocking objectivity, revealing terrors that do not fit the stereotypical form of sea monsters, sexually provocative females, retributive earthquakes, or burning skyscrapers. He pictures an entire community in the process of destroying itself, clinging festively to the very idols that corrupt it until all is lost. The victims in the meanwhile deny responsibility for the doom they have ensured.

The Last Days of Mankind was written in 1918–19 as a satirical tragedy of some eight hundred pages, with nearly five hundred characters in hundreds of scenes spread over Europe during the First World War. The play opens with the voice of a newsboy and ends with the voice of God, ironically echoing the words used by Kaiser Franz Joseph as he contemplated the destruction wrought by the war, "I didn't want it to happen." The tragedy is that of a people who unconsciously will their own destruction, who perform their daily patriotic duties in fostering the war that destroys them, deceiving themselves to the very end. Every group in European society is implicated in the catastrophe, yet the scenes are consistently banal. An angry crowd threatens an old lady who protests the use of underfed dogs to pull a cart; a priest fires an artillery weapon at the battlefront to bless it; a patriotic sermon proclaims that killing the enemy is a religious duty; a soldier berates his angry son for asking for a hot breakfast; a display of Italian shrapnel, barbed wire, and grenades is seen at a pilgrimage chapel; children play at war games; a manufacturer markets a "Hero's Grave for the Home"; leading literary figures Rilke and Werfel write martial poetry for public propaganda; a psychiatrist classifies a "patient" as a "madman" for expressing pacifist convictions; and a man is arrested for stating the truth that eight hundred thousand people had starved. These scenes of frightful inertia and festive martial celebration dangle over the catastrophic abyss much like Jonathan Edwards' sinners dancing on a string over the fires of hell, yet nowhere is there an admission of human responsibility. The Emperor Franz Joseph is pictured not as an evil conspirator but as an ineffective mediocrity: "Never before in history has a more powerful nonentity placed his stamp on all things and forms. In everything that blocks our path, in every failure to communicate, every misery, we detected his imperial beard. . . . A demon of mediocrity has decided our fate."[26] Evil here is the banal vacuum that stifles the vigor of every institution at the time of crisis.

Kraus rejected the neat moralistic formulas guaranteeing that catastrophes would punish the wicked and selectively spare the righteous. He presents scenes of indiscriminate destruction such as hungry children poking through a pile of garbage adjacent to a factory, finding an unexploded shell, and being killed by it. He avoids the petty moralism that envisions mere frivolity as triggering disasters. For instance, a love feast is pictured with officers and prostitutes. During the drunken revelry the general makes grandiose speeches extoling the heroism of his unit: "Steeled through battle, our heroic soldiers–these brave men–will march into new victories–we will not flinch. . . . I expect every one of you to fulfill your duty with complete disregard–to the last breath of man and beast." At that moment the message of the enemy's breakthrough arrives, and he flees rather than directing the resistance.

Stopping near a field hospital, he takes the tarp covering a wounded soldier to protect his staff car from the rain. Kraus' point is not that the stupid orgy precipitates the release of a moralized catastrophe, but that it reveals a more pervasive moral depravity that brings disaster on the culture as a whole. The ironic juxtaposition of idealistic rhetoric and unconscionable behavior is used to point to the moral reality. The innocent are harmed, and their loss is nonredemptive. Eden cannot be regained the day after the catastrophe is over, even though the powerful will strive to protect themselves from the consequences.[27]

Kraus predicted that when the great catastrophe of the First World War was over, no one would feel responsible. He has the "Grumbler" state: "They weren't really conscious of their actions. Austria can't be blamed for it! She merely let herself be encouraged by Germany to drag Germany into the war. And Germany drove Austria into a war she did not want. . . . Neither could really do anything about it." This evasive doubletalk is used by Kraus to show how language itself had become corrupt. He felt that the press had played a major role in sustaining the catastrophic delusions by repeating the corrupted words of public propaganda:

> In the end was the word. For the word that killed the spirit, nothing remained but to bring the deed to birth. Weaklings grew strong enough to shove us under the wheel of progress. And that was the press's achievement. . . . Not that the press set the machines of death in motion–but that it hollowed out our hearts, so that we could no longer imagine our future: that is its war guilt! And all peoples have drunk the lascivious wine of its debauchery, the kings of the earth have joined in the fornication.

Kraus developed a kind of "acoustic empiricism" to trace this corruption of language. He listened carefully to everyday speech for evidences of decay and self-deception, gleaning hundreds of authentic artifacts from articles, documents, and conversations. He saw in popular culture the evidence that "a world literally talks its way to perdition," as Max Spalter observed.[28]

Karl Kraus would be amused at the mythic empiricism of recent catastrophe films. He would likely point out that the contrived King Kong terrors are less menacing than the corruption hidden in our daily routines. He would remind us of the terrible possibility that we may enjoy and even worship what has the power to destroy us, and probably not even realize why the catastrophe occurs. Kraus' "Grumbler" concludes:

> Far greater than all the outrage of the war itself is that of people who wish to know nothing more about it. . . . For the survivors of the war, the war simply went out of fashion. . . . How easy it is to comprehend the sobering up of an epoch that never had valid experiences nor any grasp of what it had undergone—an epoch unshaken even by its own collapse! It perceived its atonement as dimly as its crime and possesses just enough self-preserving instinct to plug its ears to the heroic tunes on the phonograph, but sufficient self-sacrifice to sing along again whenever the occasion arises.

The "occasion" arose, of course, within two decades of the writing of these words, leading the Germanic peoples into the next disastrous crusade. Unlike the catastrophe films, which assume that the violent destruction of evil restores a lasting peace, Kraus accurately foresaw what the survivors of the First World War would bring upon themselves. The "Grumbler" predicts,

> That the war will turn the entire surrounding world into a huge hinterland of deceit, of debility, and of the most inhuman betrayal of God, while evil sustains itself through and beyond the war, prospering behind pretended ideals and fattening on sacrifice! That in this war, this modern war, culture is not regenerated but rather rescues itself from the hangman by committing suicide.[29]

This rejection of renewal through catastrophe was vindicated by later events, whose nature Kraus continued to document until the time of his death in 1936. His vision passes the test of time and warns us that to seek the nature of evil requires a painful look into ourselves, our institutions, and the popular language of our time. Evil is not a set of apocalyptic jaws that neatly punish the wicked and spare the virtuous before being driven away by heroes. It is rather the perpetual tendency to deceive ourselves and to blunder even when we most sincerely attempt to avoid the catastrophes our present actions are bringing.

IX
The Birth of a National Monomyth

"It is hard for us, bred on science and rationalism, to grasp how fearsome, how magical, the universe appeared to earlier societies, how full of wonders and portents it was. It could only be controlled by men and women larger than life. Heroes were necessary both as gods and as a part of the ritual that kept the external world secure and tolerable. . . . But epic heroes such as these essentially belong to rural worlds, to societies living near the wilderness. And no wonder then that they are dying, particularly in the Western world, where nature has become benign."[1]
–J. H. Plumb, "Disappearing Heroes" (1974)

For eight long chapters we have burdened our readers with the recurrent themes of artifacts embodying the American monomyth. The existence of these themes can hardly be doubted. Yet in surveying the scholarly discussion, a peculiar analytic lag is evident. Reputable scholars like J. H. Plumb have repeatedly announced the demise of mythic heroism. One wonders in Twain's terms whether these death notices may not be greatly exaggerated. We therefore provide some of the details that an obituary concerning the allegedly deceased should include. We hope the sketchy history will stimulate more exhaustive studies of the rise and development of the American monomyth.

I

The American monomyth begins and ends in Eden. Stories in this genre typically begin with a small community of hard-working farmers and townspeople living in harmony. A disruption of harmony occurs, and must be eliminated by the superhero, before the Edenic condition can be re-established in a happy ending. Thus in *Jaws* the paradisal island is first threatened and then restored to safety by Martin Brody's heroic action. The psychic center of Disneyland is the small town from which dirt and disharmony have been banned, while the nature films like *Bambi* always end with virtue's triumph in a restored Eden. The television version of the *Little House on the Prairie* begins and ends with Edenic icons, while the archetypal Heidi brings the miraculous powers of the Alpine Eden to the lonely and crippled citizens of the wicked city below. *Walking Tall* and *Death Wish* open with scenes of idyllic harmony, and use the traditional methods of the Edenic West to cope with urban crime. *Star Trek* always begins with the *Enterprise* peacefully on course, the crew efficiently at work on the antiseptic bridge. Suddenly a dangerous external threat arises to shatter this technological idyll. After the crisis is resolved, the starship is shown back on course, the computerized Eden having been restored.

In all these artifacts the state of harmony is the source from which the drama springs, as well as the goal of its resolution. The *monomythic Eden* has distinctive features: It is neither the pure state of nature, the pastoral world of small farms and plantations, nor the urban metropolis. It is a small, well-organized community surrounded by a pastoral realm whose distinguishing trait is the absence of lethal internal conflict arising from its members. The citizens are law-abiding and co-operative, without those extremes of economic, political, or sexual desires that might provoke confrontations. A cheerful atmosphere pervades the homogeneous populace, and there is no hint of a tendency on the part of the majority toward evil. If there are evil individuals in the community, they are clearly differentiated by behavior, dress, and physical appearance. The majority's only failing is impotence in the face of the evil of others.

The obvious model for this monomythic Eden is the midwestern small town. Yet small-town life in the American heartland has hardly been Edenic. Frequent crop failures, depressions, fluctuations in population, and conflicts over school, church, and civic administration have been endemic to Main Street, U.S.A. Pressures for social and moral conformity cause considerable unhappiness, and there has always been violent conflict. It is therefore unlikely that the monomythic image of a small-town paradise could have arisen from practical experience. Which raises the question: How did the myth arise?

Charles L. Sanford's study *The Quest for Paradise* suggests that "the Edenic myth . . . has been the most powerful and comprehensive organizing force in American culture." The myth arose with the discovery of the New World, long before the actual settlement of the continent. Sanford traces this quest for paradise in early tales of exploration and cites Columbus' conviction that "there is the terrestrial paradise" newly discovered in America. The "innocent qualities of Adam and Eve" were therefore attributed to the American Indians. Shortly before Columbus' last voyage, he claimed the discovery of the new heaven and new earth mentioned in the Bible, placing the discovery of America as a decisive step toward the second coming of Christ and the establishment of the millennial kingdom. This speculation fed the quest for El Dorado and stimulated Renaissance ideas about Arcadia and the recovery of the Golden Age. Erasmus' *Praise of Folly* and More's *Utopia* take up these paradisal themes. The Reformation linked the quest for paradise even more explicitly with millennial hopes. Luther's *Second Commentary on the Book of Revelation* placed current struggles with Catholicism in the penultimate phase of apocalyptic history, which would be followed shortly by a climactic battle and then the dawn of the millennial paradise. These expectations were widely shared by American Puritans. Sanford concludes:

> The most popular doctrine in the colonies was that America had been singled out, from all the nations of the earth, as the site of the Second Coming; and that the millennium of the saints, while essentially spiritual in nature, would be accompanied by a paradisaic transformation of the earth as the outward symbol of their inward state. As Mather put it, "when this Kingdom of Christ has filled all the Earth, *this Earth will be restored to its Paradise state.*"[2]

Recent studies have shown that the expectation of paradise

remained in the rather distant future for most American Puritans. Wilderness symbolized temptation, threat, and adversity to early settlers. By 1693 Mather was suggesting that "Wilderness" was the stage "thro' which we are passing to the Promised Land." The Puritans' pessimism about their own evil, and the long journey through the wilderness, tempered any tendency toward utopianism.[3]

The Edenic myth came to play a more powerful role in the next century among Enlightenment figures who abandoned the sense of omnipresent evil. Franklin and Jefferson, Sanford observes, combined the Puritan legacy of moral perfectionism with a remarkable confidence in America's Edenic potential. "The image of Paradise in the American myth of Eden has had its greatest development in the moral sphere. The superiority of the United States in quantitative achievements and political skills has consistently been blazoned forth in moral terms." Franklin seems to have been serious when he called his proposed colony in Ohio the future "paradise on earth." *The Captain America Complex* traces the secularization of this millennial zeal in the course of the nineteenth century and its attachment to the national expansion. In 1836 Thomas Cole proclaimed that ". . . we are still in Eden; the wall that shuts us out of the garden is our own ignorance and folly."[4] Such minor impediments could be dealt with by education, social reforms, and moral endeavors, to which Americans in the first half of the nineteenth century turned with enormous optimism.

The belief in America's millennial destiny, optimism about human progress, and an increasing hope in the perfectibility of man contributed to the idea of "The Garden of the World." As Henry Nash Smith defines this image of the American West, "The master symbol of the garden embraced a cluster of metaphors expressing fecundity, growth, increase, and blissful labor in the earth, all centering about the heroic figure of the idealized frontier farmer. . . ." He cites Timothy Flint's statement in 1827, describing the happy farmers raising their families ". . . in peace, plenty and privacy, under the guardian genius of our laws. . . . Farmers and their children are strong, and innocent and moral almost of necessity." The mythic image of an agrarian Eden is constantly contrasted with cities, which ". . . are the sores of the political body," as James B. Lanman put it in 1841. In 1862 this image of the Edenic Western Garden became embodied in the Homestead Act, whose strongest appeal, according to Smith ". . . . lay in the belief that it would enact by statute . . . the agrarian utopia of hardy and virtuous yeomen which had haunted the imaginations of writers about the West since the time of Crevecoeur."[5]

The power of this mythic image of the West to disguise empirical reality is illustrated by the reinterpretation of the "Great American Desert" image of the high Western plains during their settlement. The treeless region from Kansas to the Dakotas, whose sparse rainfall had seemed forever to defy cultivation, was advertised as arable after the Civil War by the Department of the Interior with the motto, "Rain Follows the Plough." Farm vegetation and newly planted trees would increase rainfall sufficiently to produce the promised Eden. David M. Emmons' study *Garden in the Grasslands* cites promotional literature that beckoned millions of immigrants to the anticipated paradise. Union Pacific Railroad ads compared settlers to Abraham, Columbus, and the Pilgrims, calling them ". . . the advance column of civilization . . . a peaceable, even tempered race, who hate war, love peace . . . honor their wives, raise honest children, live within their income, and grow rich out of Kansas soil." A Rock Island promotion explained, ". . . It is the garden spot of the world. . . . Because it will grow anything that any other country will grow and with less work. Because it rains here more than in any other place, and just at the right time," it is the ideal region to settle.[6]

It is scarcely credible today that claims about a rich and trouble-free western paradise lived on even after most original homesteaders lost their claims through adverse conditions. The myth was preserved in western novels and films depicting small communities of peaceful and industrious citizens saved from thieves and blackguards by courageous cowboys. In fact, at the very moment the Edenic myth was undergoing its most traumatic shock, during the Dust Bowl days of the Great Depression, Walt Disney was fashioning animated visions of paradise whose power is still apparent. In his classic cartoon of 1937, *The Old Mill,* a fierce storm buffets the idyllic windmill and its innocent animals just as the economic storms and dust bowl winds had been striking the midwestern Eden. A loyal pair of birds had laid their eggs in a gear hole of the unused mill, and the unusual winds drove the creaky wheel with its great gears over and over through the innocent nest. But the magic of animation preserved the myth as the baby birds magically reappear in the imperiled nest when quiet descends at the end. The same vision remains popular at Disneyland, which offers ". . . eternal fun, infinite holiday and deathlessness–in short, an urbanized Eden," to use John Seelye's words.[7]

Popular entertainments beyond Disney and the immediate scope of this study attest to the virtual omnipresence of the Eden theme. And essential to this nostalgic syndrome is a sense of loss, a conviction that the Eden Americans deserve to inhabit is now besieged by insoluble problems. This theme of a threat to paradise is embodied in the second phase of monomythic drama.

II

The action of the American monomyth always begins with a threat arising against Eden's calm. In *Death Wish,* petty criminals threaten the voyagers from Eden. In *Walking Tall,* the corruption of small-town gambling, prostitution, and bootlegging is linked to crime bosses in Nashville and New York. *Star Trek*'s challenges arise from interplanetary baddies such as Romulans, Klingons, or aggressive gods. *Playboy*'s bachelor pad is threatened by Puritanical harassments, while Amity Island's tranquillity is shattered by the marauding supershark. Spiderman and Superman contend against criminals and spies just as the Lone Ranger puts down threats by greedy frontier gangs. Thus paradise is depicted as repeatedly under siege, its citizens pressed down by alien powers. When evil is ascendant, Eden becomes a wilderness in which only a superhero can redeem the captives.

The theme of a chosen people under attack emerged in one of the earliest forms of American literature, the Indian captivity narratives. Mary Rowlandson's *The Sovereignty & Goodness of God . . . a Narrative of the Captivity and Restauration,* first printed in 1682, remained popular for a century and a half along with several similar stories, which were best sellers in Colonial America.

Rowlandson was living ". . . in prosperity, having the comforts of the world . . . ," oblivious of her shortcomings, when the Indian attack destroyed her family and carried her away into the night. Having resisted the temptations of Indian life, she was finally rescued and thus allowed to tell the story of "Israel in Babylon," to use Richard Slotkin's expression. The sense of the chosen people in an alien realm, under attack by the oppressive forces of a demonic Babylon, thus became a central theme in popular literature. "The great and continuing popularity of these narratives, the uses to which they were put, and the nature of the symbolism employed in them are evidence that the captivity narratives constitute the first coherent myth-literature developed in America for American audiences."[8]

The siege of paradise, expressed in the secular terminology of Thomas Jefferson, became central to the Declaration of Independence. "But when a long Train of Abuses and Usurpations, pursuing invariably the same Object, evinces a Design to reduce them under absolute Despotism," it is the duty of a people to revolt. The Declaration enumerates the phases of this perfidious attack by an unjust King on the innocent colonists. "He has plundered our Seas, ravaged our Coasts, burnt our towns, and destroyed the Lives of our People. . . . with circumstances of Cruelty and Perfidy, scarcely paralleled in the most barbarous Ages, and totally unworthy the Head of a civilized Nation." These attacks are pictured as totally unprovoked, evoking the mildest protestations suitable for a peaceful and law-abiding people. "In every stage of these Oppressions we have Petitioned for Redress in the most humble Terms: Our repeated Petitions have been answered only by repeated Injury."

The paradise and wilderness themes play decisive roles in the *Leatherstocking* tales, with maidens captured by aggressive Indians while peaceful frontier settlements are threatened by raiders. The Wild West shows dramatized these themes, with log cabins and stagecoaches attacked by wild Indians. The dime novels of 1860–93 analyzed by Henry Nash Smith concentrated on ". . . rescuing beautiful heroines from the Indians. When the Indians began to yield place in the dime novel to road agents or counterfeiters as the standard enemy, the hunters of the Leatherstocking type lend a hand in fighting the newer foes."[9]

At the root of this shift in the locus of evil was the inability of the western Eden to provide immunity from economic and natural disasters toward the end of the nineteenth century. Smith notes that,

> the myths of the garden and of the empire had both affirmed a doctrine of progress. . . . Neither American man nor the American continent contained, under this interpretation, any radical defect or principle of evil. But other men and other continents . . . were by implication unfortunate or wicked. This suggestion was strengthened by the tendency to account for any evil which threatened the garden empire by ascribing it to alien intrusion. Since evil could not conceivably originate within the walls of the garden, it must by logical necessity come from without. . . .[10]

A conspiratorial theory thus emerged, projecting all evil outward upon others. Whereas Mary Rowlandson had believed her suffering to be a just punishment for her own sins and those of fellow colonists, the myth of an innocent public afflicted by evil foes now began to crystallize. To confront these foes, heroic violence was required. A classic statement of this myth appeared in an early film by D. W. Griffith, appropriately titled *The Birth of a Nation.*

An opening scene of Griffith's 1915 classic is thoroughly Edenic, depicting plantation owner Ben Cameron gently stroking a pair of puppies. As Gerald Mast observes, "Significantly one of the puppies is black and the other white; also significant is the fact that a kitten soon begins to play with the pups. The animals become visual metaphors for the prewar South's happy mixture of different races and different social classes." The film pictures the Civil War as breaking this innocent idyll, having been fomented by evil abolitionists who favored miscegenation. As Mast states, "All the evil in the film is instigated by three people," mulattoes and abolitionists who seduced others into the evil of the war.[11]

The siege of innocent citizens is portrayed through a brilliant series of innovative film techniques that mark *The Birth of a Nation* as a milestone in film history. Film theorists Kinder and Houston note that *The Birth of a Nation* "developed innovations specifically suited to express a dualistic conception of the world."

Griffith skillfully blended closeups, crosscutting, iris shots, split-screen juxtapositions, and unusual camera positions to produce both realism and suspense in the conflict between stereotypical forces of good and evil. One might say that he invented mythic cuing, or at least employed its devices with unprecedented impact. He and his associates discovered ". . . the value of a detail not only as a narrative, attention-getting device, but also as a means of suggesting poetic significance."[12] Thus the plight of the innocent South at the hands of carpetbaggers and depraved blacks is conveyed by riotous street scenes, closeups of lecherous looks at white women, and scenes of war devastation. The mulatto, Gus, chases Flora Cameron to her death while the camera shifts back and forth from her desperate face to his leering eyes and pursuing body. Remarkable film-cutting techniques were used to build the suspense of a concluding scene in which Elsie Stoneman is being forced into marriage with the repulsive mulatto, Lynch, in the carpetbagger's office. Tension between absolute good and absolute evil is built by short scenes that flash from face to face and then outside to the gathering Klansmen.

The redemptive resolution provided by these galloping Klansmen derives from a tradition extending back to the Indian captivity tales. When the siege brings the innocent unbearably close to capitulation, Ben and his Klansmen arrive to kill the black militia and free all the captives. Thus the vigilantes bring justice to a threatened nation. The influence of the redemptive scheme popularized by Cody's Wild West shows is obvious. The novelty lies in the technical sophistication with which the mythic paradigm is communicated. Griffith made film into a technomythic medium immeasurably superior to the storytelling of the previous era. As Arthur Knight observes, the audience ". . . found Griffith's pictures more realistic, more convincing, more human than anything shown upon the screen at that time. . . ."[13]

The closing scene of *The Birth of a Nation* depicts Elsie Stoneman and Ben Cameron in wedding garments, symbolic of the reconciled North and South, gazing at a cloudlike image of the city of God replacing the city of man. A Christ figure replaces the warrior King who has cut the Gordian knot, confirming the resolution of Eden's siege. Gerald Mast observes, "There are several remarkable things about this closing vision–its audacity, its irrelevance, and the passionateness and sincerity of Griffith's commitment to it. . . . Exactly how is this City of God to become a reality? Certainly not by the efforts of the Ku Klux Klan alone." When one takes the emerging monomyth into account, the scene is neither irrelevant nor lacking in efficacy. As Charles Sanford reminds us, the connection between paradise and marriage has long been close in Christian symbolism: "Throughout the New Testament and in the many theological commentaries thereupon the union of the faithful with Christ in the heavenly paradise is depicted by the imagery of marriage." It is also consistent with the tradition of zealous nationalism to believe as Griffith did that righteous violence could usher in the millennial age. Although *The Birth of a Nation* did not contain the isolated, segmented superhero, the monomythic scheme of a restoration of paradise by selfless violence had fully crystallized by 1915. The film was an implicit Werther invitation to emulate the KKK in crusades to make the world safe for democracy. No wonder Woodrow Wilson was enthusiastic about its "writing history in lightning," and as Knight records, ". . . race riots and mob action followed in the wake of its presentation in many cities."[14]

III

The redemption of paradise by lone crusaders would have been unnecessary in American mythology if actual experience with democracy had matched the Edenic expectation. All the materials we have studied share the premise of *The Birth of a Nation* that democratic institutions are incapable of lifting the siege. The members of the *spectator democracy* passively witness their redemption by a superhero. The police authorities in New York are pictured as unable to stem the mugging epidemic without the assistance of vigilante Paul Kersey. The citizens of Adamsville, Tennessee, are helpless against the gambling syndicate without Buford Pusser's legendary hickory stick. Amity Island's Board of Selectmen cannot cope with the malevolent shark in *Jaws* without the services of outsiders like Quint, Hooper, and Brody. Even the humanoids on Gamma Trianguli VI are unable to free themselves from the technological monster Vaal without the intervention of Captain Kirk and his redemptive ship, the *Enterprise.*

Like so many other features of the monomyth, the theme of the defenseless City Set upon a Hill seems to have been decisively shaped by cowboy Westerns in the last third of the nineteenth century. At that time the expected western Eden was suffering repeated setbacks. The economic disorders of 1873, 1883–84, and 1893–95 were psychic shocks of formidable dimensions to those expecting a snug little nest somewhere out in the West. Henry Nash Smith describes the resulting sense of helplessness.

> . . . Since the myth affirmed the impossibility of disaster or suffering within the garden, it was unable to deal with any of the dark or tragic outcomes of human experience. Given a break in the upward curve of economic progress for the Western farmer, the myth could become a mockery, offering no consolation and serving only to intensify the sense of outrage on the part of men and women who discovered that labor in the fields did not bring the cheerful comfort promised them by so many prophets of the future of the West. The shattering of the myth by economic distress marked, for the history of ideas in America, the real end of the frontier period.[15]

Other factors, such as the corruption of the political system and the disillusionment of reformers, contributed to the psychic dilemma. But Smith seems to overlook the fact that the Westerns offered an immediate mythic solution. Contraposed against the failures of democratic institutions, the dime novels and Wild West shows offered unofficial redeemer figures on powerful horses, disinterested outsiders whose zeal for the right and sympathy for the underdog would triumph over evil.

The frontier vigilante as protector of a defenseless civilization was given substance by actual conditions in the West. Rapidly expanding exploitation of western resources and the lack of an effective national police system provided an ideal seedbed for vigilante justice. The invention of the six-gun and its successful use against the Indians of the western plains combined with the Civil War experience to produce a heavily armed citizenry. A desperado like Wild Bill Hickock, who killed dozens of men in frontier duels and ambushes, became a redeemer figure. His repeated service as a

U.S. marshal and frontier sheriff blurred the distinctions between vigilantes and public officials. As Daniel Boorstin states,

> . . . There were few if any notorious "bad men" who had not at some time or other worn the badge of the law, and risked their lives for what some men in their neighborhood called law and order. Beneath the widespread admiration for the "manhood" of the quick-on-the trigger desperado was a gnawing suspicion that the desperado himself was often . . . on the side of the right. "The 'bad men,' or professional fighters and man-killers," wrote Theodore Roosevelt in 1888 after one of his trips out West, "are of a different stamp (from the common criminal, horse thief or highway robber), quite a number of them being, according to their light, perfectly honest. These are the men who do most of the killing in frontier communities; yet it is a note-worthy fact that the men who are killed generally deserve their fate."[16]

In the western novel *The Virginian,* dedicated to Theodore Roosevelt in 1902, this theme achieved its archetypal formulation. Owen Wister's original preface introduces the romantic horseman who "rides in his historic yesterday," possessing virtues not found in the "shapeless state" of current democratic morals. "Such transition was inevitable," writes Wister, but he adds, "Let us give thanks that it is but a transition, and not a finality." In the "Rededication and Preface" of 1911, Wister relates his novel to the "half-a-century of shirking and evasion" of political responsibilities and insists, "Our Democracy has many enemies, both in Wall Street and in the Labor Unions; but as those in Wall Street have by their excesses created those in the Unions, they are the worst; if the pillars of our house fall, it is they who will have been the cause thereof."[17] In this context of a democracy besieged by mortal enemies, the unknown cowboy from Virginia and those who follow the implied invitation to imitate him provide the only viable defense.

The story begins as the narrator encounters the hero from Virginia at the Wyoming train station. "Lounging there at ease against the wall was a slim young giant, more beautiful than pictures. His broad, soft hat was pushed back; a loose-knotted, dull-scarlet handkerchief sagged from his throat; and one casual thumb was hooked in the cartridge-belt that slanted across his hips."[18] His redemptive competence is registered when he saves the narrator from a runaway horse and later shoots a rattlesnake that might have killed him. Similarly in the cowboy's first encounter with Molly Wood, the Yankee schoolteacher he is to court, he gallantly sweeps her out of a stagecoach sinking in a river. There is redemptive prefiguration in these incidents that prepares the way for his ultimate triumph over evil, personified by Trampas, who leads a gang of rustlers threatening to ruin honest ranchers like Judge Henry. After the Virginian is made foreman of the Sunk Creek Ranch, he undertakes the responsibility of tracking down the rustling gang, capturing two of its members, one of them formerly his best friend. But the frontier code demands that he renounce friendship and hang the thieves. Trampas escapes with a guileless sidekick. When the trackers approach, Trampas shoots him in the back so that he can escape on their only horse.

After an account of the lynching reaches the horrified Molly, Judge Henry visits her to explain its morality. It was [a] difficult [task] because "he had been a staunch servant of the law" while serving as a federal judge. "I am partly responsible for the lynching," he admits, but he insists there is a moral difference between ". . . burning Southern negroes in public . . . [and] hanging Wyoming cattle-thieves in private. . . ." Compared with the "semi-barbarous" practice in the South, the recent events are ". . . a proof that Wyoming is determined to become civilized." He contends that in lynching, citizens only take back the inherent powers of government they have given to the courts.

> But in Wyoming the law has been letting our cattle-thieves go for two years. We are in a very bad way, and we are trying to make that way a little better until civilization can reach us. At present we lie beyond its pale. The courts, or rather the juries, into whose hands we have put the law, are not dealing the law. They are withered hands. . . . And so when your ordinary citizen sees this, and sees that he has placed justice in a dead hand, he must take justice back into his own hands where it was once at the beginning of all things. Call this primitive, if you will. But so far from being a *defiance* of the law, it is an *assertion* of it–the fundamental assertion of self-governing men, upon whom our whole social fabric is based.

In an earlier scene, Molly had been horrified to find her schoolchildren playing the lynch game, re-enacting the hanging of

Trampas' accomplices. But the judge's words now persuade her to accept the monomythic ethic. Later she even suggests the appropriateness of vigilante violence to the Virginian as they are riding into Medicine Bow for their wedding. Trampas rides wordlessly past, and she remarks that it seems ". . . wicked that this murderer" get off when others were hanged just for stealing horses. "He was never even arrested!" says the girl. "No, he helped elect the sheriff in that county," replies the Virginian.[19]

Wister's presentation of benign western violence reflects the range war between a cattlemen's association and homesteaders in Johnson County, Wyoming. As Daniel Boorstin relates, the cattlemen's ". . . associations were of course intended to protect the cattle which bore their brands. But they were also protecting the large cattlemen's control over pieces of the open range–the public domain–which, without any legal title, they called their own." W. Eugene Hollon's definitive study *Frontier Violence* describes how the cattlemen came into conflict with small ranchers and farmers, with state and federal officials favoring the ranchers, and the local courts and juries controlled by the homesteaders. When the ranchers' lynch campaigns proved unsuccessful, they arbitrarily seized the small operators' livestock. The homesteaders retaliated with systematic thievery. Harry Sinclair Drago concludes, "It was more than range thievery undertaken for gain: it was rebellion; the oppressed striking back at its oppressors." When the ranchers imported a trainload of Texas gunmen equipped with dynamite to put down this resistance, the showdown occurred near Buffalo, Wyoming, in 1892, where federal troops finally intervened. The New York *Times* covered the story in detail, glorifying the big cattlemen's side of the struggle and praising Frank Wolcott, a wealthy cattleman born in Kentucky, whose ranch Wister visited during his first trip to the West. Wister inadvertently reveals the historical content of the novel by allowing the heroic cowboy to explain that his lynched friend ". . . knew well enough the only thing that would have let him off would have been a regular jury. For the thieves have got hold of the juries in Johnson County."[20]

Wister's distortion of the historical reality of western lynching becomes credible in the powerful mythic framework he provides, in which the besieged community is finally redeemed by a duel between Trampas and the Virginian. At the dramatic climax of the novel the rustler issues a formal challenge for a Main Street duel. The Virginian seeks the counsel of the bishop, who is to perform their marriage. The latter shares the narrator's conviction ". . . that Trampas was an evil in the country, and that the Virginian was a good. He knew that the cattle thieves–the rustlers–were gaining in numbers and audacity . . . that they elected their men to office, and controlled juries; that they were a staring menace to Wyoming. His heart was with the Virginian. But there was his Gospel that he preached, and believed, and tried to live." He reminds the Virginian of the plain command not to kill, and the latter responds: "Mighty plain to me, seh. Make it plain to Trampas, and there'll be no killin'." As they parry about the contradictory demands of religion and communal redemption, the Virginian poses the monomythic question: "How about instruments of Providence, seh?" When the cowboy refuses to give up his honor even for his future wife, the bishop says as he departs to the battle, "God bless him! God bless him!"[21]

The Virginian then confronts Molly with his painful obligation. She is appalled that he will not simply leave town when he has a chance. He explains that he gave Trampas two chances to get out of the duel:

> "I kept thinking hard of you–with all my might, or I reckon I'd have killed him right there. . . . I spoke as quiet as I am speaking to you now. But he stood to it. . . . He will have to go on to the finish now."
>
> "The finish?" she echoed, almost voiceless.
>
> "Yes," he answered very gently. . . .
>
> "If you do this, there can be no to-morrow for you and me."
>
> At these words he also turned white.
>
> "Do you mean–" he asked and could go no farther. . . . "This would be the end?" he asked.
>
> Her head faintly moved to signify yes. . . .
>
> "Good-by, then," he said.[22]

With this last in a series of renunciations in the novel, the hero goes out to his fateful duel–the first "walkdown" in American literature.[23] In an archetypal duel the bad guy draws and shoots first, but is killed by the Virginian's bullets. The hero's friends marvel, "You were that cool! That quick!" The hero returns regretfully to pack his belongings and return to a bachelor's life. But Molly's "New England conscience" relents, and she capitulates to love.

The bridal pair set off for their honeymoon, camping the first night on a peaceful mountain island, straddled by a lovely stream. "It belonged to no man; for it was deep in the unsurveyed and virgin wilderness. . . ." Their isolation is celebrated by the Virginian, "The whole world is far from here." After the first blissful night, ". . . she stretched her hands out to the island and the stream exclaiming, 'Nothing can surpass this.' He took her in his arms. . . ." In this garden encircled by the stream, symbolic of the biblical Eden surrounded by its rivers, the Virginian confesses his ancient longing: "What I did not know at all," he said, "was the way a man can be pining for–for this–and never guess what is the matter with him." Just as in *The Birth of a Nation,* the resolution of marriage and the entrance into paradise only become possible after evil has been destroyed. Once the vigilante task is completed, whether in the South or the West, the Gordian knot is cut, and the blissful marriage can ensue. The novel ends with the hero and his family ensconced in prosperity and long life. The Virginian becomes a wealthy rancher and mine owner, escaping the "cattle war" of 1892, and passing the redemptive task onto the next generation.[24]

The Virginian was one of the most influential novels of its time, becoming required reading in high schools for decades. More than two million copies were sold, and the novel became the pattern for hundreds of imitations. The success of the paradigm was due in part to the moralizing of vigilante violence by dramatic juxtaposition, impassioned arguments, and the selfless restraint of the hero. For five years the Virginian withstood the villain's provocations, reluctantly killing him at the price of renouncing sexual fulfillment. Gary Cooper played this role perfectly when *The Virginian* was made into an archetypal Western movie in 1929. Robert V. Hine has commented on the "namelessness" of the Virginian, an essential feature in the paradigm: ". . . The vagueness of his past requires the reader to judge the man solely in the present." But more than that, one suspects, it enhances the archetypal power of the story to cast an Everyman in the role of the community savior. Facing the siege of paradise, against which mere human force seems unable to prevail, only ". . . the transcendent figure, originating beyond the town," to use Peter Homan's words, is able to redeem.[25]

IV

With 1929 we enter the *axial decade* for the formation of the American monomyth. Here the unknown redeemer on a horse becomes the "Masked Rider of the Plains"; his sexual renunciation is complete; he assumes the uniform and powers of angelic avengers; and thus he grows from mere heroism to superheroism.

The development of the segmented superhero, the most distinctive feature of the monomyth, accelerates to its climax soon after the 1929 release of the sound-film version of *The Virginian.* With the technomythic advance of sound film, the embodiment of the monomythic heroism became even more compelling. The shock of the depression and the rise of unprecedented foreign threats to democratic societies provided the background for the creative advance. In this same year the comic-book version of *Tarzan* appeared. Burne Hogarth, who made Tarzan a household word in the 1930s, sets the scene: ". . . The success of 'Tarzan' owed much to the time when it was first drawn. This was a little after the start of the great depression: big corporations were crashing and misery was widespread. . . . Tarzan finds himself again, like the American people–without weapons to fight off all the perils." But Tarzan, like the many heroes who were to follow him, was more than merely human. The first of the major pulp-novel crime fighters, The Shadow, appeared in 1929. With an alter ego as Kent Allard the aviator, this mysterious figure performed super feats against the enemies of civilization in some 325 complete novels written over the next two decades. Buck Rogers was also created in 1929, and the ascetic supercop, Dick Tracy, appeared in 1931. The widely popular pulp imitators of The Shadow, such as Doc Savage, The Phantom, and The Spider, appeared in 1933. Probably the most systematic presentation of a superman appeared in Philip Wylie's novel *Gladiator,* written in 1930, which depicts a prodigy of scientist parents who proves invulnerable to machine-gun bullets. It was this figure who provided the model for Siegel and Shuster's Superman. They developed their comic superhero as a way to counter "the hopelessness and fear in the country" in 1933, but it was not marketed successfully until 1938.[26]

A decisive factor in the axial decade was the emergence of serialization in the new and more powerful technomythic media. Comic books and radio programs required a heroic format with traditional appeals of adventure and redemption but without marital resolution at the end. Sexual renunciation had to become permanent: If the hero rode off with his bride into the golden sunset, it would entail devising a new redeemer figure for the next episode. Once a hero became involved in family and business complexities, he would have to pass the redemptive torch to the next candidate. The new media offset this problem by allowing a presentation of heroic action more spectacular than any made credible before. Heroes could fly across the frames of comic strips with impunity, or thunder on their mounts at incredible speeds across the sound-effects stages of radio programs. The augmented capabilities ensured the resolution of otherwise insoluble crises. Miraculous redemption thus came to replace the blissful union of married partners as a fitting expression of Eden's restoration.

In *The Lone Ranger,* the new, permanently segmented superhero sprang to life in serial form. The program was developed by a Detroit radio station in 1933 to meet the requirements of a regular time slot on a new network. The station owner, George Trendle, wanted a cowboy who would play the role of a "guardian angel," a hero who would be the "embodiment of a granted prayer." The radio version of *The Lone Ranger* ran to 2,956 episodes, ending only in 1954. It has since been replayed many times, as well as appearing in comic books, television programs, and films. The genesis episode reveals both the continuity and the development beyond the Virginian archetype. A voice announces, "This is the legend of a man who buried his identity to dedicate his life to the service of humanity and country. . . . Early settlers in the West had to be brave men and women. . . . There was danger on every side, wild beasts, savage Indians, and the Cavendish gang." Having established the theme of a hero with secret identity who defends humanity from danger, the narrator turns to Butch Cavendish, who orders his gang to open fire on a helpless wagon train: "Wipe them out to the last man!" Later a group of Texas Rangers follows them into a desolate canyon, where they are betrayed by their guide. Just before the ambush begins, the birds are heard twittering in the trees as Captain Daniel Reid asks his younger brother to care for his family if tragedy overtakes them. The Edenic scene is broken by gunfire from the outlaws, which falls upon the trapped Rangers until night. Young Reid wakes up four mornings later in a cave, where he had been carried by an Indian, who introduces himself:

"Me . . . Tonto. . . ."

Reid asks, "What of the other Rangers? They were all my friends. One was my brother."

Tonto replies, "Other Texas Rangers—all dead. You only Ranger left. *You lone Ranger now.*" The two men discover they had been boyhood friends. The youthful Reid had saved Tonto's life, thus providing a prefiguration of his redemptive capabilities, in the style of *The Virginian.* Reid and Tonto resolve to track down the Cavendish gang and bring them to justice. Jim Harmon describes the scene: "Marked for death by a huge outlaw organization, he decided to disguise himself with a mask, a mask made from the black cloth of a vest in his brother's saddlebags—cloth that had borne the silver star of justice." The narrator intones the litany: "In the Ranger's eye there was a light that must have burned in the eyes of knights in armor, a light that through the ages must have lifted the souls of strong men who fought for justice, for God!"[27] The young man gives voice to his zealous decision:

"I'll be—the Lone Ranger!"

As in the story by Owen Wister, it is a Southerner who comes West to play the role of the national redeemer. In this instance the unification of the symbol system is portrayed by the deep midwestern voice of the Lone Ranger rather than by a marriage to a Vermont schoolteacher. The requisite selflessness in his campaign is portrayed by the dedication of the proceeds from his secret silver mine to pay the expenses for his crusade. The Lone Ranger renounces both wealth and love. In his friendship with Tonto, there is a remarkable degree of racial reconciliation, differing drastically from the implacable hatred between Indians and the Texas Rangers.[28] Tonto not only becomes the constant companion and follower of the Lone Ranger, but also takes up the crusading ideology, which had played such havoc with the American Indians. A more striking symbol of co-optation could scarcely be imagined, but it provides a powerful confirmation of the white man's vigilante code.

Of equal importance symbolically is the taming of the great white stallion, Silver, after the Lone Ranger saved it from death in a battle with a "giant buffalo." The powerful horse responds instinctively to the sound of its name and accepts the gentle mastery of its savior. The narrator describes the wondrous scene.

"As the halter touched Silver, he trembled as if from a chill. Every instinct told him that he must flee at once to preserve his freedom. Yet he stood his ground. It wasn't gratitude that kept him there. It was something stronger. Some mysterious bond of friendship and understanding. He heard the man's voice and he liked it."

"Silver, Silver, we're going to be partners!" says the Lone Ranger.

Tonto is amazed, "Him let you use halter!"

"Give me the saddle."

Tonto replies, "Oh, no horse like that take saddle."

The Lone Ranger then states the mythic point as he places the saddle on the magnificent horse: "There never was a horse like this. Now Silver, we're going to work together."

The narrator reiterates the theme: "No hooves had ever beat the plains like the thundering hooves of that great horse, Silver!" The opening lines of the radio program henceforth feature Silver as a full member of the redemptive team. He not only responds to his master's voice without being trained, but seems to "understand" the vigilante work in which he is engaged. The peculiar capabilities of radio sound effects make it possible to render Silver virtually human, whinnying his assent to utterances of Ranger truth. He is the first in a remarkable line of redeemer animals in American popular culture.

The speed of the incomparable horse provides the Lone Ranger with his crucial element of the superhuman: rapid mobility, the most characteristic and coveted form of freedom in America, the ability to transcend space and time. The need for such speed is displayed in an early episode by the Lone Ranger's inability to overtake Butch Cavendish with his former steed. "My next horse must be faster," the Lone Ranger says, in order to take the culprit alive and bring him to justice. This theme is touched on but not fully exploited by Wister's references to the Virginian's horse, Monte. But in the Lone Ranger series, Silver develops into a symbol of tireless endurance and strength, allowing the vigilante to accomplish miraculous feats that raise him above the merely heroic level of the Virginian.

Extralegal violence and personal vengeance are essential to the vigilante ideology, but in the Lone Ranger's instance there is an elaborate effort to downplay objectionable features of lynch justice. The Masked Rider is not acting as a law-enforcement officer, despite the black mask of cloth that had borne the star of justice. But he invariably turns his captured crooks over to the authorities for punishment. The program always began with loud pistol shots interspersed with the "William Tell Overture," yet the Lone Ranger never killed anyone. With superhuman accuracy his silver bullets struck the hands of threatening bad guys, neutralizing their evil powers. In an elaborate extension of the ideology of cool zeal, which seeks to relieve the vigilante from guilt in the exercise of vengeance,[29] the Lone Ranger's powers ensured that minimum injury was inflicted. Just as in the later theory of nuclear deterrence, unlimited power is celebrated as the ultimate defense, because it presumably will never have to be used destructively. Magical silver missiles will keep the foe from aggression, incurring no blame on selfless redeemers. All one needs to escape the ambiguity of violent power is more power. Thus *The Lone Ranger* program answers the objections posed by Molly and the bishop in *The Virginian*. The vigilante has become the saint, not merely through superior virtue but also because of superhuman power.

The Werther invitation implicit in the program was articulated when the Lone Ranger found his brother's long-lost son and explained the "great heritage" he was to carry forward.

> [Your forefathers] . . . have handed down to you the right to worship as you choose, and the right to work and profit from your enterprise. They have given you a land where there is true freedom, true equality of opportunity, a nation that is governed

> by the people, by laws that are best for the greatest number. Your duty, Dan, is to preserve that heritage and strengthen it. [Strains of "America the Beautiful" grow louder.] That is the heritage and duty of every American.

In a program broadcast during 1950 the invitation is even more sharply formulated, as a dying government agent tells the Lone Ranger: "Listen to me–carry on. And train someone to carry on in the twentieth century when–when you join your Ranger pals–and me. . . ." The Lone Ranger replies, "Dan Reid is going to meet the twentieth century as a man."[30] The appeal to the audience is to take up the vigilante task with similar manliness.

The final, monomythic extension of powers into the superheroic occurred toward the end of the axial decade. *Superman* began to appear as a feature in the June 1938 *Action Comics.* By the fourth issue, the sales curve indicated that something significant had occurred. Within a few years, millions of copies were selling each month, revolutionizing the comic-book industry and making a permanent alteration in the American hero pattern. It was, as Les Daniels puts it, ". . . an instant triumph, a concept so intense and so instantly identifiable that he became perhaps the most widely known figure ever created in American fiction." Ted White refers to the "magnificent sense of wonder" with which these pages were received by readers. Episodes climaxing with "Look! The bullets bounce right offa him!" virtually replaced the ordinary development of plots. The August 1939 issue of *Action Comics* stresses this theme:

> Leaping over skyscrapers, running faster than an express train, springing great distances and heights, lifting and smashing tremendous weights, possessing an impenetrable skin–these are the amazing attributes which Superman, savior of the helpless and oppressed, avails himself of as he battles the forces of evil and injustice.[31]

As with the Lone Ranger, these extraordinary powers made it possible to carry out vigilante violence without incurring blame. Speeding getaway cars could be stopped dead by Superman's arms, without splattering anyone on the windshield. The actual effects of boundless power are denied, since Superman never kills anyone. If crooks are hurt or killed, it is their own fault. The steel-sinewed fists of Superman can be as gentle as Disney's mill wheel, knocking them unconscious without raising welts on their jaws. Siegel and Shuster's fantasy was even better than silver bullets, because their superhero never even had to fire at the enemy. His bulletproof body could close with adversaries and bring them to a flawless form of vigilante justice.

In the first years of comic-book life, Superman's power of flight was limited to prodigious leaps. When the first motion-picture cartoons appeared, ". . . he gained the power of pure flight," which was subsequently taken over by the comics. As we have noted before, the mythic advance goes hand in hand with technomythic breakthroughs, in this instance related to animation techniques. The transcending of human capabilities had reached its apex. When combined with the appealing structure of the plebeian alter ego, Clark Kent, a beguiling fantasy world took form. The redemptive god with superhuman strength is disguised as Everyman, and thus the bounds of democratic ordinariness are broken. For the first time in modern, secularized America, superhuman powers become widely distributed in fantasy. But the transformation of the redeemer paradigm that surfaces in *The Birth of a Nation* and *The Virginian* exhibits two remarkable features: a transcending of human muscular powers, and a completion of the segmentation pattern. Like its serialized counterpart, the Lone Ranger, Superman's sexual segmentation is permanent.

V

Following the phenomenal success of Superman comics in 1938, the axial decade closes with a proliferation of superheroes. The masks, uniforms, miraculous powers, and secret alter egos combine with sexual renunciation and segmentation to complete the formation of the monomythic hero. Batman, Sandman, Hawkman, and The Spirit all spring to life in 1939. Flash, The Green Lantern, The Shield, Captain Marvel, and White Streak follow in 1940. Sub-Mariner, Wonder Woman, Plastic Man, and Captain America are born the following year. The opening captions of these comic superhero tales reveal the degree to which the monomythic definition of mission, character, and powers was permanently crystallized by the axial decade. Episode 1 of *Batman* in May 1939 introduces the disguised isolate as ". . . a mysterious and adventurous figure fighting for righteousness and apprehending the wrongdoers, in his lone battle against the evil forces of society . . . his identity remains unknown." The beginning issue of Captain Marvel comics is announced in these monomythic terms: "Whiz Comics proudly presents THE WORLD'S MIGHTIEST MAN–POWERFUL CHAMPION OF JUSTICE–RELENTLESS ENEMY OF EVIL." In this story Billy Batson is confronted by a divine personage looking suspiciously like "The Ancient of Days" in old Sunday school material. "All my life," the figure says, "I have fought injustice and cruelty. But I am old now —my time is almost up. You shall be my successor merely by speaking my name. You can become the mightiest man in the world—Captain Marvel!" "Shazam!" "Blam!" "Captain Marvel, I salute you. Henceforth it shall be your sacred duty to defend the poor and helpless. Right wrongs and crush evil everywhere."[32] Thus a new superhero takes up the redemptive task from a senile religious symbol, offering in the fantasy life of every schoolboy an opportunity to be transformed by the magic word into the all-powerful redeemer.

The connection of these materials with the American religious heritage relates to the displacement of the redeemer myth. Only in a culture preoccupied for centuries with the question of salvation is the appearance of redemption through superheroes comprehensible. The secularization process in this instance does not eliminate the need for redemption, as the Enlightenment had attempted to do, but rather displaces it with a semihuman process. Powers that the culture had earlier reserved for God and his angelic beings are transferred to an Everyman, conveniently shielded by an alter ego. Even the most explicit references to the mythology of the ancient world are conditioned by this new superhero paradigm. This can be documented in materials created long after the axial decade. The television version of *Isis* began in 1975 with the mysterious-sounding lines:

> "O mighty queen," said the royal sorceress, "with this amulet you and your descendants are endowed by the goddess Isis with the powers of the animals and the elements. You will soar as the

The Lone Ranger emerged in the 1930s as an exemplary monomythic hero—selfless, sexless, and benignly violent in dispensing justice. His silver missiles unerringly deterred enemies without harming them.

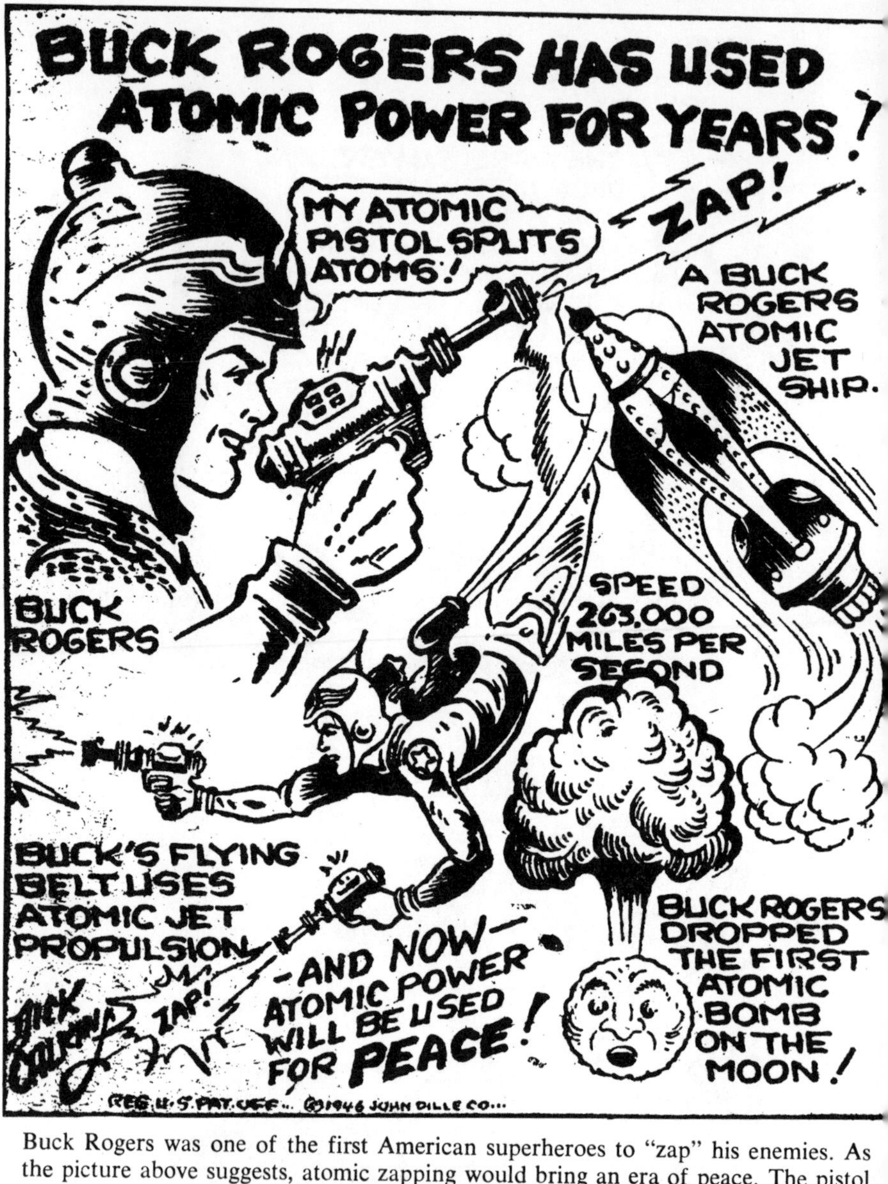

Buck Rogers was one of the first American superheroes to "zap" his enemies. As the picture above suggests, atomic zapping would bring an era of peace. The pistol is as benevolent as the Lone Ranger's silver bullets.

ANNOUNCING the NEW
U-235
ZAP
ZAP!
BUCK ROGERS ATOMIC
PISTOL
Buck Rogers zooms out of the stratosphere with the original Daisy ATOMIC PISTOL. It's big —10 inches long. It "ZAPS" with a loud bang. It flashes through the red windows of the "Fission Rate Indicator." Body, barrel, grip, jacket and trigger guard of silvery steel. Bell muzzle, fins, trigger and front sight blued steel. No sharp edges. Lasting metallic copper finish.
$1.00
Licensed by John Dille, Chicago
Length . . . . 10 inches
Weight . . . . 13 ounces
Packing . . . . 60 pieces
Weight per shipping case . . . . 50 pounds
Retail price, each . . shown at left
DICK CALKINS

An advertisement for Buck's atomic gun in *Daisy* magazine (1948). A mail-order purchase helped youngsters identify with this mythical role and do a little zapping of their own.

Even secular redeemer figures assume religious roles. Here we see the comic book Flash sustaining religious faith through miracles of mobility.

The Virginian, played here by Gary Cooper, was one of the last American redeemers to be permitted a honeymoon in the woods.

Contemporary underground comics ridicule the monomythic ideal of selfless heroism. Sexual restraints are abandoned and ungrateful females are zapped—but these comics remain true to the monomythic plot.

Zap comics undertook, in the 1960s, to ridicule and destroy the establishment's faith in its superheroes. The American businessman is stereotyped in monomythic fashion as thoroughly degenerate and worthy of destruction.

Mr. Natural is the underground version of the selfless candidate with unknown origins and nothing to hide. Does his appealing campaign style shape current elections in America?

falcon soars, run with the speed of gazelles, and command the elements of sky and earth."

But as the narrator extends the context, it is clearly the familiar redemption scheme with a segmented superheroine in disguise.

> Three thousand years later a young science teacher dug up this lost treasure and found she was heir to the secrets of Isis. And so, unknown to even her closest friends . . . became a dual person –Andrea Thomas–teacher–and Isis–dedicated foe of evil, defender of the weak, champion of truth and justice.[33]

The references to ancient gods and amulets may sound archaic to some, but the format was shaped during the axial decade of the twentieth century.

As the superhero genre was elaborated in the years following the axial decade, the displacement of traditional religious symbols was frequently articulated. A *Flash* episode of August 1971 seems archetypal. A gang of urban thugs have taken over a church to store and divide their loot; when the faithful nuns pray for relief, one of their oppressors pours scorn on the thought of divine intervention.

> Haw! Whatcha doin'? Askin' your own top man to help you? No Way! Nothin's gonna stop us from keepin' this loot!

The gang then accuses the nun's brother of being an informer. Flash arrives just in time to save him from death as they throw him off the roof of a tall building. The boy decides to go straight, but the chief has hidden the loot. He confides his problem to Sister Anne, who says she will pray for help. Flash overhears the conversation and comments:

> There's only one way of quickly finding that hidden loot . . . and that's *scientifically!*

He becomes a rapidly moving radar unit, systematically projecting grids over the city and searching until he finds the cave where the loot is hidden. He saves the informer and his girlfriend from retaliation by secretly warding off hostile bullets and making clubs disintegrate while increasing the strength of the good guy's fists. The young man tells his girlfriend after triumphing over the crooks, "Might makes right!" The nuns receive control of their church again; the juvenile delinquents are reformed, and as Vic recounts the events, he says, ". . . It all seems like a miracle!" Barry Allen, alias Flash, mutters to himself, "Made possible by the miracle of superspeed!"

In the final scene, Sister Anne is expressing her thanks to God for deliverance. As Barry acknowledges that it had been "a *kind* of miracle," the caption reads: "Perhaps, Barry–but to those who believe, 'the moment of a miracle is like unending lightning.' " The miraculous intervention of the modern superhero has confirmed the faith of the naïve sister. She thinks God still works in mysterious ways, and if this story is right, he does–through the jet-age counterpart of the Lone Ranger's speedy horse.[34]

The superheroes therefore provide a secular fulfillment of the religious promise articulated in the endings of *The Birth of a Nation* and *The Virginian.* They cut Gordian knots, lift the siege of evil, and restore the Edenic state of perfect faith and perfect peace. It is a millennial, religious expectation, at least in origin, fulfilled by secular agencies. The discrepancy, of course, is that superhuman powers have to be projected onto ordinary citizens, transforming them into superheroes. Moreover, total power must be pictured as totally benign, transmuting lawless vigilantism into a perfect embodiment of law enforcement. That such fantasies suddenly become credible is the abiding legacy of the axial decade. Although they had not yet appeared in the minds of their creators, Kirk and Spock, Kersey and Pusser, Brody and Bronson were already defined. They were ready to play out their roles of redeeming the American Dream, along with their nonviolent cohorts from Heidi and Mary Poppins to Lassie and Flipper. All that remained was for the subplots to vary and the scenes to change. Henceforth, materials for mass audiences would have to undergo mythic alchemy to fit the new monomythic consciousness. A mythic paradigm as potent as Hercules or Odysseus had been born, spawning its offspring in a popular culture that would soon encircle the world. It would not be long until the American monomyth became the subculture of Planet Earth, massaging the consciousness of youth and evoking Werther effects everywhere.

By the end of the axial decade the audience was ready to accept this secular displacement of religion, this new form of redemption whose religious component was submerged into adolescent fantasy life. E. E. Smith's vivid description of the mind-set at the end of the axial decade is equally applicable for today. Asked to define the meaning of the First International Science Fiction Convention to its participants in 1940, he did so in terms that are disarmingly religious.

> What brings us together and underlies this convention is a fundamental unity of mind. We are imaginative, with a tempered, analytical imagination which fairy tales will not satisfy. . . . Science fiction fans form a group unparalleled in history, in our close-knit . . . organization, in our strong likes and dislikes, in our partisanship and loyalties . . . there is a depth of satisfaction, a height of fellowship which no one who has never experienced it can even partially understand.[35]

Although Smith was careful to point out that science fiction fans would never comprise more than a fraction of the population, and that outsiders would have trouble grasping the basis of their fervor, the attitude of credulity and the yearning for fantasy redemption was certainly widespread. A revolution in religious consciousness had occurred, enabling the emergence of formal and informal pop religions in which the various superheroic rites could be conducted. Fandom was the new form of religious community, and in the alter ego feature of the superhero fantasies, every worshiper could become a god.

VI

In retrospect, the monomythic superhero is distinguished by disguised origins, pure motivations, a redemptive task, and extraordinary powers. He originates outside the community he is called to save, and in those exceptional instances when he is resident therein, the superhero plays the role of the idealistic loner. His identity is secret, either by virtue of his unknown origins or his alter ego, his motivation a selfless zeal for justice. By elaborate conventions of restraint, his desire for revenge is purified. Patient in the face of provocations, he seeks nothing for himself and withstands all temptations. Sexual fulfillment is renounced for the duration of the mission. The purity of his motivations ensures moral infallibility in judging persons and situations. When threatened by violent adversaries, vigilantism is the answer, restoring justice and thus lifting the siege of paradise. To accomplish this mission without incurring blame or causing undue injury to others, superhuman powers are required. The aim of the superhero is unerring, his fists irresistible, and his body incapable of suffering fatal injury. In the most dangerous trials he remains utterly cool and thus divinely competent. When confronted by insoluble personality conflicts within the community, nonviolent manipulation is employed. With wisdom and coolness equal to the vigilante counterpart, the Heidi-redeemer brings happiness to a desperate Eden.

In these conventions the monomyth betrays an aim to deny the tragic complexities of human life. It forgets that every gain entails a loss, that extraordinary benefits exact requisite costs, and that injury is usually proportionate to the amount of violence employed. The bold figures of Superman and Flash and the dramatic hoofbeats of the great horse Silver may seem to lack ambiguity. But the paradoxes abound. The American monomyth offers vigilantism without lawlessness, sexual repression without resultant perversion, and moral infallibility without the use of intellect. It features a restoration of Eden for others, but refuses to allow the dutiful hero to participate in its pleasures. The Lone Ranger's laughter was one sound effect never heard after the first program. The monomythic hero claims surpassing concern for the health of the community, but he never practices citizenship. He unites a consuming love of impartial justice with a mission of personal vengeance that eliminates due process of law. He offers a form of leadership without paying the price of political relations or responding to the preferences of the majority.

The tapestry of the American monomyth is woven in bold and stirring colors. Its radiant, electronic aura dazzles the beholder's eye and conceals the discordant clash of its components. The intricately crafted message of paradise redeemed by heroes larger than life has appeals far deeper than reason, particularly to a culture believing itself besieged by ruthless foes. To borrow words from the unbelieving J. H. Plumb, the world of the American monomyth is truly ". . . fearsome . . . magical . . . full of wonders and portents. . . ."[36] All things considered, the scholar's obituary for "disappearing heroes" was indeed premature. Can it be that the technomythic portraits in radio, film, television, and comics are so artful that even highly sophisticated minds fail to detect the new heroic presences? Are the dramas of redemption so true to our most earnest hopes that they acquire the semblance of reality? Perhaps if the monomyth is truly alive and well, it reveals a side to scientific, modern man seldom imagined in the dreams of reason that stirred the century in which the American nation was founded. It is surely appropriate now, as we enter our third century of national life, to cope with this pervasive mythic legacy.

X
Zapping the American Monomyth

> ". . . A change to a new type of music is something to beware of as a hazard of all our fortunes. For the modes of music are never disturbed without unsettling . . . the most fundamental political and social conventions."[1]–Plato, *Republic* (ca. 360 B.C.)

> "The art of a free society consists first in the maintenance of the symbolic code; and secondly in fearlessness of revision . . . to secure that the code serves . . . purposes which satisfy an enlightened reason."[2]–Alfred North Whitehead, *Symbolism* (1927)

The critical task of examining and assessing the American monomyth recalls Plato's concern that the arts must develop social discipline. He had concluded that the lives of artists and their audiences acquire the qualities of the dramas, music and poetry being performed. Participation in "good" art he saw as beneficial since ". . . rhythm and harmony find their way to the inmost soul and take strongest hold upon it, bringing with them and imparting grace. . . ." Such art enters one's soul ". . . like a breeze bearing health from happy regions. . . ." But it was equally possible that corrupted art, ignored by inattentive leaders, would bring significant evils to the republic. Plato warned against allowing citizens to be ". . . bred among symbols of evil, as it were in a pasture of poisonous herbs, lest grazing freely . . . they little by little and all unawares accumulate . . . a mass of evil in their own souls."[3] Plato's intuition that art shapes behavior led to the first philosophical justification for censorship and its corollary suggestion that artists exercising their capabilities irresponsibly should be exiled from the republic.

Our study lends some plausibility to Plato's sense of the latent force in artistic creations. Materials like *Death Wish, Jaws,* and *Walking Tall* suggest the need to assess the Werther effects evoked by monomythic entertainment. Is it possible to measure the impact of such materials on their audiences? Can we discern the influence of the American monomyth on such disparate forces as the counterculture and the scholarly establishment? What forms of political and sexual relationships does it encourage? Is it possible to solve the problem defined by Plato once and for all, by zapping the monomyth? These threatening questions, which hardly lend themselves to cool discussion or precise answers, draw us into a no-man's-land where the crossfire is intense.

I

It was concern about the effect of entertainment upon public morals that led to the creation of production codes for movies, comics, and television. Prior to the application of sophisticated testing methods, the early period of study and debate was inconclusive. Hollywood censors seemed sure that sexual displays would inspire imitations, but had more difficulty interpreting crimes and the heroic retributions that followed. Alarming stories were told, but cause-and-effect relations were impossible to establish. For instance, Murray Schumach reports a case in the censors' files involving a ". . . youth who murdered his teen-aged date while they were necking in a car shortly after seeing a movie."[4] The fact that the film was Disney's *Snow White and the Seven Dwarfs* seemed to lend little plausibility to the belief that it had stimulated the crime.

In recent years several dozen studies of "imitative aggression" have been conducted, most of which point to Werther effects, at least for some individuals. Psychiatrists have reported instances of "cinematic neuroses" in which insomnia, anxiety, and paranoia arose after seeing films like *The Exorcist* or *Jaws.* In 1975 a seventeen-year-old girl was admitted to a western Kansas hospital with stiff neck, trembling hands, and seizures: "She would jerk her arms spasmodically and scream 'Sharks! Sharks!' " A Chicago psychiatrist reported admitting six patients for mental hospitalization "straight from the theater."[5] Plato would have expected such disorders, but they appear surprising to a culture convinced of the bubble-gum fallacy.

Recent investigations and audience reactions have moved conceptually beyond isolated horror stories. The National Commission on the Causes and Prevention of Violence, established by presidential decree in 1968, applied the resources of the social sciences with unprecedented vigor. Among the reports sponsored by the Commission, the one authored by George Gerbner and Larry Gross has special relevance to the monomythic materials conveyed by American television. They began by studying the "message content" of current television, noting particularly its patterns of victimization. Women in the programs were more likely to be victimized than men, and the latter are pictured as likely to get away with fatal violence, especially when they play redemptive roles. Having established a television version of social reality, the researchers created a questionnaire that tested, in effect, the extent to which television "cultivated" its world view among viewers. Subjects were classified according to the amount of television they watched, their ages, and their formal education. They were asked questions like "During any given week, what are your chances of being involved in some kind of violence?" "What percent of all crimes are violent crimes–like murder, rape, robbery, and aggravated assault?" "What is the likelihood that you will be the victim of a crime during the next year?" Light viewers or nonviewers tended to select answers representing the actual probability of such victimization, while heavy viewers tended to select answers congruent with the monomythic world of television. The latter gave answers that ". . . exaggerate danger and violence and law enforcement in the real world and generally project assumptions that would underlie a heightened sense of fear and risk." The study also revealed that television diminished and distorted the effects of higher education, particularly among women, who are so frequently pictured as victims in monomythic dramas. Women ". . . consistently reported higher estimates of violence and law enforcement than men."[6]

An even more striking result from the Gerbner-Gross study was the emergence of a "TV generation," citizens under thirty years of age whose fearful estimates about their world far exceeded those of older groups. "Respondents under 30 show greater readiness to choose the 'television answers' at all levels of viewing than the older respondents. Young light viewers responded like older heavy viewers. . . . It seems evident . . . that those under 30 have grown up in a world in which television was an increasingly pervasive aspect of the cultural environment."[7] This research confirms the operation of what we have called mythic selectivity in comprehending reality: Perception of the real world is decisively shaped by the monomythic paradigm.

There is also considerable evidence to suggest that the encounter with violent forms of entertainment encourages emulation. Although the term "Werther effect" was not employed, the final report of the National Commission noted ". . . the vast majority of experimental studies . . . have found that observed violence stimulates aggressive behavior, rather than the opposite. Moreover, the stimulation of aggressive responses from exposure to filmed aggression is more likely to occur when the witnessed aggression occurs in a justified rather than in an unjustified context." Researchers have also shown that even when imitative behavior does not occur immediately, the mood of television watchers in daily life is affected by the type of material viewed. Heavy viewers of crime programs exhibit higher levels of hostility and anger toward others than those watching comedy and variety programs.[8] Since monomythic material provides moralization for hostile and aggressive behavior, its presence in such large quantities in popular entertainment is cause for serious alarm.

II

Various efforts to counter the alarming tendencies of monomythic values have been made, the most strenuous emerging from the under-thirties generation of the 1960s. Leading the attack on the Edenic image of America, the selfless hero paradigm, and the pattern of sexual renunciation, is comic-book artist Robert Crumb. His *Zap Comics* reached a wide audience in 1968, the first of a considerable number of underground comics that have had "a sizable effect" on their readers and the comic business. The title expresses a penchant for total war against what is perceived to be a repressive American mythology; to "zap" means to ". . . destroy or kill with a burst of gunfire, flame, or electric current . . . to attack with heavy firepower." This slang term was popularized, if not invented, in the Buck Rogers comics, where it depicted the firing of his atomic pistol. In its wider application, "zap" becomes the current equivalent for cutting Gordian knots. *Zap Comics* sequences by Gilbert Sheldon, Rick Griffin, Victor Moscosco, and S. Clay Wilson share Robert Crumb's purpose ". . . to fuck the American bourgeoisie."[9] Their aim is to destroy the credibility of the establishment's symbol system, to reveal its hypocrisy and destructive propensities. The use of crude drawing styles, obscene language, pornographic details, and stereotypical ugliness is intended to produce mythic shock waves comparable in effectiveness to futuristic ray guns or the miraculous powers of Captain Marvel.

In depicting "Mr. Natural," a bald, bearded guru resembling the godlike figure who passed the redemptive mission onto Billy Batson, turning him into Captain Marvel, Crumb has created the ultimate putdown of redeemer figures. The flavor of Mr. Natural has been nicely captured by Les Daniels, who describes him as ". . . an ancient wise man who wavers between inspiration and charlatanry. . . . Surviving on contributions for which he offers nothing in return except the opportunity to search fruitlessly for truth in his presence. . . . On a few occasions he has proved himself capable of performing something that could pass for a miracle." In an early encounter with "Flaky," Mr. Natural turns up to ". . . sit around and talk about your problems." He instructs his friend how to overcome sexual hangups: "Whatever it is that's happening, it keeps on happening no matter what! Right?" With this enigmatic word to let it all hang out, Mr. Natural helps himself to an enormous sandwich from Flaky's refrigerator and stalks off with reminders about how grateful his friend should be for such long-suffering help. In "Mr. Natural Takes a Vacation," he is surrounded by crowds of eager fans, hoping for mystic self-realization in the form of a kick in the pants. He escapes to an inner sanctum, only to find a groupie who says, "All I want is to fulfill your needs." He performs a sexual favor for her while being interrupted by phone calls asking for redemptive advice, and when his roommate disturbs his rest that night by seeking counsel, Mr. Natural escapes to a raft, where he has ". . . only the elements to contend with."[10] Thus Crumb's effort to overcome monomythic heroism remains indebted to the tradition of the segmented superhero in a natural paradise.

The campaign to zap the tradition of selfless, renunciatory superheroes, who solve problems in Heidi style or destroy enemies with atomic pistols, develops in a more recent episode into a paranoid broadside against the Edenic dream. Crumb opens with a citation from Revelation about the battle of Armageddon and proceeds to depict current American dilemmas in grotesque fashion. John Q. Public sits bitching in front of his television set: "Three hundred years ago this was a virgin land . . . it didn't take 'em long to mess it up . . . all th' goddamn pimps, panderers, pickpockets and plutocrats." So he storms off to a topless bar to get what he's "entitled" to have. Everyone Crumb hates is pictured in suitably degenerate form–the drugged youth, the motorcycle gangs, the capitalists, the revolutionaries, and the glad-handers. After the cartoonist falls into "apathy and indifference" because his simple solutions to global problems are inadequate, he cheers up a friend by saying, "Tomorrow is gonna be a beautiful sunny day, only I'd forget about trying to get a tan . . . it ain't healthy!" The final frame has a leering figure in a "pussy wagon" with swastikas for eyes saying "Ain't it a gas!" as he runs over a fat woman. The caption reads, ". . . And that's life in Modern America!"[11]

Zap's campaign against components of the American monomyth drifts into a moral swamp where values are debased, relationships perverted, and human hopes denied. Yet Crumb and his colleagues retain an implicit belief in the efficacy of apocalyptic violence, a rigid segmentation of sex, and radical stereotyping–characteristic features of the American monomyth. Clinton R. Sanders comments on the function of these underground comics, suggesting that they provide cohesion for a ". . . group of people who feel alienated from the dominant culture and who are seeking social support for their anger and disgust . . . [providing a] . . . wall which separates the 'friends' from the 'enemies.'"[12] The depiction of such zealous stereotypes in the powerful and grotesque cartoon style of Crumb and others prepares its audience to applaud the brutal but morally justified destruction of the baddies.

The campaign to zap monomythic values was elaborated in the musical *Hair,* whose circulation and popularity surpassed most artifacts within the mainstream of the culture. Clive Barnes of the New York *Times,* a member of the very establishment skewered by the work, applauded the play: "The Kids are fun and they have a sharp-honed spontaneity and engaging honesty." The plot moves smoothly through every monomythic convention, its action beginning in an Edenic setting with an Indian totem pole, a dirt floor, and the good Tribe of the Counter Culture. The directorial instructions describe the assembly as ". . . a search for a way of life that makes sense to the young, that allows the growth of their new vision . . . to find an alternative to the unacceptable standards, goals, and morals of the older generation, the establishment." The aim of the drama is "to turn on the audience" to increased "understanding, support, and tolerance," in order to restore a troubled world to its paradisal status, thus producing ". . . a better, saner, peace-full, love-full world."[13] Except for the lack of inhibitions, one would think it was a gathering of Heidi-redeemers, inviting the audience to restore the Eden it had betrayed.

The disruption of paradise comes in the form of "Mom" and "Dad," a single pair of actors who change costumes to represent the carbon-copy villains of corrupt institutions. Dad appears as the school principal, equipped with whip and gun, while Mom loses her self-control and begins to rape Claude after lecturing him on proper values. Dad speaks for them both in expressing his pleasure that "in two months my son will be in Vietnam and is going to be killed, and I'm proud of him." Ritual cleansing of this corrupt establishment is provided when the Tribe takes up a vigilante campaign against symbols of American virtue. Custer, Grant, Teddy Roosevelt, and Abraham Lincoln are attacked by the blacks, while Le Roi Jones shouts, "I cut yo' up. I hate you and your white mothers. I hope you all die and rot. You're all for shit." The white leaders are cut down, and a happy slave sings "Emancimotherfuckin'-pater of the slave" with his foot on Lincoln's chest, followed by "Happy Birthday, Abie Baby," satirizing the Gettysburg Address.[14] These are the scenes of "fun" and "engaging honesty" calculated to turn audiences on to "peace-full . . . visions of loveliness." The stereotyping and the reliance on zealous retribution are thoroughly monomythic.

There is even a redeemer figure in *Hair:* Claude, like his monomythic counterparts, comes to the Edenic community from far away, in this instance from Manchester, England. Despite these promising origins, Claude is victimized by the establishment and forced into the Army. He is a suffering Christ-figure, casually stating, "I am the Son of God," and proclaims, "I'm going to spread it around the world brother. . . . So everybody knows what I got," namely, "hair." After the apocalypse an Edenic future is in store for his followers:

> Total beauty/ Total health
> No government and no police/ No Wars/ No Crime/ No Hate
> Just happiness and love

Claude dies before bringing the promised Eden. The only redemption he achieves before the fatal trip to Vietnam is to seduce the reluctant Sheila, alienated after being raped by Berger while the Tribe casually watches. Their refrain at his being shipped away is a powerful Werther invitation to destroy the establishment that so callously disregards the savior, whose body will be crucified in battle.[15]

Just as in the conclusions of the *Walking Tall* films, an image of innocent suffering is presented that demands vengeance. Who will come forward to fire the zap guns now?

III

If the counterculture tends to be trapped by monomythic conventions when it attempts to zap dominant cultural values, there remains a substantial majority who would defend the American monomyth as a healthy embodiment of religious ideals and democratic dreams. Millions of viewers and readers of pop materials resonate pleasurably to messages of miraculous redemption in secular as well as religious guise. One might have guessed that the churches and synagogues, as traditional custodians for salvation messages, would have sniffed out the monomyth and denounced it as a dangerous form of secularization. Their oversight is best exemplified in the ecclesiastical reaction to the religious films. During the decades following Cecil B. DeMille's classic *King of Kings,* with its powerful earthquake scene, Hollywood produced *Ben-Hur, The Robe, The Crusades, David and Bathsheba, Samson and Delilah, Sodom and Gomorrah, The Ten Commandments,* and *The Bible,* as well as many lesser-known epics. These movies portrayed the sensational and sentimental aspects of the religious tradition; yet they evoked little prophetic wrath from the churches. Coyly described as "lust in the dust" films by insiders, they evoked anger from the religious community only when they provided too much lust and too little dust. Momentarily, institutional religion saw itself bathed in electronic auras as these films appeared. Who could really carp at the enjoyment of the religious thrills that had become rare in traditional forms of worship?

Symbolizing the public's reverent faith in Hollywood's religion, the American Bicentennial Freedom Train contained no forbidding religious relics from Cotton Mather or Jonathan Edwards. But it did include the staff used by Charlton Heston while playing Moses in *The Ten Commandments,* along with Cecil B. DeMille's script. Henry Wilcoxon's helmet from *The Crusades* was included, alongside items like John Wayne's eyepatch from *True Grit*. There were no images of American religious art or architecture, but Philco's Cathedral-style radio receiver from 1935 was present. Can it be that religious sensibility has itself become monomythic, failing to recognize the pop creeds because its understanding of the biblical tradition is so closely linked with the American monomyth? John Huston's film *The Bible,* released in 1966 and given its world television premiere at Christmastime in 1975, is an instructive case.[16]

The Bible scarcely lives up to its title, as it only relates a selection of episodes from the first half of Genesis. But even these are presented monomythically, implying they are somehow typical of the whole biblical message. Screenwriter Christopher Fry regularly juxtaposes biblical quotes with his own, all unctuously intoned by director Huston, and visually cued so that monomythic messages are reinforced throughout. This process can most clearly be discerned in the episodes featuring Adam and Eve, Cain and Abel, Noah, the Tower of Babel, and Abraham.

Huston and Fry simplify the issue of man's fall in Eden, equating knowledge of good and evil with sexual pleasure. The temptress Eve, sensuously fondling the forbidden fruit and victimizing guileless Adam, single-handedly effects the downfall of the human race by leading him away into the bushes. Not even medieval pulpiteers stated it quite so baldly. Mythic alchemy is also decisive in the Cain and Abel episode. While the Bible is mysteriously silent on the reason for divine displeasure with Cain's offering, the camera reveals him greedily withholding sacrificial grain for his own basket. This cardinal flaw of selfishness establishes the stereotype that explains his becoming a murderer and fugitive.

The film then leaps eagerly forward to the story of Noah, a splendid opportunity to depict a catastrophe in the popular style. Huston casts himself as the clownish patriarch who follows the directive to build the Barnum & Bailey ark. His mocking neighbors are shown in all their sexily attired, skullbone-bejeweled, foul-mouthed degeneracy, in contrast to the piety of Noah and his family. Huston and Fry invent temptations for Noah to resist: procrastination; nocturnal labor to evade public attention; using the pitch on his own house's leaky roof; everything but bedtime invitations from Mrs. Noah. When the flood begins, Noah enjoys the wailing of the wicked in his snug ark. His wife asks if it is the sound of the wind. "No, it is the chaff which the wind driveth away," is the biblical-sounding response invented for this scene of Tertullian ecstasy. Aboard the ark, miracles of animal virtue occur. In this peaceable kingdom, carnivores drink milk, and lions lie down with lambs. After the waters have covered the earth, his family requests some sensible guidance from the helmsman, but Noah refuses to put out a rudder, apparently considering obedience to God and the use of intellect incompatible. In the happy debarkation, Noah waves a silly farewell to the animals and turns a befuddled face toward the rainbow, a gospel according to P. T. Barnum having replaced the symbol of divine covenant not to destroy the world again. But Huston and Fry refrain from depicting the biblical story of Noah's drunken revel and disgrace, which would have revealed his flawed humanity all too clearly.

In the cinematic account of the Tower of Babel, a strutting King Nimrod, berouged and surrounded by degenerates, stands at the top of his proud tower and defiantly shoots an arrow heavenward—an incident found nowhere in Scripture. But it provides a retributive explanation of the avenging wind that destroys the rigging, hurls people to earth, and leaves the King impotent. In contrast, the Book of Genesis relates a more sober account of nationalistic pride on the part of the Babylonians: "Come, let us build ourselves a tower with its top in the heavens, and let us make a name for ourselves . . ." (Gn. 11:4). The resultant alienation of competing tongues and tribes embodies insights considerably more relevant to America in 1966 than this monomythic farce. A nation that has for decades made a fetish of its skyscrapers, while being mired in a war of pride in Asia, might have reflected critically upon its enterprises, rather than fantasizing that Babylon fell because of a fag King.

The film's culmination is the story of Abraham, a righteous superhero, portrayed, in the absence of Charlton Heston, by George C. Scott. Virtually every monomythic theme is introduced in this interminable episode. Anachronistically spouting passages from the Song of Songs, Ava Gardner, in the role of his wife Sarah, seduces Abraham; such aggressive lust implicitly explains the punishment of her barrenness. When Abraham must bed down with the ravishing Hagar to produce an heir, his stoic devotion to duty is edifying. When he wages war to free his captive nephew, he dispatches enemies with superheroic efficiency. The divine emissaries then roam the streets of Sodom to find the ten righteous men requisite for God's mercy. They encounter scenes of appalling perversion: whips crack; women scream; a reluctant maiden is forced to submit to a rapist goat, thus fixing the theme of feminine victimization. When an atomic holocaust destroys Sodom, as in all catastrophe films because of sexual offenses, the audience has been well prepared to welcome this divine retribution.

The climax of the Abraham story features the superhero's renunciation of affection, obeying the command to sacrifice Isaac. Huston and Fry invent a tirade on the theme of righteous retribution, which Abraham delivers while passing through Sodom and Gomorrah on the way to the mountain. He is at the point of applying the knife to his son as vultures wheel overhead, when Isaac is delivered in the nick of time by the voice of God. The film cribs a few lines from Isaiah, written a thousand years after Abraham's time, as God says, "Behold, I have tried thee like metal in a furnace. I have chosen thee in a furnace of affliction." Lapsing back into Genesis with unvarying tabernacular tones, the voice continues, "Now will I multiply thy seed as the stars of the heaven, as the sand which is by the seashore, innumerable." Thus a biblical story of tested faith becomes monomythic drama in which the righteous are predictably rewarded and the wicked punished. A divine agency redeems the innocent from death on schedule after they renounce the claims of affection.

Religious audiences accepted the monomythic *Bible* as if it somehow distilled scriptural truth. The film was welcomed as innocuous, according to the *Christian Advocate*'s reviewer; "Children won't be harmed by it—that's something."[17] Thus a religious tradition that might suitably stand in judgment on the new electronic creed falls prey to its spell.

Defenders of the monomyth are also to be found at the highest levels of the literary and academic communities. In a recent *Horizon* essay, for example, Walter Karp asserts that cowboy Westerns are repositories for democratic values. "In the Western the old republican spirit lives on in a kind of suspended animation. . . . It is Republicanism turned into ritual." He suggests that Americans like Westerns because they ". . . want to see the bright stage of an American polis where each life touches all lives, where each person's actions affect the common fate, where everyone is a citizen and everybody matters. That is a free man's ideal." Karp admits that the central convention of the Western is redemption by the lone cowboy but defends it because the public is impotent to deal with tyranny and corruption. The "good" people in the Westerns are not pictured as "repositories of virtue," he writes:

> They attend citizens meetings at the church and wring their hands in dismay, but they cannot rid themselves . . . of the usurper. . . . Yet they cannot accept servility either, for they are free men. . . . Their haplessness embodies a profound and rather

> bleak political truth. Machiavelli, in his *Discourse on Livy,* insisted that a truly corrupted republic cannot save itself by its own exertions. There is simply not enough civic virtue left in such a republic to restore the reign of civic virtue.

Karp suggests that the Western plots embody a ". . . Madisonian skepticism, the refusal to rely on, or even believe in, men of high public virtue . . ." and that the public expects the cowboy redeemer to have a private motive for his action. "He wreaks ruthless private vengeance, and the town, as a result, is set free"[18]; so public quibbling is really out of order.

This is truly a strange version of democracy from so sophisticated a mind. Karp has accepted the premises of the monomyth almost to the same degree as *Hair* and *Zap*. Despite his erudite and historical language, his essay reveals the yearning for monomythic redemption. In citing Machiavelli's contention that a truly corrupted republic cannot save itself, he implies that political salvation is attainable. His claim that ". . . only through violence and insurrection can free men rid themselves of entrenched corruption" makes it sound as if vigilantism actually ushers in a "reign of virtue." Behind this conclusion lies the acceptance of the "goodguy" and "badguy" stereotypes that precede redemptive destruction. Karp disparages the possibility of collective responsibility or constitutional limitations, reducing democracy essentially to a public yearning for violent redemption. His emphasis on the lone redeemer seems directly contradictory to the republican ideals of ". . . each person's action affecting the common fate, where everybody is a citizen and everybody matters." In this version of the "free man's ideal" the public becomes a passive spectator, while the cowboy "wreaks vengeance." The Western veils these antidemocratic implications so effectively that many academic Penelopes would have to work overtime to unravel its technomythic confusions.[19]

IV

In contrast to the defenders of monomythic redemption, we contend that the American monomyth is an escapist fantasy. It encourages passivity on the part of the general public and unwise concentrations of power in ostensible redeemers. It betrays the ideals of democratic responsibility and denies the reliance on human intelligence that is basic to the democratic hope.

As a first step in understanding this escapist fantasy, we turn to Freud's suggestion about the wish-fulfilling function of art. Normal daydreams, he suggested, have crude qualities that compel a person to shield them from critical examination. Artists have the peculiar genius of elaborating daydreams in such a way that they lose their personal, grating character. An artist draws upon unfulfilled cravings from his own experience that are widely shared by his audience, providing vicarious gratification and momentary relief from troubling conditions. "In fantasy," Freud writes, ". . . man can continue to enjoy a freedom from the grip of the external world, one which he has long relinquished in actuality." The relevance of this insight is visible when one turns to a recent artist's explanation of his audience appeal. Clint Eastwood, one of the superstars who enacts the role of the cool, violent redeemer, says, ". . . It's not the bloodletting or whatever that people come to see in the movies. It's vengeance. Getting even is very important with the public. They go to work every day for some guy who's rude and they . . . have to take it. Then they go see me on the screen and I just kick the shit out of him."[20] Assuming Eastwood is correct, his screen action amounts to a vicarious gratification for audience members who confront abuses of power in real life. Since they are afraid to cope with such situations on their own initiative, they gain a sense of release through seeing Eastwood do it for them. This allows them to avoid the nasty business of taking responsibility for their own justice.

There is a peculiar logic to the political daydream in which daily ambiguities and struggles "east of Eden" are redeemed by a fantasy in which total solutions are offered. The monomyth instructs both the public and the superhero how to respond to evil, and their actions are thought to become effective when properly ritualized. There is a vast contrast here with Western culture's distinctive approach to responsibility as embodied, for instance, in the writing of Karl Kraus. It assumes that creative responses are dictated by novel circumstances, while each is held accountable both for actions and consequences.

Ritualized, monomythic responsibility begins when evil is denied within oneself or one's group and projected outward. That the "other side" alone is guilty of evil is conveyed by conventions of character and plot, assisted by subtle devices of mythic cuing. Just as the spectator democracy is not held responsible for causing evil in monomythic drama, it is not called upon to cope with it. Since the monomyth depicts the public as devoid of creative intelligence, its laws and institutions as incorrigibly corrupt, and evil as immensely powerful, the task of coping is transferred to redeemer figures.

Superheroes possess powers unattainable by others, and are capable of resisting stylized temptations to forsake their redemptive tasks. Repressing their own needs, the heroic figures act only in response to external provocation, never in expression of their own desires. They accept the ritualized responsibility of the duel forced upon them by incorrigible foes, or the communal dilemmas that only their manipulative wisdom can solve. Fate works in behalf of the violent heroes, so that villains are generally destroyed by their own attempts to perpetrate wickedness or escape apprehension. The community's inability to act ensures that it bears no guilt for the redemptive violence. There are no dirty hands in paradise. But when redemption comes in Heidi-style, the solutions are so clean and desirable that there is no need for such mythical conventions, though they tend to be carried over from the more dominant genre of the violent hero. A frequent motif is the redeemer's lack of community with those he rescues, which prevents their sometimes unsavory methods from staining the City Set upon a Hill. Moreover, superheroes are too large to be integrated with any merely human community, and their mission prevents permanent sexual or familial responsibilities. Families are too demanding to accommodate redemptive crusades, and parenthood permanently jeopardizes the guise of perfect wisdom or competence. Sex is inescapably selfish to some degree, thus threatening the credibility of selfless superheroes who transcend normal needs. Therefore, the typical monomythic hero departs in a ritual fashion once the mission is accomplished: Mary Poppins flies away, Superman becomes the despicable Clark Kent, and the cowboy disappears over the horizon.

In summarizing these features of monomythic heroism, one can understand why Gerbner and Gross suggested that television violence, in addition to inspiring imitative behavior on the part of some, might have the predominant effect of encouraging passivity. "Fear may be a more critical concomitant of a show of violence than aggression. . . . Acceptance of violence and passivity in the face of injustice may be consequences of great social concern."[21] Given the requirements of the redeemer role–total selflessness, sexual renunciation, isolation from the community, and cool courage in face of impossible odds–very few are audacious enough to respond directly to Werther invitations. The rest are taught to applaud passively from the grandstand, convinced they are too impotent to cope with evil. Monomythic drama has the character of a tranquilizer, exchanging the sense of communal alarm and obligation for a fantasy of Edenic resolution achievable only by superhumans.

The effect of this monomythic copout is to encourage the very centralization of power that democratic theorists have considered to be the greatest potential danger to the political order. Superhuman leaders in monomythic dramas are granted unlimited powers to accomplish the impossible task of restoring paradise. They can make and enforce the laws as they see fit, like Kirk in his powerful starship, without waiting for the cumbersome voice of a democratic majority. They can evade due process of law like Paul Kersey, and command brutal powers of coercion like Buford Pusser. Symbolic of this careless concentration of power in the hands of superheroes is the sale of Buck Rogers' atomic pistols to comic-book readers after the Second World War so that in fantasy each could zap his enemies with force as destructive as that used against Hiroshima and Nagasaki, all for the sake of an Edenic "peace."

The question of who should be entrusted with such incredible power is answered by the monomythic conventions about the selfless superhero, but democratic theorists would pose decisive objections. As Karl Popper has suggested, democratic thinkers shun the traditional and authoritarian question "Who should rule?"–in current slang, "Who should zap?"–because it presupposes we can identify the "good ones." Experience indicates it is very difficult to find persons in whom total powers can be entrusted, and our most perceptive tradition about human nature informs us that power inevitably corrupts. Therefore, Popper argues, ". . . we must ask whether . . . we should not prepare for the worst leaders, and hope for the best." He suggests replacing the question of who should be empowered with "How can we so organize political institutions that bad or incompetent rulers can be prevented from doing too much damage?"[22] The answer for the American constitutional system lies in finding ways to check power rather than hoping that superheroic force will somehow redeem a "corrupt republic." One-man crusades against evil, so perfectly exemplified in the American monomyth, hardly qualify as standing within the tradition of democratic sentiment.

The results of surrendering personal responsibility to savior figures are evident in some of the greatest tragedies of the twentieth century. Ernest Becker has called such surrender "The Demonic" of our time. By this he refers to those tendencies of human action that defeat the possibility for survival and the equitable development of human potential.

> In the realm of human affairs, The Demonic is real. It is engendered by the acts of men, or better . . . by the *failure* of men to act. Specifically, it comes into being when men fail to act *individually* and *willfully,* on the basis of their own *personal, responsible* powers. The Demonic refers specifically to the creation of power by groups of men who blindly follow authority and convention, power which engulfs them and defeats them.

Democracy attempts to cope with The Demonic by envisioning each person as "an end in himself and a responsible, self-reliant point of authority to which power leaders and power institutions are beholden." In particular, democracy fears those entrusted with power: "It knew that the leader had to be controlled by responsible and willful masses of men, precisely because he will be corrupted by power into making decisions that are self-defeating. Whether he knows it or not, or admits it or not, the leader needs to be curbed, needs the broadest base of self-limiting decisions."[23]

A basis in traditional democratic theory for the limitation of power was a belief in the diffusion of intelligence among the citizenry. Individuals acting on their own judgments could assert a collective responsibility superior in wisdom to the inspirations of individual saviors. Without denying that democracy often fails to live according to its own mythic heritage, one can clearly see that the monomyth betrays deep antagonism toward the creative exercise of reason on the part of the public as well as the individual. Careful deliberation, knowledge of law, and mastery of book learning are usually presented in monomythic materials as indicators of impotence or corruption. In the exercise of redemptive power, purity of intention suffices. Heroes are either static, innately possessing all the wisdom they need, or they learn all they require from a single incident. The public and its representatives are pictured as too stupid to survive confrontations with evil. Even Lassie, Flipper, Benji, and Herbie the Volkswagen are pictured as possessing the moral wisdom lacking in the democratic community.

So hostile is monomythic material to individual intelligence that one of its most durable conventions is to use "brains" as a distinguishing trait of evil persons. In his study of comic superheroes, Oswald Wiener noted that intelligence is normally presented as a violation of the principle of equality—not the principle of equality before the law, but the leveling equality of mediocrity. Whenever intelligence exceeds the norm of mediocrity, ". . . this evil superiority must be compensated for: through hatefulness, through weaknesses, and through despicable and weakening neuroses."[24] Wiener cites numerous supervillains marked by the stereotype of intellect: Egghead, Brainiac, Brainstorm, Madthinker, and others. The mad, wicked scientist is now a standard figure in science fiction and children's cartoons, appearing for instance on *Superfriends* with the line, "I want to use my device 'X'—to rule the world!" The only acceptable form of science, it seems, is in the service of redeemer figures, who rarely possess any intellectual abilities. Isolated from the radiance of the superheroic aura, intellect is presented as simply a power for amplifying evil.

In summary, the American monomyth rejects democratic values at a number of crucial points. It conveys a pessimism about democratic institutions and public responsibilities, a messianic expectation that society can be redeemed by a single stroke, and an impatience with constitutional processes. In its repeated celebration of the evasion of collective responsibility, the monomyth has become a ritual of The Demonic. So skillful, so eloquent and moving are its materials that they are probably the most effective sources of the erosion of democratic credibility today. Conscious attacks by antidemocratic propagandists seem sporadic, stupid, and ineffective by comparison.

V

One of the pathological features of the American monomyth is its endorsement of sexual segmentation. In films like *Jaws* and *Earthquake,* the presence of temptresses provided the occasion for the repressive channeling of love into violent retribution. In *Death Wish* we saw the transformation of sexual impulses into the retributive revolver of the vigilante. This theme was inverted by the counterculture in the motto, "Make love, not war!" *Zap Comics* and its underground bedfellows constantly stress that the violent ills of the WASP establishment result from sexual repression. In Zap's initial "Whiteman" episode, for instance, the middle-aged, white protagonist confesses that "my real self deep down inside . . . craves only one thing! SEX! I'm so virile! (slurp) I read *Playboy!* (drool)." Everywhere Whiteman goes he reveals a contemptible and dangerous obsession with the reality he attempts to control. He walks down the street saying, "Got to get a grip on myself! I'm a grown man! An intelligent adult! With responsibilities! I'm an American! . . . A real hard charger! Step aside, buddy!" He aggressively pushes someone off the sidewalk, then finds himself caught in a traffic jam, exclaiming, "I need a drink! Oh, no! Here it comes again! . . . Those illicit desires! Only . . . choke. This time it isn't sex! This time it's something horrible! . . . I want to . . . KILL, destroy, cut, slice, maim!"[25]

Zap's protest against the pathology of sexual repression, linking it with stereotypical forms of violence, does not reduce brutality but extends it into sex itself. In a "Wonder Wart-Hog" episode, there is an attempt to satirize the Superman fantasy, with its complete repression of sexual gratification. The alter ego of the grotesque Wonder Wart-Hog is Philbert Desanex, a mild-mannered reporter for the *Morning Mungpie.* Like Clark Kent, his frustrations arise from thwarted passions for Lois Lamebrain's Playmate body. As "Hog-vision" allows him to fantasize her eight-breasted nude body, Philbert muses, "Ignore *me,* will you? What if I ripped off my Philbert Desanex disguise and said, 'I'm Wonder Wart-Hog! Let's fuck!" Aware of Philbert's interest, Lois prefers he wouldn't stare so much: "He's so uncool!" After failing to get a scoop, the frustrated Philbert discovers Lois in the stockroom and makes a pass. Realizing his Wonder Wart-Hog identity, she faints and he undresses her. When she awakens, she mocks his organ. "Ha Ha Ha Ha Ha Your 'thing!' It's all little and curly like a piggie's tail!" The angered superhog says, "Well, I can still use my *snout.*" He inserts the ten-inch, nobbed proboscis to the accompaniment of brutal captions like "Snort, Rip, Root, Ravage." When he sneezes, Lois's body is blown to pieces. In the final scene, the editor lambastes the hapless reporter. "Desanex, where have you been? You missed the news story of the century! The nude body of Lois Lamebrain was mysteriously found in the middle of a downtown street, literally blown apart at the seams!"[26]

In this story, sexual hangups are transcended in that desires are not repressed, but the outcome hardly overcomes sexual segmentation. In the place of sexual union there is savage retribution against a woman who rejects the advances of a repulsive hero. Wonder Wart-Hog may not be meant as anything more than bubble-gum entertainment for an audience enjoying a little explicit sexuality, but in attempting to improve upon the attitudes of its repressive culture, *Zap*'s images make one prefer a little Puritan restraint. The casual mutilation of a sexual partner, even in mere cartoon imagery, promises little in the way of liberation. Yet this form of liberation has now become habitual in underground materials where rape, torture, and murder are presented with gleeful nonchalance.

In 1929 Aldous Huxley wrote an essay, "Fashions in Love," describing the death of the taboos surrounding sex. He concluded, "Love has ceased to be the rather fearful mysterious thing it was, and becomes a perfectly normal, almost commonplace activity. . . . A strenuous offensive against the old taboos and repressions is everywhere in progress." But Huxley, certainly no prude, posed the question, "What new or what revived mythology will serve to create those restraints without which sexual impulse cannot be transformed into love?"[27] Huxley penned these hopeful lines at the beginning of the axial period for the development of the American monomyth. But far from encouraging transformations into love, it has created new restraints against sexual integration. In this respect the monomyth and its countercultural inversions are more ferocious in the rejection of human affections than Puritanism, which always retained an ideal of married love.

Without attempting the difficult task of creating alternative myths, we should indicate some of the sexual values omitted in monomythic vision. The most conspicuous and perhaps most logical omission is the experience of intimacy. In sexual love the "two become one flesh," overcoming their lonely separateness. Mutual responsiveness, trust, and sharing that can grow out of permanent sexual relationships are among the most commonly sought values in human experience. That the institution of marriage, a permanent covenant to secure such values, proves durable in spite of its current pressures is evidence of the persistent yearning for such experiences. Successful channeling of sexuality is doubtless the key to creativity in the lives of many persons. As Rollo May suggests, "Eros is the drive toward union with what we belong to–union with our own possibilities, union with significant other persons . . . in relation to whom we discover our own self-fulfillment."[28]

Monomythic heroes suppress their needs in order to achieve a selfless perfection that lacks any need for personal fulfillment. They display a static personality structure, lacking need for development and thus transcending the nurturing values of sexuality. Furthermore, the achievement of redemption through destruction or manipulation sidesteps procreative and companionate dimensions that usually accompany the attainment of realistic goals. Monomythic heroism is marked by nullification rather than creation. Charles Manson, who styled himself in the heroic mold of an exterminating angel, felt that sexual gratification was subordinate to his mission. If one can believe his words, he said that his sexual relationships became a means of cultivating the loyalty of disciples. "I don't need broads. Every woman I ever had, *she* asked *me* to make love to her. I never asked them. I can do without them." Manson had internalized the monomythic ideal of sexual segmentation, providing some justification for his accusation against American culture that "I am what you have made of me."[29]

VI

Despite the distortions of the monomyth, its vision may contain important fragments of truth. Its hostility toward human sexuality conveys the awareness that love often takes tragic and destructive forms. As Rollo May puts it, ". . . Sexual love has the power to propel human beings into situations which can destroy not only themselves but . . . other people. . . ."[30] He mentions the mythic figures of Helen and Paris, Tristan and Iseult as embodiments of the insight that sexual love can ". . . seize man and woman and lift them up into a whirlwind which defies and destroys rational control." In compelling attention to the danger of neglecting responsibilities for gratification and of sexual exploitation, the monomyth's partial insights deserve to be taken with some seriousness.

The monomythic concern for human evil must also be incorporated into any realistic grappling with the problems of community. Its failures lie in the partial identification of who is evil, its melodramatic exaggeration of evil traits, its facile belief in selective punishment, and the assignment of a retributive role to nature and to superheroes. Monomythic materials overplay the role of conspiracy in accounting for evil, overlooking the propensities within each member of the chosen community.

The yearning for figures larger than life mirrors the eternal need for leaders who will stand forth and assume lonely and unpopular tasks. The monomyth smudges this point by depicting leaders who win universal acclamation by the completion of their task. The anti-elitist bias, expressed through the hint that anyone can become a superhero, embodies a respect for widely distributed human potential, a worthy democratic theme. But the type of leadership a democracy requires does not promise total solutions but undertakes the more limited human task of coping. As Reinhold Niebuhr suggested, democracy is a system offering "proximate solutions for insoluble problems." Basic human dilemmas and conflicts cannot be eliminated by a process of destructive purgation.[31]

The monomythic convention of allowing the redeemer to disappear from the redeemed community is perhaps a sad recognition that ". . . no prophet is acceptable in his own country" (Lk. 4:24). The deaths by assassination of so many American leaders and the constant effort by some to torture those who attain distinction suggest that heroic stature is an affront to the impotent few whose sense of significance stems from destructive urges. The classical monomyth was somewhat more promising at this point because it allowed reintegration into the hero's community at the conclusion of his adventure.

Finally, the Edenic inclinations of the monomyth point toward the human need for intimate relationships with the forces of nature, requiring a balance between the demands of urban, industrial life and the sustenance of the physical environment. The difficulty lies in the lack of balance in monomythic vision. In his essay "Nature Nostalgia and the City," John McDermott shows that the mixture of the urban, the pastoral, and the primitive in America's yearning for paradise results in falsifying the essential qualities of each:

> . . . We lament the city as being without nature. On the other hand, the nature . . . , about which we are nostalgic, is stripped of its most forbidding qualities; loneliness, unpredictability, and the terrors of the uninhabitable. . . . For the most part, the nature envisioned by urban and suburban man is one that has been domesticated by the very qualities of the city which we take to be unnatural. . . . Under the press of nostalgia, however, we strip both nature and city of ambivalence, in a bizarre reversal of the wilderness and paradise theme.[32]

McDermott forcibly reminds us that the American monomyth blocks the celebration of experiences that make urban life attractive and locks its adherents into a nostalgic yearning that can never be satisfied.

Reviewing the elements of truth in the monomyth compels the recognition that it has valid roots in experience, however selective or partial its interpretation. It is unlikely that a powerful fantasy could otherwise arise and be sustained through generations. Even slender shreds of evidence confer credibility when shaped by the wish of the faithful and the eloquence of technomythic presentation. So believable does the monomythic creed remain that its mere recital renders most improbable statements credible. It seems to immunize audiences to any sort of critical response. Ronald Reagan, for example, has given a speech for years in which he declares that Washington has become as much a foreign threat for Americans as the London of 1776. "The coils woven in that city are entrapping us all, and, as with the Gordian knot, we cannot untie it. We have to cut it with one blow of the sword." The ending of *The Birth of a Nation* seems lodged in his consciousness as the appropriate way to deal with grand conspiracies. In his announcement of presidential candidacy for 1976, Reagan diagnosed the "Gordian knot" tied through "a buddy system that functions for its own benefit. . . ." The solution lies in choosing ". . . leaders who are independent of the forces that brought us our problems: the Congress, the bureaucracy, the lobbyists, big business, and big labor." As John Nordheimer noted, "It was obvious he viewed himself as a man not sullied by long years in Washington, an outsider not trapped by the 'buddy system.' " Even Jimmy Carter, who usually exhibits a greater sense of complexity, fell into the monomythic rhetoric at campaign time, attacking the ". . . confused, bloated, bureaucratic mess in Washington. . . . I'm not a member of Congress, so I'm not responsible for letting that horrible mess develop."[33]

This sort of selfless, heroic stance is so commonplace that it is echoed constantly by the New Left. In a "Nuttin' but Nuttin' " episode of *Zap,* Mr. Natural enters a presidential campaign in opposition to "Oscar Myer, the Wiener Czar." "The story behind the Oscar Myer power grab involves a series of manipulations by the General Motors group. This ambitious midget must be stopped," proclaims cartoonist Crumb. Another opponent is Mr. Zip, "Big Brother himself!," whose words are "I promise to stamp out misfits, creeps, and slobs!" A KKK candidate is pictured next. But the final frame of the campaign sequence provides mythic, wish-fulfilling assurances. "But don't worry! Mr. Natural's gonna be campaigning too!" He is depicted being carried about in a bathtub with the shower on and a sign stating, "Here's Mr. Natural with today's health tip" as he spouts unprintables. He is clean despite his profane language because he has nothing to hide. He has not been corrupted by "buddies" or special interests. Monomythic politics makes strange bathfellows as Ronald Reagan and Jimmy Carter play Mr. Natural with origins in the clean, redemptive region beyond the wicked city. Another amusing example of monomythic expectations for the American presidency is Mrs. Betty Ford's report of public reactions to the disclosure that she and the President share the same bedroom. Letters arrived ". . . from all across the country from people who feel it's very immoral for us to be using the same bedroom. . . . I guess if you're President, that part of your life is–I guess you're supposed to become a eunuch."[34]

In a more somber vein, former President Nixon spoke of the need to "rekindle spiritual growth . . . to knit our people together" during the Bicentennial year. But he was pessimistic about achieving such unity without the threat of a foreign attack. "We are so cynical, so disbelieving–that it may take the shock of an invasion–in Korea or in Thailand. If American lives are threatened, we may regain our sense of belief in our country and our need for strength. We are a compromised country at the moment." The call to Demonic integration was never more casually issued or blandly received. Nixon concluded the December 1975 interview with comments on President Ford that confirm this vision of public surrender of responsibility: ". . . He's okay. Right now, he is too accessible. A congress or a parliament can paralyze leadership. You can't get caught up in absurdities."[35] Thus the yearning of The Virginian and his admirers to provide redemption outside the constitutional system lives on among those who have exercised the highest levels of authority. Democratic values seem absurd when they impede the resurrection of pride through zealous crusades.

VII

Gazing at the American monomyth and its effects is admittedly a disturbing experience. Once its electronic radiance has been dimmed through critical short-circuitry, the mood of entertainment passes, and one feels a sinister presence. It is therefore tempting to embark on a zapping crusade as Frederick Wertham did during the 1950s in his campaign against comic books.[36] The result of that crusade, in fact, was the codification of monomythic values in the Comics Code Authority, whose conventions paralleled those of the movie industry. Its "Seal of Approval" on a comic book dealing with serious themes was a guarantee that tales of miraculous victories over powers of pure evil were to be found within. The belief that "badness" could be purged from comic books by a single stroke was thoroughly monomythic. But the American mythic system is not the result of a conspiracy localized in a guilty few whose behavior can be controlled by law. Most Americans, including ourselves, have resonated to the articulation of the monomyth and feel the pull of its assumptions even when attempting to reject them. The seductive appeal, even after one discounts its escapist elements, is rooted in a form of moral idealism, developed through generations of popular creation and restatement. It is foolish to believe that monomythic values can quickly be dispelled.

The American monomyth is one of those vexing issues that calls for the virtues of democratic coping rather than redemptive crusading or "problem solving." It requires a public examination of popular materials with all the critical intelligence that can be mustered. There is sufficient common sense even among those indoctrinated by the monomyth to make a careful diagnosis possible. New forms of technomythic criticism are needed to discern and evaluate the messages so glamorously displayed in popular materials, sensitizing audiences to the new forms of mythic eloquence, and providing rabbit tests for the gestation of Werther effects.

In carrying out this task, we should be aware that other nations have crucial insights to contribute and a vital stake in the outcome. Popular American entertainments have increasingly become international commodities. Between 1960 and 1970, nearly eighty countries introduced television systems; ninety-five countries now import serialized programs. Heroes like Mannix, Perry Mason, Kojak, Cannon, Porky Pig, and Mickey Mouse reach some four hundred million people in both industrialized and developing countries. British film critic David Robinson reports these words from a fellow countryman: "Everybody likes American films, but with me, things British often irritate me, whereas for anything American, I feel an unreasoned, impassioned loyalty such as one is usually supposed to have for the land of one's birth." Other foreign observers are responding more critically, in some instances with insights unlikely to be suggested by Americans habituated to the world of the monomyth. For instance, *Der Spiegel* printed articles about catastrophe films like *Jaws* that reflected an awareness of mythic elements overlooked by most American reviewers.[37] The tempering of the American monomyth will be easier if we can escape the provincialism to which we are prone and begin to look into the mirror others can hold up for us.

It is a sobering thought that America is spreading its monomyth to the rest of the planet through the powerful new technomythic media. It is also sobering to note that a new era of international vigilantism coincides with the international dispersion of monomythic artifacts. Crime rates in the United States are mounting in a way parallel to acts of idealistic piracy and terrorism elsewhere. In many lands there is a paralysis of political responsibility accompanied by curiously passive and nostalgic publics. Violent redemption is promised by masked gunmen, whether Japanese, Palestinian, German, or American, in a worldwide pattern of monomythic behavior. Friedrich Hacker, an Austrian who has practiced psychiatry in Los Angeles, commented about international patterns in the justification of violent aggression.

> Never before was mankind so inventive in preparing and refining symbols of its enemies and in producing and intensifying its feelings of clear conscience. . . . Everywhere and always, everyone is fully justified, whether in the ruling palaces or underground, whether in seats of power or in the slums, on every continent, in the First, Second, and Third Worlds.

Hacker believes that the mass media have popularized this verbal weaponry that now endangers the world. The media rationalize unlimited violence through the conviction that the enemy's evil requires his extermination and that of any other person who can conveniently be reached. He concludes that ". . . the secret message of the mass media" inspires destructive heroics on a worldwide scale. It is as if Joseph Campbell's "hero" has become an anonymous killer in search of an enemy "with a thousand faces."[38] We suspect that further studies would confirm connections between the new forms of international terrorism and the American export of monomythic entertainments.

Sifting through monomythic materials, one encounters the traditional notion that America somehow has a responsibility to the rest of the world. This is no moment to discard that belief, though we would insist that the attempt to act on it should take democratic forms. The critical evaluation of America's role as an international purveyor of mythic fantasies calls for the "fearlessness of revision" referred to by Whitehead. But it should be combined with "a reverence for symbols"[39] which recognizes that the monomyth has roots in centuries of creative American dreaming. Ultimately the monomyth will have to be temperately reshaped by those who have enjoyed and fully understood its appeals. We must discard its skepticism about merely human agencies and its preference for final solutions. Above all, coping with the monomyth demands creators and performers who understand the implications it contains and resolve to give their work a more responsible content. The same technomythic means that have given the monomythic premises their credibility can be turned to the celebration of democratic and sexually integrated alternatives. But we should avoid the illusion that we shall ever live entirely without myths or transcend the human condition of "seeing through a glass darkly." Democracy has its own necessary myths concerning the wisdom of the majority, the efficacy of individual reason, the enhancement of due process, and the advancement of equality. Even these hallowed myths of democracy must be subject to public scrutiny. Rather than yearning for a final vision that contains the whole truth, we must move through mythic sifting and renewal toward insights capable of sustaining life and love on a planet that seems to spin ever more fatefully. It is not too late in history to hope for an abundance of entertainments worthy of a free society entering our experience "like a breeze bearing health from happy regions."[40]

Notes

Introduction

1. "Welcome Home, Jaime," ABC (Jan. 14 and 21, 1976).
2. John G. Cawelti, *The Six-gun Mystique* (Bowling Green: Bowling Green University Popular Press, 1971), pp. 12, 28.
3. Joseph Campbell, *The Hero with a Thousand Faces* (New York: Meridian, 1956), p. 30.
4. See McLuhan's chapter "The Medium Is the Message," in *Understanding Media: The Extensions of Man* (New York: McGraw-Hill, 1964) and his book with Quentin Fiore, *The Medium Is the Massage* (New York: Random House, 1967).
5. Harvey Cox, *The Seduction of the Spirit: The Use and Misuse of People's Religion* (New York: Simon and Schuster, Touchstone Book, 1973), p. 267.

Chapter I

1. David Gerrold, *The World of Star Trek* (New York: Ballantine, 1973), p. 222.
2. Interview with Joseph Thesken, *The Press Democrat* (Santa Rosa, Calif., July 30, 1975); in a similar vein, Gene Roddenberry discussed ". . . the near fanatical cult that continues to follow the series. . . ." He described his reactions to the *Star Trek* conventions: "It is scary to be surrounded by a thousand people asking questions as if the events in the series actually happened" (Sioux City *Journal,* March 31, 1976).
3. Herbert J. Gans, *Popular Culture and High Culture : An Analysis and Evaluation of Taste* (New York: Basic Books, 1974), sent. 2, p. 32; sent. 5, p. ix; sent. 6, p. x; sent. 7, p. 35.
4. Sent. 4, ibid., pp. 33–34; sent. 6, Donald T. Lunde, *Murder and*

Madness (Stanford: Stanford Alumni Association, 1975), p. 1; sent. 7–8, Gans, *Popular Culture,* p. 51.

5. Ibid., pp. 57–58.
6. Sent. 2, Jacqueline Lichtenberg, Sondra Marshak, and Joan Winston, *Star Trek Lives!* (New York: Bantam, 1975), p. 50; sent. 6–7, ibid., pp. 78–79.
7. Sent. 3, Stephen E. Whitfield and Gene Roddenberry, *The Making of Star Trek* (New York: Ballantine, 1968), p. 256; sent. 6–11, Gerrold, *World of Star Trek* (New York: Ballantine, 1973), p. 32; sent. 12, Gerrold, loc. cit.
8. Sent. 2, ibid., pp. 222, 251; caps, parenthesis, and italics in original; sent. 4, ibid., p. 6; sent. 5, cf. Robert Jewett, *The Captain America Complex: The Dilemma of Zealous Nationalism* (Philadelphia: Westminster, 1973); sent. 7–8, David Halberstam, *The Best and the Brightest* (New York: Random House, 1972); Lichtenberg, Marshak, and Winston, *Star Trek Lives!,* p. 40.
9. Sent. 4–5, ibid., p. 99; sent. 12, Gerrold, *World of Star Trek,* p. 257; sent. 13–14, Lichtenberg, Marshak, and Winston, *Star Trek Lives!,* p. 100; sent. 15–16, Gerrold, *World of Star Trek,* p. 256.
10. Richard Slotkin, *Regeneration Through Violence: The Mythology of the American Frontier, 1600–1860* (Middletown: Wesleyan University Press, 1973), pp. 14–24.
11. Sent. 5–6, Brian Ball, *Space Guardians* (New York: Pocket Books, 1975), p. 74; sent. 9, ibid., p. 66.
12. Sent. 5, Joseph Campbell, *The Hero with a Thousand Faces* (New York: Meridian, 1956), p. 387; sent. 7–8, Campbell, loc. cit.; sent. 10, cf. James Blish, *Star Trek 7* (New York: Bantam Books, 1972), pp. 1–27; story by Gilbert A. Ralston and Gene L. Coon. The narrative of Blish's adaptation of this *Star Trek* episode has been summarized. Blish's dialogue differs only in minor details from the actual television program.
13. Erich von Daniken, *Chariots of the Gods* (New York: Bantam Books, 1971).
14. Sent. 2–3, Gerrold, *World of Star Trek,* p. 48; italics in original; sent. 7, Whitfield and Roddenberry, *Making of Star Trek,* p. 213.
15. Sent. 4, Campbell, *Hero with a Thousand Faces,* p. 101; sent. 7, Whitfield and Roddenberry, *Making of Star Trek,* p. 23; sent. 8, ibid., p. 202.
16. Sent. 7, Campbell, *Hero with a Thousand Faces,* p. 121; sent. 8, ibid., p. 109.
17. Sent. 5–7, Whitfield and Roddenberry, *Making of Star Trek,* p. 217; sent. 9–13, Lichtenberg, Marshak, and Winston, *Star Trek Lives!,* p. 41; sent. 15, ibid., p. 151.
18. Ibid., p. 80.

19. Sent. 5–11, Ball, *Space Guardians,* p. 113; sent. 15–18, ibid., p. 133; sent. 21–24, pp. 134–35, ibid.
20. Sent. 8, Ernest Lee Tuveson, *Redeemer Nation: The Idea of America's Millennial Role* (Chicago: The University of Chicago Press, 1968); sent. 12, Gerrold, *World of Star Trek,* p. 251.
21. Lichtenberg, Marshak, and Winston, *Star Trek Lives!,* p. 74; italics in original.
22. Sent. 2–3, Ball, *Space Guardians,* p. 11; sent. 6, ibid., p. 140.
23. Sent. 5, James Blish, *Star Trek 8* (New York: Bantam Books, 1972), screenplay by Lee Cronin, p. 5; sent. 10, ibid., p. 9; sent. 13, ibid., p. 30. See note 12, above.
24. Sent. 2, Whitfield and Roddenberry, *Making of Star Trek,* p. 43; sent. 3, ibid., p. 380; sent. 4, ibid., p. 383; Lichtenberg, Marshak, and Winston, *Star Trek Lives!,* p. 1; sent. 5–8, ibid., p. 47; sent. 10–11, ibid., pp. 203, 170.
25. Karl Popper, *Conjectures and Refutations* (New York: Harper & Row, 1968), p. 127.
26. Sent. 3, 8–9, Lichtenberg, Marshak, and Winston, *Star Trek Lives!,* p. 119.
27. Ibid., p. 159.
28. Sent. 2–3, E. B. White's citation in Douglass Cater, "The Intellectual in Videoland," *Saturday Review* (May 31, 1975), p. 14; sent. 14, Howard Koch, *The Panic Broadcast* (New York: Avon, 1970), picture section, p. 16a.
29. Sent. 2, Cater, *Saturday Review* (May 31, 1975), p. 14; sent. 4–5, 8, Cater, op. cit., p. 16.

Chapter II

1. Clyde Kluckhohn, *Mirror for Man* (New York: McGraw-Hill, 1949), p. 247.
2. *The Education of Henry Adams* (Boston: Houghton Mifflin, 1961), p. 387.
3. James Blish, *Star Trek 6* (New York: Bantam Books, 1972), pp. 49–68; story by Max Erlich and Gene L. Coon. See Note 12, Chapter 1.
4. Sent. 5, Lichtenberg, Marshak, and Winston, *Star Trek Lives!,* p. 149; sent. 7, ibid., p. 87, italics in original; sent. 8, ibid., p. 112.
5. Ibid., p. 79.
6. Sent. 3–5, ibid., p. 43; sent. 9, ibid., p. 149.
7. Sent. 3–7, ibid., pp. 120–21; sent. 10–11, ibid., pp. 62–63.
8. Sent. 2–3, ibid., pp. 144–45, italics in original; sent. 4, ibid., p. 212.
9. Sent. 1–2, ibid., p. 16; sent. 4–8, ibid., p. 19; sent. 9, ibid., p. 20.
10. Sent. 2–4, ibid., p. 129; sent. 6–7, ibid., p. 132; sent. 9, pp. 190–91.

11. Gans, *Popular Culture and High Culture,* p. 32.
12. Sondra Marshak and Myrna Culbreath, *Star Trek: The New Voyages* (New York: Bantam Books, 1976), presented a collection of stories of the fanzine type. Gene Roddenberry lifted up the devotional quality of this writing in his Introduction, p. x: "Eventually we realized that there is no more profound way in which people could express what *Star Trek* has meant to them than by creating their own very personal *Star Trek* things . . . it was their *Star Trek* stories that especially gratified me . . . all of it was plainly done with love."
13. Sent. 2–3, Lichtenberg, Marshak, and Winston, *Star Trek Lives!,* p. 222; sent. 5–6, ibid., p. 256; italics in original.
14. Sent. 1–3, ibid., p. 269; details about *Kraith* publication plans are reported as of July 1975; sent. 5, Gene Roddenberry confirmed this inference in an interview that took place after the completion of our manuscript: "I'm not a guru and I don't want to be. . . . It frightens me when I learn of 10,000 people reading a 'Star Trek' script as if it were scripture. I certainly didn't write scripture. . . ." Sioux City *Journal* (Mar. 31, 1976); sent. 7, Lichtenberg, Marshak, and Winston, *Star Trek Lives!,* p. 273.
15. Sent. 2–5, ibid., p. 107, italics in original; sent. 6, ibid., pp. 107–8.
16. Sent. 2, ibid., p. 7, italics in original; sent. 3, Norman Vincent Peale, *You Can Win* (New York: Abingdon, 1938).
17. Sent. 3–4, Gerrold, *World of Star Trek,* p. 182; sent. 5, Lichtenberg, Marshak, and Winston, *Star Trek Lives!,* p. 78; sent. 6–8, Gerrold, *World of Star Trek,* p. 182.
18. Sent. 3–4, the stories in Marshak and Culbreath, *Star Trek: The New Voyages,* are all written by females but are introduced by the stars of the television programs whose presence is used to prove that the gods are real, so to speak. The editors claim, p. xvi, "Here are not merely bold knights and fair damsels, but flesh-and-blood men and women of courage and achievement . . . if this be our new Camelot, even more shining–make the most of it." An excellent example of the Spock sexual fantasy in the volume is "The Enchanted Pool" by Marcia Ericson, pp. 66–79; sent. 7–9, Lichtenberg, Marshak, and Winston, *Star Trek Lives!,* p. 238, parenthesis in original.
19. Sent. 2–4, Gerrold, *World of Star Trek,* p. 184; sent. 5–9, ibid., pp. 182–83.
20. Sent. 3–4, cf. Horace Newcomb, *TV: The Most Popular Art* (Garden City: Anchor Press/Doubleday, 1974), pp. 178–82, for a discussion of voluntary behavior alterations provoked by television, revealing the need for analytic categories.
21. Stuart Pratt Atkins, *The Testament of Werther in Poetry and Drama* (Cambridge: Harvard University Press, 1949), p. 2.

22. Sent. 2, Walter Kaufmann, *Without Guilt and Justice: From Decidophobia to Autonomy* (New York: Delta, 1975), p. 161; sent. 5–8, Atkins, *Testament of Werther,* p. 2.
23. Sent. 4, ibid., p. 64; it is also revealing that Goethe assigned the date of his own birthday to that of his character, Werther. Cf. the Foreword by Herman Weigand in *The Sorrows of Young Werther* (New York: New American Library, Signet Classics, 1962), p. viii; sent. 7, we find unconvincing Marshall McLuhan's denial that the story content of the new media has any effect on behavior: "The effect of the movie form is not related to its program content," he writes in *Understanding Media: The Extensions of Man* (New York: McGraw-Hill, 1964), p. 18. McLuhan continues: "Program and 'content' analysis offer no clues to the magic of these media or to their subliminal charge . . . the formative power in the media are the media themselves. . . ." pp. 20–21.
24. Sent. 6, Gans, *Popular Culture and High Culture,* p. 36; sent. 8–9, ibid., p. 33.
25. Rowland Evans, Jr. and Robert D. Novak, *Nixon in the White House: The Frustrations of Power* (New York: Random House, 1971), p. 252.
26. Sent. 2–3, Vincent Bugliosi, *Helter Skelter: The True Story of the Manson Murders* (New York: Bantam Books, 1975), p. 247; sent. 5–6, ibid., p. 331; sent. 12–19, ibid., p. 528; there is also evidence to suggest that Manson's behavior was shaped by his reading of Robert Heinlein's novel *Stranger in a Strange Land.* Ed Sanders reports in *The Family* (New York: Avon, 1972), p. 33: "Initially, Manson borrowed a lot of terminology and ideas from this book. . . . Manson was, however, to identify with the hero of the book, one Valentine Michael Smith (Manson's first follower's child was named Valentine Michael Manson)—a person, who in the course of building a religious movement, took to killing or 'discorporating' his enemies."
27. Sioux City *Journal* (Sept. 6, 1975).

Chapter III

1. Joseph Campbell, *The Hero with a Thousand Faces* (New York: Meridian, 1956), p. 25.
2. Cited by Arthur Schlesinger, Jr., *Violence: America in the Sixties* (New York: Signet Books, 1968), p. 52.
3. Cf. Rollo May, *Power and Innocence: A Search for the Sources of Violence* (New York: W. W. Norton, 1972), the thesis of which was related to the problem of mythic coherence in his presenta-

tion of March 14, 1975, at the Symposium on Violence at Kearney State College, Kearney, Nebraska.

4. *Variety* magazine's compilation "All Time Box Office Champions" indicates that *Death Wish,* with $8.8 million in rentals through 1975, has been an extremely popular film; cf. p. 44 (Jan. 7, 1976).
5. Sent. 3, cf. Henry Tudor, *Political Myth* (New York: Praeger, 1972), p. 17; sent. 4, cf. Ernst Cassirer, *Philosophy of Symbolic Forms,* Vol. II, *Mythical Thought,* tr. R. Manheim (New Haven, Conn.: Yale University Press, 1966), pp. 153 ff.; Mircea Eliade, *Myth and Reality,* tr. W. R. Trask (New York: Harper & Row, Torchbook, 1968), pp. 1–20; Mircea Eliade, *Myths, Dreams and Mysteries: The Encounter Between Contemporary Faiths and Archaic Realities,* tr. P. Mairet (New York: Harper & Row, Torchbook, 1967), pp. 13–20; sent. 7–8, Tudor, op. cit., p. 35; sent. 10–14, Slotkin, *Regeneration Through Violence,* pp. 6–7.
6. Sent. 1–4, Jewett, *Captain America Complex,* pp. 90–98; sent. 6–8, Michael T. Marsden, "Savior in the Saddle: The Sagebrush Testament," *Focus on the Western,* ed. J. Nachbar (Englewood Cliffs: Prentice-Hall, 1974), p. 100.
7. Sent. 1–2, Victor Turner, "Myth and Symbol," *Encyclopedia of the Social Sciences,* Vol. X, pp. 576–77; sent. 5, C. G. Jung develops this connection rather one-sidedly, emphasizing that all myths are symbolic projections of internal, unconscious dilemmas experienced by individuals. Turner seems more convincing in giving attention to the role of culture in the transmission and function of myths; cf. Jung, *Psychological Reflections: An Anthology of Writings,* selected and ed. J. Jacobi (New York: Harper & Brothers, 1961); sent. 7, Ernest Becker, *Angel in Armor: A Post-Freudian Perspective on the Nature of Man* (New York: Braziller, 1969), p. 183.
8. Sent. 2–3, ibid., pp. 183–84; sent. 6–8, Lunde, *Murder and Madness,* pp. 4, 41.
9. Clarence M. Kelley, *Uniform Crime Reports for the U. S. 1974* (U. S. Government Publication No. 027-001-0013), Tables 2 and 4.
10. John G. Cawelti, *The Six-gun Mystique* (Bowling Green: Bowling Green University Popular Press, 1971), p. 60.
11. Cf. James Mooney, *The Ghost Dance Religion and the Sioux Outbreak of 1890* (Chicago: University of Chicago Press, 1896, 1965).
12. Sent. 3–4, Steven Whitney, *Charles Bronson Superstar* (New York: Dell, 1975), pp. 192–93; sent. 5, "Periscope," *Newsweek* (Dec. 1, 1975).

13. Sent. 5–6, Brian Garfield, *Death Wish* (New York: David McKay, 1972), p. 109; sent. 8–14, ibid., pp. 34–35.
14. Sent. 5–7, ibid., p. 166; sent. 9–11, ibid., p. 169; sent. 12–14, ibid., pp. 177–78, italics in original.
15. Sent. 3–4, Whitney, *Charles Bronson Superstar,* p. 193; sent. 5, (New York: Manor Books, 1975).
16. Whitney, *Charles Bronson Superstar,* p. 155.
17. Ibid., p. 157.

Chapter IV

1. George Herbert, *The Works of George Herbert,* ed. F. E. Hutchinson (Oxford University Press, 1941), p. 352.
2. "Hugh Hefner's 20th Anniversary *Playboy* Interview" (Jan. 1974).
3. Jules Feiffer, *The Great Comic Book Heroes* (New York: Bonanza Books, 1965), p. 21.
4. Herbert Richardson has used the term "segmentalization" to describe a form of sexual renunciation ". . . related to the emergence of self-consciousness . . . ," which in his opinion constitutes a kind of evolutionary necessity. We do not wish our equally infelicitous term "segmentation" to be understood in Richardson's sense, cf. *Nun, Witch and Playmate: The Americanization of Sex* (New York: Harper & Row, 1971), pp. 20–24.
5. James Steranko, *History of Comics* (Reading: Supergraphics, 1970), Vol. I, p. 39, cited from an early *Superman Comic;* italics omitted.
6. Feiffer, *Great Comic Book Heroes,* p. 20.
7. Steranko, *History of Comics,* Vol. I, p. 40.
8. Cf. Les Daniels, *Comix: A History of Comic Books in America* (New York: Bonanza Books, 1971), pp. 18 ff.
9. Sent. 2, Reinhold Reitberger, Wolfgang Fuchs, *Comics: Anatomy of a Mass Medium* (Boston: Little, Brown, 1972), cf. pp. 120–21; sent. 8, Ted White, "The Spawn of M. C. Gaines," *All in Color for a Dime,* ed. R. A. Lupoff and D. Thompson (New York: Ace, 1970), p. 27.
10. Sent. 2, cf. ibid., p. 37; sent. 3–4, Dick Lupoff, "The Big Red Cheese," *All in Color for a Dime,* ed. R. A. Lupoff and D. Thompson (New York: Ace, 1970), p. 64; sent. 5–6, ibid., p. 78; sent. 7, Don Thompson, "OK, Axis, Here We Come!" *All in Color for a Dime,* p. 129; Daniels, *Comix,* p. 139; Stan Lee, *Origins of Marvel Comics* (New York: Simon & Schuster, 1974), pp. 154 ff.; sent. 8, Steranko, *History of Comics,* Vol. I, p. 72; Vol. II, p. 61.
11. Sent. 3, Philip José Farmer, *Doc Savage: His Apocalyptic Life*

(New York: Bantam Books, 1975), p. 155; sent. 5–6, ibid., p. 54; sent. 8–10, ibid., p. 55.

12. Feiffer, *Great Comic Book Heroes,* p. 21.
13. Sent. 2–3, *Playboy Philosophy* (Chicago: HMH Publishing, 1963–64), Vol. IV, p. 164; sent. 4, ibid., Vol. IV, p. 179; sent. 5, ibid., Vol. IV, p. 164.
14. Sent. 2, ibid., Vol. IV, p. 164; sent. 8, ibid., Vol. I, p. 1.
15. Sent. 3, *Playboy* (Aug. 1975), p. 130; sent. 4, *Playboy* (July 1975).
16. *Playboy Philosophy,* Vol. I, p. 17.
17. *Playboy* betrays no awareness of its Superman premise, and in fact publishes materials like "Clark Ghent's Schooldays" by Robert S. Wieder (May 1975). Clark is portrayed as an iron superstud who gets girls pregnant and uses his X-ray vision to leer at naked women through the gymnasium wall.
18. Sent. 5–6, *Playboy* (Apr. 1975), p. 83.
19. *Playboy* (Feb. 1975), pp. 123–31.
20. Al Capp, "The Model," *Playboy* (Apr. 1975), p. 153.
21. *Playboy* (July 1975), pp. 86–88.
22. *Playboy Philosophy,* Vol. I, p. 5.
23. Sent. 4, ibid., Vol. I, p. 4; sent. 9, reprinted from *Playboy* (Jan. 1974); sent. 11, Frank Brady, *Hefner* (New York: Ballantine, 1975), p. 220.
24. *Playboy Philosophy,* Vol. IV, pp. 180–81.
25. Sent. 3–4, *Playboy* (Apr. 1974), p. 88; sent. 6, *Time* (March 20, 1972), p. 54; sent. 7, detail derived from a survey of *Playboy* articles by Pat Spang, "Playboy vs. Playgirl," paper for the seminar Pop Culture and Americanism (Morningside College, spring semester, 1975).
26. Morton Hunt, *Sexual Behavior in the 1970's* (Chicago: The Playboy Press, 1974).
27. Richard Todd, "Gathering at Bunnymede," *The Atlantic Monthly* (Jan. 1972), p. 87.
28. *Playboy Philosophy,* Vol. IV, p. 179.
29. Sent. 2–6, Rollo May, *Power and Innocence: A Search for the Sources of Violence* (New York: W. W. Norton, 1972), pp. 114–15; sent. 8, *Playboy Philosophy,* Vol. IV, p. 164; sent. 10, *Playboy* (Apr. 1975), p. 144.
30. *Playboy Philosophy,* Vol. IV, p. 162.
31. *Playboy* (Apr. 1975), p. 95.
32. *Playboy* (May 1975), pp. 84, 86, 168.
33. Sent. 3, Norman Mailer, "The Time of Her Time," *The Long Patrol* (New York: World, 1971), p. 255; we are indebted to Kate Millett, *Sexual Politics* (New York: Avon, 1971), pp.

14–16, for drawing attention to this aspect of Mailer's work; sent. 5–9, *Long Patrol,* p. 246–47.

34. Sent. 2–3, ibid., pp. 248–50.
35. Sent. 2, ibid., p. 250; sent. 3, ibid., p. 253; sent. 5–9, ibid., pp. 260–62.
36. Sent. 1, ibid., p. 439; sent. 5–6, ibid., p. 456; sent. 12–14, ibid., pp. 465–66.
37. Sent. 3–4, *Love's Labour's Lost, The Complete Plays and Poems of William Shakespeare,* ed. W. A. Neilson and C. J. Hill (Boston: Houghton Mifflin, 1942), Act I, Scene 1, lines 9–10; sent. 5, ibid., Act I, Scene 1, line 25; sent. 6–7, ibid., Act I, Scene 2, lines 177–81.
38. Sent. 4–5, ibid., Act IV, Scene 3, lines 6–7; sent. 7–10, ibid., Act IV, Scene 3, lines 299–304, 327–32; sent. 13–14, ibid., Act IV, Scene 3, lines 216–18.
39. Sent. 5–6, ibid., Act IV, Scene 3, lines 366–69.
40. Friedrich Nietzsche, *Thus Spake Zarathustra: The Portable Nietzsche,* ed. and tr. W. Kaufmann (New York: Viking, 1954), p. 190.

Chapter V

1. Henry Nash Smith, *Virgin Land: The American West as Symbol and Myth* (Cambridge: Harvard University Press, 1950), p. 107.
2. Line derived from the movie *Walking Tall* (Bing Crosby Productions Film, 1973); cf. Doug Warren, *Walking Tall* (New York: Pinnacle, 1973), p. 16.
3. John Burke, *Buffalo Bill: The Noblest Whiteskin* (New York: G. P. Putnam's Sons, Capricorn Books, 1973), p. 95.
4. Sent. 1–6, ibid., cf. pp. 23–35; sent. 9, ibid., p. 48.
5. Smith, *Virgin Land,* pp. 106–7 and note 19.
6. Sent. 4, Burke, *Buffalo Bill,* p. 45; sent. 6–8, Dixon Wecter, *The Hero in America* (Ann Arbor: University of Michigan Press, 1963), p. 355.
7. Cited by Burke, *Buffalo Bill,* pp. 289–92.
8. Cited by Wecter, *The Hero in America,* p. 357.
9. Sent. 3, cf. Don Russell, *The Lives and Legends of Buffalo Bill* (Norman: University of Oklahoma Press, 1960), pp. 88–89 for a cautious evaluation of Buffalo Bill's claim; sent. 5–8, excerpt from *Buffalo Bill: Story of the Wild West,* repr. W. A. Wilbur, *The Western Hero: A Study in Myth and American Values* (Menlo Park, Calif.: Addison-Wesley, 1973), p. 31; sent. 13, cf. Russell, *Buffalo Bill,* pp. 185–87; sent. 15, Russell, ibid., p. 188, notes that

Cody associated his wound with this expedition, but that he probably confused it with a verified graze wound in 1869.

10. Sent. 4, ibid., p. 230; sent. 5, cf. ibid., pp. 221–35, for a discussion of the varying accounts; sent. 4–5, Burke, *Buffalo Bill*, p. 123; sent. 8, Wecter, *Hero in America*, p. 359; sent. 9–10, Smith, *Virgin Land*, p. 108.
11. Sent. 3, 7, cf. Burke, *Buffalo Bill*, pp. 120–21; sent. 8–10, ibid., p. 11.
12. Sent. 4, ibid., p. 143; sent. 5, ibid., cf. p. 195; sent. 7, cf. Russell's reprinting of the 1893 program, pp. 376–77; sent. 9–11, Robert V. Hine, *The American West: An Interpretive History* (Boston: Little, Brown, 1973), pp. 277–78.
13. Sent. 3, Wecter, *Hero in America*, p. 359; sent. 5–6, Burke, *Buffalo Bill*, p. 164; sent. 7–10, ibid., pp. 12–13.
14. Sent. 2, cf. Jewett, *Captain America Complex*, pp. 42–45; sent. 4–5, cf. Burke, *Buffalo Bill*, p. 143.
15. Ibid., p. 231.
16. Sent. 1, Kent Ladd Steckmesser, *The Western Hero in History and Legend* (Norman: University of Oklahoma Press, 1965), p. 241; sent. 3–4, cf. Cawelti, *Six-gun Mystique*, p. 78: "With such a hero, the creators of Westerns were able to express some sense of ambiguity about these ideals and yet at the same time to reaffirm the essential benevolence of American progress."
17. Don Russell, "Cody, Kings and Coronets," *The American West*, Vol. VII, No. 4 (1970), p. 62.
18. Pauline Kael, "The Street Western," *The New Yorker* (Feb. 25, 1974), p. 100.
19. Sent. 1, 12–14, W. R. Morris, *The Twelfth of August* (New York: Bantam Books, 1974), pp. 45–50, 88; sent. 2–8, cf. Charles Thompson, "The Saga of the Hem Stitched Sheriff," Nashville *Tennessean* (Aug. 24, 1969), and Kathy Sawyer, "Everybody's Out to Get Buford Now," Nashville *Tennessean: Sunday Magazine* (Aug. 12, 1973).
20. Sent. 2–5, Charles Thompson, "The Slowest Gun in the West," Nashville *Tennessean* (Aug. 31, 1969); sent. 7, Morris, *Twelfth of August*, p. 102; cf. Kathy Sawyer, "Everybody's Out to Get Buford Now"; sent. 10, Charles Thompson, "The Slowest Gun in the West."
21. Sent. 3, ibid., p. 142; sent. 7, Doug Warren, *Walking Tall* (New York: Pinnacle Books, 1973), p. 138.
22. Kael, "The Street Western," p. 102.
23. Sent. 1, Sawyer, "Everybody's Out to Get Buford Now"; sent. 2, Kael, "The Street Western," p. 105; cf. Thompson, "Saga of the Hem Stitched Sheriff"; sent. 6, "Pusser Film Stood Too Tall to Let it Die," Nashville *Tennessean* (Dec. 1, 1973); cf. Robert Kol-

lar and Kirk Loggins, "Hundreds View Body of Pusser," Nashville *Tennessean* (Aug. 23, 1974); sent. 7, Kael, "The Street Western," p. 106.

24. Sent. 4, Evidence regarding the crash is discussed by John Pope, "Crash Kills Buford," Nashville *Banner* (Aug. 21, 1974); sent. 10, Morris, *Twelfth of August,* p. 174.
25. The statement from the Prologue is printed in Webster Carey's novelistic *Part 2 Walking Tall,* based on the original screen play by Howard B. Kreitsek (New York: Bantam Books, 1975), no page number, italics and elision in text. Regarding Pusser's enjoyment of brutality, cf. Morris's account in *Twelfth of August,* pp. 159–62, and Charles Thompson, "Saga of the Hem Stitched Sheriff."
26. Details about the advertising campaign are found in "Pusser Film Stood Too Tall to Let it Die."
27. Sent. 6, Carey, *Part 2 Walking Tall,* p. 37.
28. Sent. 2, citation from Nashville *Banner,* printed on the jacket of Morris, *Twelfth of August;* sent. 4–5, ibid., pp. 163–64; Sawyer, "Everybody's Out to Get Buford Now"; sent. 9–13, cited by Morris, op. cit., p. 122; sent. 14, details on Pusser's heavy armaments are provided by Thompson, "Saga of the Hem Stitched Sheriff."
29. The sermon is cited by Bill Hance, "His Action Was Fast, Hard," Nashville *Tennessean* (Aug. 21, 1974).
30. Michael Straight, *Carrington* (New York: Knopf, 1960).
31. Citation from John R. Milton, *Three West: Conversations with Vardis Fisher, Max Evans, Michael Straight* (Vermillion: University of South Dakota Press, 1970), pp. 130–31; details about Straight's research methods are provided on pp. 113 ff.
32. Sent. 5–14, ibid., pp. 159–60; sent. 17–18, Paul A. Hutton has provided a careful documentation of this point in his examination of the Custer legends in recent films: "Thus from a symbol of courage and sacrifice in the winning of the West, Custer's image was gradually altered into a symbol of the arrogance and brutality in the white exploitation of the West. The only constant factor in this reversed legend is a remarkable disregard for historical fact." "From Little Big Horn to Little Big Man: The Changing Image of Western Hero in Popular Culture," *The Western Historical Quarterly* (Jan. 1976), p. 45.
33. Straight, *Carrington,* pp. 373–74.
34. Sent. 5–7, "RIPOFF Boosting Nebraska," Sioux City *Journal* (Jan. 23, 1976); sent. 10, Milton, *Three West,* p. 138.

Chapter VI

1. Johanna Spyri, *Heidi* (Racine: Western Publishing, Whitman Book, 1970; original German, 1884), p. 210.
2. Sent. 6–7, Steven Marcus, *Dickens: From Pickwick to Dombey* (New York: Basic Books, 1965), p. 142; sent. 10, Charles Dickens, *The Old Curiosity Shop* (Boston: Houghton Mifflin, 1894), p. 329; sent. 11, cf. Marcus, *Dickens,* p. 151; sent. 12, Dickens, *Old Curiosity Shop,* p. 536.
3. Sent. 6, Charles Dickens, *Dombey and Son* (Boston: Houghton Mifflin, 1894), Vol. II, p. 416; sent. 9, ibid., p. 421.
4. Ibid., p. 445.
5. Sent. 2–4, A. E. Dyson, *The Inimitable Dickens: A Reading of the Novels* (London: Macmillan and St. Martin's Press, 1970), p. 173; sent. 5–7, J. Hillis Miller, *Charles Dickens: The World of His Novels* (Bloomington: Indiana University Press, 1969), p. 240; sent. 8, ibid., p. 241.
6. Charles Dickens, *Hard Times* (New York: Signet, New American Library, 1961), p. 94.
7. Sent. 3, cited by H. R. Hays, *The Dangerous Sex: The Myth of Feminine Evil* (New York: Pocket Book, 1966), p. 213; sent. 8, ibid., p. 219.
8. Sent. 2, Edwin Percy Whipple, "Introduction," Dickens, *Old Curiosity Shop,* p. xix; sent. 3–5, cf. May Hill Arbuthnot, Zena Sutherland, *Children and Books* (Glenview: Scott, Foresman, 1972, 4th ed.), p. 96.
9. Sent. 7–8, Spyri, *Heidi,* p. 33; sent. 11–12, ibid., p. 44.
10. Sent. 3–5, ibid., p. 61; sent. 8, ibid., p. 76; sent. 10–13, ibid., p. 89.
11. Ibid., pp. 90, 94.
12. Sent. 5–7, ibid., p. 123; sent. 10, ibid., p. 127.
13. Sent. 3–5, ibid., p. 143; sent. 7–8, ibid., p. 212.
14. Ibid., pp. 159–63.
15. Sent. 7–9, ibid., p. 191; sent. 11–12, ibid., pp. 204–5; sent. 17–20, ibid., p. 210, italics in original.
16. Untitled *Little House on the Prairie* episode, NBC (June 4, 1975).
17. Untitled *Little House on the Prairie* episode, NBC (June 11, 1975).
18. "Ebenezer Sprague," *Little House on the Prairie,* NBC (Sept. 24, 1975).
19. Laura Ingalls Wilder, *On the Way Home* (New York: Harper & Row, 1962), p. 1.
20. Lewis K. Parker, "Big Hearts, Big Hit. In a 'Little House,'" *Read: The Magazine for Reading and English* (Middleton, Conn.:

Xerox Education Publications, Vol. XXV, Sept. 3, 1975), p. 13.
21. Ibid., pp. 12–13.

Chapter VII

1. Mortimer J. Adler, *Art and Prudence: A Study in Practical Philosophy* (New York: Longmans, Green, 1937), p. 581; the citation is critically evaluated by Max Horkheimer in his essay "Art and Mass Culture," *Critical Theory* (New York: Herder and Herder, 1972), p. 281.
2. Mildred Houghton Comfort, *Walt Disney: Master of Fantasy* (Minneapolis: T. S. Denison, 1968), p. 123.
3. Sent. 2, Hortense Powdermaker, *Hollywood: The Dream Factory* (Boston: Little, Brown, 1950), p. 58; sent. 4–6, ibid., p. 61; sent. 9–12, ibid., p. 59; sent. 13, ibid., p. 55; sent. 14, ibid., p. 67.
4. Sent. 3–6, Murray Schumach, *The Face on the Cutting Room Floor* (New York: Da Capo Press, 1974), pp. 280, 282–83; sent. 13–14, Christopher Finch, *The Art of Walt Disney: From Mickey Mouse to the Magic Kingdoms* (New York: Harry N. Abrams, New Concise Edition, 1975), p. 52.
5. Sent. 2, Finch, op. cit., p. 53; sent. 3, cited by Leonard Maltin, *The Disney Films* (New York: Crown, 1973), p. 5; sent. 6–8, Fritz Moellenhoef, "The Remarkable Popularity of Mickey Mouse," *The History of Popular Culture,* ed. N. F. Cantor and M. S. Werthman (New York: Macmillan, 1968), p. 611.
6. Richard Schickel cites this detail in *The Disney Version* (New York: Avon, 1969), p. 75.
7. Ibid., p. 204; one realizes how thoroughly Disney banished sex when one compares his work with that of the Warner Brothers' "Looney Tunes" cartoons. Cf. Joe Adamson, *Tex Avery: King of Cartoons* (New York: Popular Library, 1975), who discusses the sexual content of "Red Hot Riding Hood" (1943), "Swing Shift Cinderella" (1945), "Wild and Wolfy" (1945), and "Uncle Tom's Cabaña" (1947).
8. Sent. 4–6, *Kinder- und Hausmärchen, Gesammelt durch die Brüder Grimm* (Munich: Bardtenschlager, n. d.), pp. 195–96, in our translation. Cf. the similar version in the Marian Edwardes translation, "Snow-Drop," *Anthology of Children's Literature,* ed. E. Johnson, C. E. Scott, and E. R. Sickels (Cambridge: Houghton Mifflin, 1948, 2nd ed.), pp. 86–89; sent. 7–17, *The Wonderful Worlds of Walt Disney: Fantasyland* (New York: Golden Press, 1965), p. 113.
9. Sent. 1, Maltin, *Disney Films,* p. 56; sent. 6, ibid., p. 55.

10. Sent. 2–7, ibid., p. 7; sent. 8, Burne Hogarth, *Tarzan of the Apes* (New York: Watson-Guptil, 1972), pp. 27–28.
11. Robert D. Feild, *The Art of Walt Disney* (New York: Macmillan, 1942), p. 31.
12. Ibid., p. 38.
13. Pamela L. Travers, *Mary Poppins* (New York: Harcourt, Brace and World, 1962); *Mary Poppins Comes Back* (New York: Harcourt, Brace and World, 1963); *Mary Poppins Opens the Door* (New York: Harcourt, Brace and World, 1943); *Mary Poppins In the Park* (New York: Harcourt, Brace and World, 1952); *Mary Poppins From A to Z* (New York: Harcourt, Brace and World, 1962).
14. Sent. 2, Judith Crist as cited by Leonard Maltin, *Disney Films,* p. 230; sent. 5–6, *Walt Disney's Stories from Other Lands* (New York: Golden Press, 1965), p. 6; sent. 9, Maltin, *Disney Films,* p. 232.
15. J. Glenn Gray, *The Warriors: Reflections on Men in Battle* (New York: Harper & Row, Torchbook, 1967), p. 31.
16. Cited by Feild, *Art of Walt Disney,* p. 122.
17. Sent. 3–6, Bob Thomas, *Walt Disney: The Art of Animation* (New York: Simon & Schuster, 1958), p. 56; sent. 9, Finch, *Art of Walt Disney,* p. 66.
18. Sent. 6–7, Maltin, *Disney Films,* p. 61; sent. 12–18, ibid., p. 63; sent. 21, cited by Schickel, *Disney Version,* p. 233.
19. Sent. 2–4, cited by Robert Batchelder, *The Irreversible Decision, 1939–50* (Boston: Houghton Mifflin, 1962), p. 172; Batchelder also reports the results of the U. S. Strategic Bombing Survey, undertaken by the Department of Defense after the end of the war. It showed that bombing of civilian populations was of minimal and even negative military value, p. 186; sent. 6–11, Maltin, *Disney Films,* p. 70; sent. 12, Siegfried Kracauer, *From Caligari to Hitler* (Princeton: Princeton University Press, 1947), p. 300.
20. The most serious attempt to study the social effects of Disney's work has been written by South American scholars Ariel Dorfman and Armand Mattelart, *How to Read Donald Duck: Imperialist Ideology in the Disney Comic* (New York: International General, 1975; tr. and Introduction D. Kunzle).
21. Cited by Schickel, *Disney Version,* p. v.
22. Cited ibid., p. 187.
23. Sent. 3, "Good Times," Advertising Supplement to the Los Angeles *Times* (June 13, 1975); sent. 5, Schumach, *Face on the Cutting Room Floor,* p. 285.

Chapter VIII

1. *The Macmillan Book of Proverbs, Maxims and Famous Phrases,* ed. B. Stevenson (New York: Macmillan, 1948), p. 2,026.
2. Cited by Harry Sohn, *Karl Kraus* (New York: Twayne, 1971), p. 49.
3. Sent. 4, cited by Charles L. Sanford, *The Quest for Paradise: Europe and the American Moral Imagination* (Urbana: University of Illinois Press, 1961), p. 173; sent. 6, *Variety*'s compilation "All Time Box Office Champions," (Jan. 7, 1976), indicates that recent catastrophe films have been among the most popular in history. *Jaws* grossed $102,650,000 in its first year of distribution, making it filmdom's greatest money earner. *Towering Inferno, Airport, The Poseidon Adventure* and *Earthquake* rank among the top twenty films in history.
4. Sent. 4–6, George Fox, *Earthquake: The Story of a Movie* (New York: Signet, 1974), p. 96; sent. 8, ibid., p. 27; sent. 10, ibid., p. 9.
5. Sent. 3, ibid., p. 79; sent. 8–12, ibid., p. 19.
6. Cf. Jewett, *Captain America Complex,* pp. 218–42, for an account of the impact of the Deuteronomic principle of retribution on American nationalism and literature.
7. Sent. 4–5, Fox, *Earthquake*, p. 70; sent. 8–9, ibid., p. 123.
8. Schumach, *Face on the Cutting Room Floor,* p. 45.
9. Sent. 8, in *The Responsive Chord* (Garden City: Anchor Press/Doubleday, 1973), Tony Schwartz, creator of more than four thousand radio and television commercials, recommends what we have called "cuing" as an ideal of visual communication: "The critical task is to design our package of stimuli so that it resonates with information already stored within an individual and thereby induces the desired learning or behavior effect," p. 24. Schwartz, however, does not develop a theory of mythic content.
10. Hollis Alpert, *Saturday Review* (July 12, 1975), p. 51.
11. Schumach, *Face on the Cutting Room Floor,* p. 282.
12. Carl Gottlieb, *Jaws Log* (New York: Dell, 1975), p. 69.
13. Stan Lee, *The Origin of Marvel Comics* (New York: Simon & Schuster, 1974), pp. 133–36.
14. Ibid., p. 150.
15. Ibid., p. 167.
16. Sent. 2, Heb. 9:22; sent. 5–10, "The Epic of Creation," *Larousse Encyclopedia of Mythology* (New York: Prometheus, 1959), p. 51.
17. Sent. 3–4, Ps. 58:10–11; sent. 6, 2 K. 9:30; sent. 8, 1 K. 22:38.

18. Sent. 6–7, *The Ante-Nicene Fathers: Translations of the Writings of the Fathers down to A.D. 325,* ed. A. Roberts and J. Donaldson, Vol. III, *Latin Christianity: Its Founder, Tertullian,* tr. S. Thelwall (Grand Rapids: Eerdmans, 1957), p. 91; cf. Walter Kaufmann's discussion of the passage in his notes to Friedrich Nietzsche, *On the Genealogy of Morals* (New York: Random House, Vintage, 1967), pp. 49–52, n. 2; sent. 9, cf. n. 1 above.
19. Sent. 4–7, cited by William Ruehlmann, *Saint with a Gun* (New York: New York University Press, 1974), p. 97; sent. 10, John Cawelti, "The Spillane Phenomenon," *Journal of Popular Culture,* Vol. III, No. 1 (1969), p. 16.
20. Lunde, *Murder and Madness,* p. 59.
21. Sent. 2, Peter Benchley, *Jaws* (New York: Bantam Books, 1974), pp. 15, 291; sent. 3, ibid., p. 17; sent. 6, ibid., pp. 144–45; sent. 8–10, ibid., p. 217; sent. 11, ibid., pp. 30–31.
22. Sent. 5, ibid., p. 94; sent. 9–12, ibid., p. 293.
23. Ibid., p. 93.
24. Cited by Gottlieb, *Jaws Log,* pp. 151–52.
25. Zohn, *Kraus,* p. 46.
26. Sent. 2, Karl Kraus, *Die Letzten Tage der Menschheit* (Munich: Deutscher Taschenbuch Verlag, 1964), Vol. II, p. 309. All translations from this work have been made by the authors. Sent. 9–10, ibid., Vol. II, p. 79.
27. Sent. 2, ibid., Vol. II, p. 262; sent. 6–7, ibid., Vol. II, p. 235.
28. Sent. 3–7, Vol. I, p. 325; sent. 10–15, ibid., Vol. II, p. 230; sent. 16–18, Zohn, *Kraus,* p. 71.
29. Sent. 5–8, Kraus, op. cit., Vol. I, p. 6; sent. 13–14, ibid., Vol. I, p. 171.

Chapter IX

1. J. H. Plumb, "Disappearing Heroes," *Horizon,* Vol. XVI, No. 4 (Autumn 1974), pp. 50–51.
2. Sent. 1, Sanford, *Quest for Paradise,* p. vi; sent. 3–5, ibid., pp. 39–40; sent. 10, cf. William Haller, *The Rise of Puritanism* (New York: Columbia University Press, 1938), pp. 174–75, 269 ff.; Conrad Cherry, *God's New Israel: Religious Interpretations of American Destiny* (Englewood Cliffs, N.J.: Prentice-Hall, 1971), pp. 25–30; Winthrop S. Hudson, *Religion in America: An Historical Account of the Development of American Religious Life* (New York: Charles Scribner's Sons, 1973, 2nd ed.), pp. 18–22; sent. 11–12, Sanford, op. cit., pp. 82–83, italics omitted.
3. Sent. 3, Roderick Nash, *Wilderness in the American Mind* (New Haven: Yale University Press, 1967), p. 26; sent. 4, Daniel J.

Boorstin, *The Americans: The Colonial Experience* (New York: Random House, 1958), p. 29.

4. Sent. 3–4, Sanford, *Quest for Paradise,* p. 117; sent. 5, ibid., p. 125; sent. 6, Jewett, *Captain America Complex,* pp. 31–46; sent. 7, cited by Nash, *Wilderness in the American Mind,* p. 97.
5. Sent. 3, Smith, *Virgin Land,* p. 123; sent. 4–5, ibid., p. 140; sent. 6, ibid., p. 142; sent. 7, ibid., p. 170.
6. Sent. 4, *Garden in the Grasslands: Boomer Literature of the Central Great Plains* (Lincoln: University of Nebraska Press, 1971); sent. 5–8, ibid., pp. 34–36.
7. John Seelye, "The Mouse in the Machine," review of Christopher Finch's *The Art of Walt Disney, The New Republic* (Dec. 22, 1973), p. 24.
8. Sent. 2, Slotkin, *Regeneration Through Violence,* pp. 95–112; sent. 3, ibid., p. 104; sent. 6, ibid., p. 95.
9. Smith, *Virgin Land,* p. 95.
10. Ibid., p. 187.
11. Sent. 2–3, Gerald Mast, *A Short History of the Movies* (New York: Pegasus, 1971), p. 85; sent. 5, ibid., p. 86.
12. Sent. 2, Marsha Kinder and Beverle Houston, *Close-Up: A Critical Perspective on Film* (New York: Harcourt Brace Jovanovich, 1972), p. 20; sent. 5, Fred Silva, *Focus on the Birth of a Nation* (Englewood Cliffs: Prentice-Hall, 1971), p. 11; sent. 8–9, cf. Lewis Jacobs' compilation of Griffith's shots in this concluding scene, "D. W. Griffith: *The Birth of a Nation,*" *Focus on Birth of a Nation,* ed. F. Silva, p. 166; Marshall McLuhan overlooks these technomythic advances of early filmmakers when he claims that movies ". . . would prove unacceptable as mass audience films if the audience had not been preconditioned by television commercials to abrupt zooms, elliptical editing, no story lines, flash cuts." *The Medium Is the Massage* (New York: Random House, 1967), p. 128.
13. Arthur Knight, *The Liveliest Art: A Panoramic History of the Movies* (New York: New American Library, 1957), p. 34.
14. Sent. 3–5, Mast, *Short History of the Movies,* p. 86; sent. 8, Sanford, *Quest for Paradise,* p. 14; sent. 9, Jewett, *Captain America Complex,* pp. 176–214; sent. 12, Knight, *Liveliest Art,* p. 35.
15. Smith, *Virgin Land,* p. 188.
16. Sent. 3, Daniel J. Boorstin, *The Americans: The Democratic Experience* (New York: Random House, 1973), pp. 34–41; sent. 6–9, ibid., pp. 36–37.
17. Sent. 2–3, Owen Wister, *The Virginian: A Horseman of the Plains* (New York: Grosset & Dunlap, 1911, 3rd ed.), pp. x–xi; sent. 5, ibid., p. vii.
18. Ibid., p. 4.

19. Sent. 2–4, ibid., pp. 432–37; sent. 6–13, ibid., pp. 438–39; sent. 17–19, ibid., p. 450.
20. Sent. 2, Boorstin, *Democratic Experience,* p. 27; sent. 3, W. Eugene Hollon, *Frontier Violence: Another Look* (New York: Oxford University Press, 1974), p. 152; sent. 7, Harry Sinclair, *The Great Range Wars: Violence on the Grasslands* (New York: Dodd, Mead, 1970), p. 275; sent. 9, Hollon, op. cit., p. 161; Neal Lambert, "Owen Wister's Virginian: The Genesis of a Cultural Hero," *Western American Literature,* Vol. VI (1975), p. 101; sent. 10–11, Wister, *Virginian,* p. 414; for an extensive discussion of the relation between the novel and Wister's life, cf. Sanford E. Marowitz, "Testament of a Patriot: The Virginian, the Tenderfoot, and Owen Wister," *Texas Studies in Literature and Language,* Vol. XV, No. 3 (1973), pp. 551–75.
21. Wister, *Virginian,* pp. 471–74.
22. Ibid., pp. 476–79.
23. Max J. Herzberg, *Readers Encyclopedia of American Literature* (New York: Crowell, 1962), pp. 1,183.
24. Sent. 2–7, Wister, *Virginian,* pp. 487–96; sent. 11, ibid., p. 506.
25. Sent. 1–2, Robert V. Hine, *The American West: An Interpretive History* (Boston: Little, Brown, 1973), p. 270; Roy W. Meyer, "B. M. Bower: The Poor Man's Wister," *The Popular Western,* ed. R. W. Etulain and M. T. Marsden (Bowling Green: Bowling Green University Popular Press, 1974), pp. 25–37; Leslie A. Fiedler, *Love and Death in the American Novel* (New York: Criterion, 1960), p. 255; sent. 5, cf. Robert Warshow, "Movie Chronicle: The Westerner," *Focus on the Western,* ed. J. Nachbar (Englewood Cliffs: Prentice-Hall, 1974), p. 49; sent. 6, Hine, op. cit., p. 270; sent. 8, Peter Homans, "Puritanism Revisited: An Analysis of the Contemporary Screen-Image Western," *Focus on the Western,* p. 84.
26. Sent. 5–7, Burne Hogarth, *Tarzan of the Apes* (New York: Watson-Guptil, 1972), p. 22; sent. 8–9, Steranko, *History of Comics,* Vol. I, p. 19; sent. 13, ibid., Vol. I, p. 37; sent. 15, Des Moines *Register* (Nov. 10, 1975).
27. Sent. 3, Jim Harmon, *The Great Radio Heroes* (Garden City: Doubleday, 1967), p. 202; sent. 7–9, "The Adventures of the Lone Ranger," *Decca Records* (DL 75125); sent. 11 ff., loc. cit.; Harmon, op. cit., pp. 196–97.
28. Cf. Hollon, *Frontier Violence,* pp. 42 ff.
29. Cf. Jewett, *Captain America Complex,* pp. 90–98; John G. Cawelti, *The Six-gun Mystique* (Bowling Green: Bowling Green University Popular Press, 1971), pp. 60–61.
30. Sent. 2–6, *Decca Records* (DL 75125); sent. 8–11, Harmon, *Great Radio Heroes,* pp. 212–13.

31. Sent. 5, Daniels, *Comix,* p. 11; sent. 7, Ted White, "The Spawn of M. C. Gaines," *All in Color For a Dime,* ed. D. Lupoff and D. Thompson (New York: Ace, 1970), p. 26; sent. 9, Feiffer, *Great Comic Book Heroes,* p. 18.
32. Sent. 7–8, ibid., p. 26, italics omitted; sent. 9–18, ibid., p. 68, caps omitted.
33. "Shazam–Isis," CBS (Nov. 1975).
34. *Flash Comics* (Aug. 1971).
35. E. E. Smith, "What Does This Convention Mean?," *All Our Yesterdays: An Informal History of Science Fiction Fandom in the Forties,* ed. H. Warner, Jr. (Chicago: Advent, 1969), p. 96.
36. Sent. 4, cf. caption citation for this chapter; sent. 5–8, H. L. Nieburg comes to similar conclusions in *Culture Storm: Politics and the Ritual Order* (New York: St. Martin's Press, 1973), p. 15: "But modern man is immersed in a universe of magic and ritual that he ethnocentrically considers 'scientific' and 'rational.' He thinks himself the most advanced product of human history standing at a pinnacle of self-understanding, mastery of his environment, and free from delusion and superstition. This pose has always been characteristic of man whatever his condition. Advanced civilization is greatly augmented by technology and large-scale organization, but it remains as saturated with ritual as any primitive society. Magic, faith, and arbitrary mental constructs encompass the needs of modern man."

Chapter X

1. Plato, *Republic, The Collected Dialogues of Plato,* ed. E. Hamilton and H. Cairns, tr. P. Shorey (Princeton: Princeton University Press, Bollingen Series LXXI, 1961), p. 666 (424c).
2. Alfred North Whitehead, *Symbolism: Its Meaning and Effect* (New York: Macmillan, 1927, 1959), p. 88.
3. Sent. 3, Plato, *Republic,* tr. Shorey, p. 646 (401c); sent. 4, *The Republic of Plato,* tr. F. M. Cornford (New York: Oxford University Press, 1956), p. 90 (401c), selected because of the clarity of the translation; sent. 6, tr. Shorey, p. 646 (401b-c).
4. Schumach, *Face on the Cutting Room Floor,* p. 37.
5. Dolores Katz, "Some Movies Can Scare You Right into the Hospital," Des Moines *Register* (Dec. 8, 1975).
6. Sent. 3, George Gerbner and Larry Gross, *Trends in Network Drama and Viewer Conception of Social Reality, 1967–1973* (*Violence Profile,* No. 6, Annenberg School of Communications, University of Pennsylvania, Dec. 1974); sent. 5, ibid., pp. 38–40; sent. 8–12, ibid., pp. 41–48.

7. Ibid., p. 48.
8. Sent. 2–3, *To Establish Justice, to Insure Domestic Tranquillity: The Final Report of the National Commission on the Causes and Prevention of Violence* (New York: Bantam Books, 1970), p. 169.
9. Sent. 3, cf. Daniels, *Comix,* p. 166; sent. 4, *American Heritage Dictionary of the English Language,* ed. W. Morris (Boston: Houghton Mifflin, 1969), p. 1,487; sent. 6, David Kunzle, "Self Conscious Comics," *The New Republic* (July 19, 1975), p. 27.
10. Sent. 2–3, Daniels, *Comix,* pp. 170–71; sent. 4–7, "Mr. Natural 'Visits the City,'" *Zap,* No. 1 (Nov. 1967); sent. 8–10, "Mr. Natural Takes a Vacation," *Zap,* No. 4 (1969).
11. "Let's Talk Sense About This Here Modern America," *Arcade: The Comics Revue* (Summer 1975).
12. Clinton R. Sanders, "Icons of the Alternate Culture: The Themes and Functions of Underground Comix," *Journal of Popular Culture,* Vol. VIII, No. 4 (Spring 1975), p. 849.
13. Sent. 1, *Hair* played 1,750 days in New York and had extensive runs in many cities of the world; cf. *The World Almanac and Book of Facts* (New York: Newspaper Alliance Association, 1976), p. 554; sent. 2, Clive Barnes, "Theater: 'Hair' Moves into Toronto," New York *Times* (Jan. 13, 1970), p. 39; sent. 4–5, Gerome Ragni, James Rado, *Hair: The American Tribal Love-Rock Musical* (New York: Pocket Books, 1969), pp. viii–ix.
14. Sent. 2, ibid., pp. 28, 59; sent. 3, ibid., p. 114; sent. 5–9, ibid., pp. 153–54.
15. Sent. 3, ibid., p. 176; sent. 4, ibid., pp. 192–93; sent. 6, ibid., pp. 78–79; sent. 7, ibid., p. 204.
16. *The Bible: In the Beginning . . . ,* Dino de Laurentiis' production of 1966 was directed by John Huston; it ranks high in *Variety*'s "Box Office Champions," with earnings of fifteen million dollars (Jan. 7, 1976).
17. William Henzlick, *The Christian Advocate* (Nov. 17, 1966), p. 20.
18. Sent. 3–6, Walter Karp, "What Westerns Are All About," *Horizon,* Vol. XVII, No. 3 (Summer 1975), p. 39; sent. 9–15, ibid., p. 39.
19. Karp's conspiratorial worldview surfaces in *Indispensable Enemies: The Politics of Misrule in America* (New York: Saturday Review Press, 1973), which claims that an oligarchy behind the American political parties is responsible for every evil in society today, including an aggressive foreign policy, governmental waste, and the crime rates of alienated citizens. The parties that play the role of indispensable enemies are in collusion with each other to divide the spoils. Karp proves this by oracular claims

rather than historical evidence: "The war to make the world safe for democracy Wilson launched for no other reason than to make oligarchy safe at home. . . . The immediate background to America's entry into the Second World War was Roosevelt's determination to bury the New Deal and crush yet another popular movement for reform," p. 252.

20. Sent. 5, Sigmund Freud, "Wish Fulfillment and the Unconscious," *A Modern Book of Aesthetics,* ed. M. Rader (New York: Holt, Rinehart and Winston, 1973, 4th ed.), p. 124; sent. 7–11, cited by William Ruehlmann, *Saint with a Gun: The Unlawful American Private Eye* (New York: New York University Press, 1974), pp. 98–99; the appeal of such roles to democratic leaders is symbolized by the fact that President Richard Nixon, at the height of his popular acclaim in August of 1972, appointed Clint Eastwood to a seven-year term on the National Council of the Arts. Patrick Agan explained that this appointment was ". . . in recognition of his clear and unmistakable contribution to motion pictures and also as a tribute to his huge success with the public." *Clint Eastwood: The Man Behind the Myth* (New York: Pyramid, 1975), p. 136.
21. Gerbner and Gross, *Trends in Network Drama,* p. 8.
22. Karl Popper, *The Open Society and Its Enemies* (Princeton: Princeton University Press, 1950), pp. 119–20.
23. Ernest Becker, *Angel in Armor: A Post-Freudian Perspective on the Nature of Man* (New York: Braziller, 1969), pp. 111–14.
24. Oswald Wiener, "der geist der superhelden," (no caps in original), *Vom Geist der Superhelden: Comic Strips,* ed. H. D. Zimmermann (Berlin: Geb. Mann Verlag, 1970), our translation, p. 97.
25. *Zap,* No. 1 (Nov. 1967).
26. *Zap,* No. 4 (1969).
27. Aldous Huxley, *Collected Essays* (New York: Bantam Books, 1959), pp. 73–75.
28. Rollo May, *Love and Will* (New York: W. W. Norton, 1969), p. 74.
29. Bugliosi, *Helter Skelter,* pp. 634, 561.
30. May, *Love and Will,* p. 110.
31. Reinhold Niebuhr, *The Children of Light and the Children of Darkness: A Vindication of Democracy and a Critique of its Traditional Defense* (New York: Charles Scribner's Sons, New Foreword edition, 1960), p. 118.
32. John McDermott, "Nature Nostalgia and the City: An American Dilemma," *The Family: Communes and Utopian Societies,* ed. S. TeSelle (New York: Harper & Row, 1971), pp. 11–12.
33. Sent. 7–8, cited by Peter Goldman et al., "Can Reagan Stop Ford?," *Newsweek* (Nov. 24, 1975), p. 31; sent. 10–12, cited by

John Nordheimer, "Reagan Enters Campaign, Seeks a Curb on Spending," New York *Times* (Nov. 21, 1975), p. 20; sent. 13–14, Patrick Anderson, "Peanut Farmer for President," New York *Times* magazine (Dec. 14, 1975), p. 15.

34. Sent. 2–10, "Nuttin but Nuttin," *Zap,* No. 1 (Nov. 1967); sent. 13, it is worth noting that this kind of campaign strategy was developed by Richard Nixon and his staff at about the time of the *Zap* episode. Joe McGinniss cited the "advertising proposition" for Nixon's presidential primary in 1968: "There's an uneasiness in the land. A feeling that things aren't right. That we're moving in the wrong direction. That none of the solutions to our problems are working. That we're not being told the truth about what's going on. The trouble is in Washington. Fix that and we're on our way to fixing everything. . . . Richard Nixon will know what has to be done–and he'll know the best way to get it done. We'll all feel a whole lot better knowing he's there in Washington running things instead of someone else," *The Selling of the President* (New York: Pocket Books, 1968), pp. 180–81; sent. 15–16, Myra MacPherson, "The Blooming of Betty Ford," *McCall's* (Sept. 1976), p. 120.
35. William Fine, "Sunday With Richard Nixon," *Ladies' Home Journal* (Dec. 1975), pp. 50 ff.
36. Frederick Werthan, *Seduction of the Innocent* (New York: Rinehart, 1954).
37. Sent. 3–4, Wieland Schulz-Keil, "Bonanza ist Ueberall," *Die Zeit,* No. 49 (Dec. 5, 1975), p. 15; sent. 6, David Robinson, "The Movies," *The Saturday Review* (Dec. 13, 1975), p. 71; sent. 8, cf. *Der Spiegel,* No. 9 (Feb. 24, 1975), No. 30 (July 21, 1975); the problematic qualities of American superhero comics have stirred considerable controversy in Western Germany. Cf. Dagmar V. Doetinchem and Klaus Hartung, *Zum Thema Gewalt in Superheldencomics* (Berlin: Basis Verlag, 1974); Wiltrud Ulriche Drechsel, Jörg Funhoff and Michael Hoffmann, *Massenzeichenware: Die gesellschaftliche und ideologische Function der Comics* (Frankfurt: Suhrkamp Verlag, 1975); Hans Dieter Zimmermann, ed., *Vom Geist der Superhelden: Comic Strips* (Berlin: Gebr. Mann Verlag, 1970).
38. Sent. 7–8, Friedrich Hacker, *Aggression: Die Brutalisierung der modernen Welt* (Hamburg: Rohwohlt, 1973), p. 21, our translation; sent. 11, Hacker's more recent study, *Terror: Mythos—Realität—Analyse* (Vienna: Molden Verlag, 1973), provides a comprehensive analysis of contemporary terrorism; cf. especially Chap. V, "Macht und Ohnmacht des Schreckens;" sent. 12, Joseph Campbell, *The Hero with a Thousand Faces* (New York:

Meridian, 1956); the transformation of Campbell's thesis was suggested by Robert Stone in a letter to the authors.
39. Cf. note 2 in this chapter.
40. Cf. note 1 in this chapter.

Glossary

American monomyth–an archetypal plot pattern emerging in American popular culture in which a community threatened by evil is redeemed through superheroism.

axial decade–the period from 1929 to 1941 in which traditional dramatic motifs coalesced to create the American monomyth.

bubble-gum fallacy–the ascription of trivial, diversionary qualities to popular entertainments while denying their mythical aspects and formative influences.

classical monomyth–an archetypal plot pattern in folktales and classical myths, deriving from pagan rites of initiation in which a hero leaves home, undergoes trials, and returns as an adult.

Heidi-redeemer–a superheroic figure who miraculously saves individuals or communities by psychological manipulation or other nonviolent means.

icon–a visual image capable of evoking uncritical devotion.

iconic photography–the use of a mythical paradigm to shape a visual image into an object of uncritical devotion.

monomythic Eden–a benign community in close proximity to a pastoral realm, dwelling in harmony until attacked by evil.

myth–an uncritically accepted story that provides a model to interpret current experience, disclosing the meaning of the self, the community, and the universe.

mythic–pertaining to the processes of expressing or accepting myths.

mythical–a trait of mythic beliefs or dramatic expressions or of a story expressing the character of a myth.

mythic alchemy–the transmutation of previously created cultural materials to match a compelling mythical paradigm.

mythic cuing–the communication of mythical content without direct verbal articulation through the juxtaposition of visual and aural fragments.

mythic denial–the verbal or symbolic refusal to acknowledge a crucial but problematic feature of a mythical story.

mythic massage–a process of dramatizing a mythical story in a way that leads an audience to accept its efficacy as a realistic pattern for coping with current experience.

mythic paradigm–a story exemplifying with special clarity all of the features common to a group of similar myths.

mythic selectivity–a process of presenting dramatic details that conform to a mythical paradigm.

myth of mythlessness–the unexamined belief that scientific culture has transcended mythical forms of thought.

pop religion–a system of beliefs, rituals, and devotional acts associated with fandom, deriving its central symbols and objects of worship from the realm of popular entertainments.

pop theology–the effort to elaborate, explain, celebrate, and defend the beliefs and behavior enjoined by a pop religion.

pseudo-empiricism–the use of technology and surface realism to simulate the scientific credibility of mythical materials.

redemption–the decisive rescue of individual or community from the threat of evil.

saga–a traditional adventure story in which a hero's strength and wits are tested.

sexual renunciation–a hero's rejection of sexual relations, or his impassive participation for instrumental reasons, in either case for the sake of a redemptive mission.

sexual segmentation–the separation of sexual relationships from the most important personal values of a hero, making permanent sexual commitments impossible.

spectator democracy–a recurrent motif of monomythic drama in which citizens and institutions are passive observers of superheroic redemption.

technomythic critical theory–an analysis designed to elucidate popular entertainments whose mythical content has been rendered credible by sophisticated technology.

Tertullian ecstasy–an experience of release, often with a vicarious sexual component, occasioned by witnessing the punishment of transgressors, particularly those violating sexual norms.

Trekkie–a devoted follower of the *Star Trek* series.

Werther effect–an alteration of behavior that results from encountering an artifact of popular culture.

Werther invitation–a symbolic exhortation for members of an audience to conform their behavior to a mythical paradigm from popular culture.

Acknowledgments

This book has exorbitantly consumed the resources, time, and valued opinions of several dozen people. Without our students at Morningside, we would never have discovered the materials needed to carry through our project. Monte Albert, Dan Anderson, Terry Feenstra, Barb Gist, Steve Heaton, Karen Isbell, Lyle Johnston, Rachel Lieder, Sandy McCulloch, John McWhorter, Pat Spang, and Inge Zibers all made significant contributions. Friends and colleagues have been generous beyond measure in providing critical appraisal. Robert Bataille, Francis Brockman, Linda Busby, Larry Graham, Jan Hodge, Michael Husband, James N. Jordan, Hubert G. Locke, David McCreary, Carroll McLaughlin, David Nelson, John Nelson, Jean Schmidt, Harlan Soper, Robert V. Stone, Frank Terry, Bernard Timberg, and Jane Vallier have helped with the style and logic of the manuscript throughout. Robert and Eloise Weisinger made a systematic contribution to the entire manuscript. Pauline Kael, Raymond Newell, and the staff of the Nashville *Tennessean* gave special assistance in the research on Buford Pusser. Staff members at libraries have repeatedly offered assistance, especially Joan Ayers, Orpha Jerman, Charles Lemaster, Vernon Martin, and Mary Stodden. Peter Koller and Gabriele Sinigoj at the University of Graz provided material unavailable in the United States. Larry Fuller generously shared archival material on several occasions. Mary Corliss of MOMA helped locate movie stills. Maxine Percell, our typist, prevented numerous catastrophes and rectified even more. Above all, we must acknowledge the patient efforts of our fine editor at Doubleday, Cathleen Jordan. Without her, *The American Monomyth* probably wouldn't have gone anywhere.

Jewett and Lawrence

February 1976

Index